FRAMED

FRAMED

The 'True' Story of the Theft of Picasso's Weeping Woman

STUART ROSSON

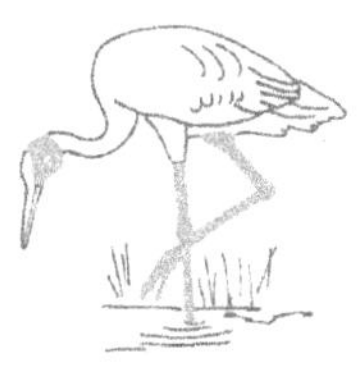

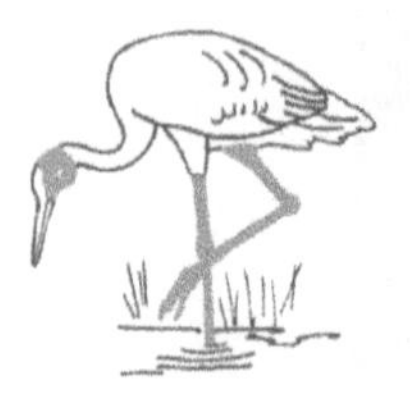

Published by Brolga Publishing Pty Ltd
ABN 46 063 962 443
PO Box 452
Torquay Victoria 3228
email: markzocchi@brolgapublishing.com.au

National Library of Australia
Cataloguing-in-Publication data

Stuart Rosson, author. ISBN: 978-0-6458158-6-3 (paperback)

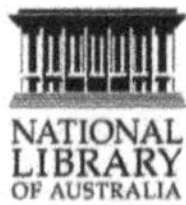

A catalogue record for this work is available from the National Library of Australia

Printed in Australia
Cover design and typeset by WorkingType Studio

ACKNOWLEDGMENT OF COUNTRY

The author wishes to acknowledge the Djaara (my character, Jack's mob), traditional owners of Dja Dja Wurrung lands, where part of this story is set; and respectfully acknowledge the Martiinga kuli – the Dja Dja Wurrung ancestors – for their connection and care of country over millennia.

Further respect and acknowledgment are paid to the traditional custodians of Wurundjeri and Wadawurrung lands, to their elders and leaders past, present and emerging who hold the memories, traditions, and culture of their communities.

In addition respect is paid to all Aboriginal, Torres Strait Islander, and Māori people and acknowledgement of the importance of their ongoing connection to land, sea, sky, and community throughout the Kulin nation and beyond.

In loving memory of my brother,
Peter Rosson: 1954–2002

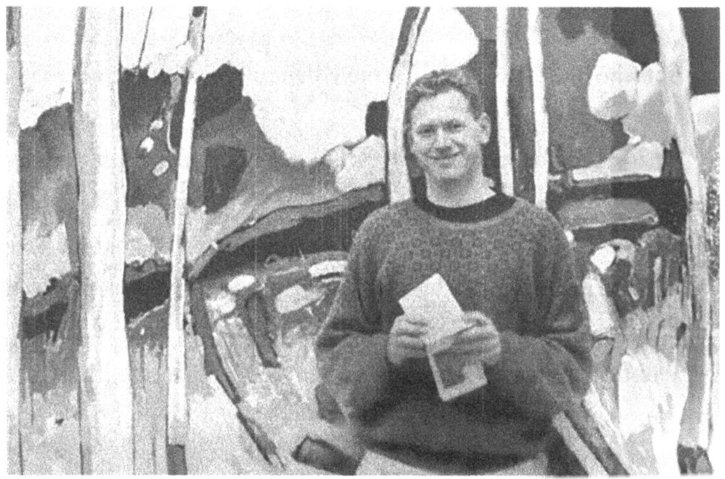

In the mid-1980s Peter Rosson (re-named Daniel Hardman for the purposes of this fictional account) was a wildly successful Melbourne artist, known for by-passing the nepotism of contemporary dealers and galleries, and selling paintings direct to the public.

In early 1986 he had a sell-out exhibition in which over thirty of his extraordinary Ash Wednesday expressionist landscapes sold for a total equivalent to ninety thousand dollars in today's money.

In August 1986, he and his partner, Margaret Casey, were framed for the theft of Picasso's Weeping Woman from the National Gallery of Victoria, which had occurred some three weeks earlier.

The so-called evidence touted by the investigating police at the time, was a hand-drawn artist's sketch, of dubious providence, depicting a woman with an uncanny likeness to Peter's partner Margaret, holding a wrapped package identical to the one widely viewed on television several days earlier, when police had finally recovered the Picasso from a railway station locker.

It was a little too pat. It was a set-up. And within forty-eight hours, when fingerprints and typewriter faces didn't match up, the police knew they'd been had....

But who had produced this convenient piece of 'evidence'... This artist's sketch?

No one seemed to know, and the police certainly weren't saying.

But what is known, is that within weeks, the investigation into Australia's biggest ever art heist – a crime which attracted massive media and public interest here and world-wide, and during which a group calling themselves 'The Australian Cultural Terrorists', repeatedly threatened and ridiculed the police and the state government – was dropped.

The crime remains unsolved to this day.

Thirty-five years later, when a documentary team gained access to the police archive containing Rosson and Casey's police file, the file box – once the dust was blown off and it was opened – was found to be empty.

Rosson's career as an artist never recovered from the taint of being implicated in the Picasso theft, and sixteen years later, in 2002, he took his own life.

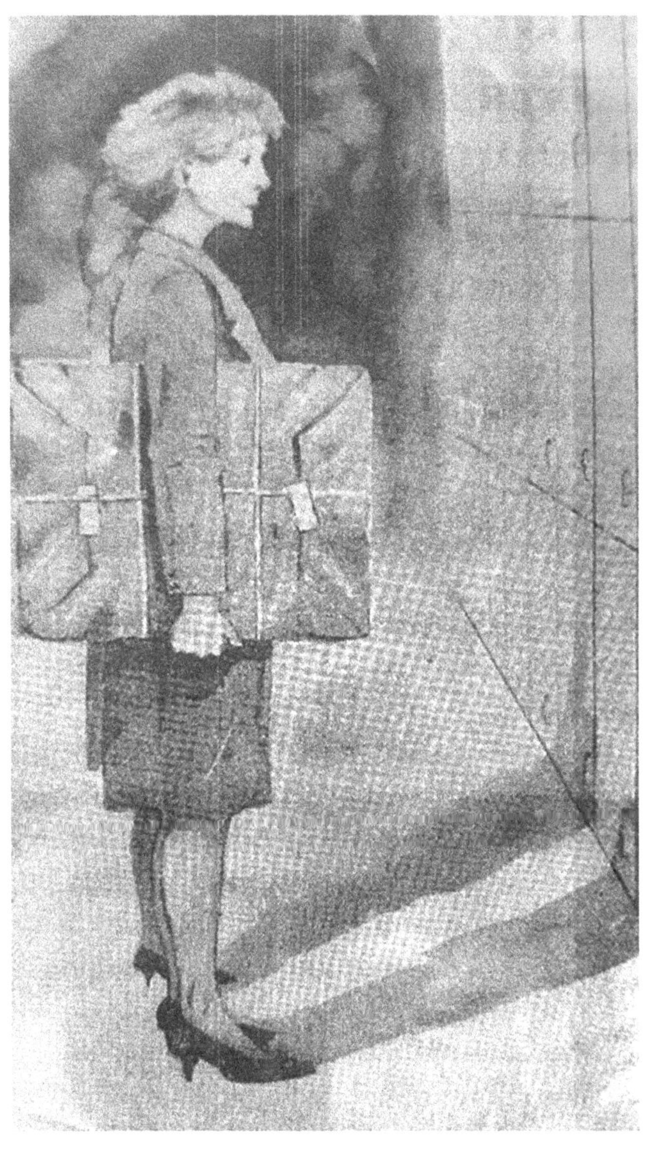

The artist's sketch, as reproduced in The Age *newspaper*

Rewind to September 1989:

Frustrated after two years of trying to identify the informer who had attempted to frame him, and facing the increasingly harsh reality that his career was tanking and he was apparently 'black-listed' by the mainstream art establishment, Peter and his new wife, retreated to the coast to re-group.

There we shared a duplex rental – a kind of family compound.

We went surfing a lot, and Pete talked about the Picasso affair... A lot.

It had been a deeply traumatic experience, especially in light of the damage done to his career. But Pete had learned much in his attempts to get to the bottom of what had happened. And he had plenty of theories too, which I heard repeatedly as we traversed the coast, looking for waves.

Many of Pete's theories seemed a little outlandish at the time, but with the passage of time, some have begun to seem quite plausible...

Framed is my brother's story; based in part on the known facts of the Weeping Woman fiasco, and drawing on some of his colourful theories about what had transpired. But mostly it is fiction. My characters Daniel and Audrey are perhaps all too easily identifiable as my brother and his partner, Margaret. But the other characters are imaginary – perhaps coloured somewhat by the stories my brother told me – but nonetheless invented to fit a fictional plot, and not intended to resemble any real person in any way.

Note: The quotes in italics in each of the chapter headings are taken from Angry Buddha – a hitherto unpublished book written by my brother.

I believed it was the artist's job in society
To engage in a search for the truth of things
With the materials available.
I thought artists were in search of meaning
And a beautiful way of expressing this meaning, or truth;
A unique addition to the society in which they lived and worked
An attempt at something;
Not a sanctioned proof, declaration or decoration.
I thought the artist might even locate the comedy in life
As they lived the life of the Fool
And struggled toward the light.
Perhaps I was wrong.
In this essay I am going to tell the truth
As I saw it once
Before I didn't care anymore.
Angry Buddha 2001

ONE

Melbourne – Friday night, May 9th, 1986

'But, like Picasso, I figured the best art I could fake was my own.'
Angry Buddha 2001

They were like cats. Travis thought so anyway, as he watched them from the makeshift bar. Big, fat cats, all five of them. Torn apart mice all day, and now here they were, licking their fur – all self-satisfied and feline smug – sitting in the high backed chairs Travis had lugged in from the storeroom, balancing their cards on their big respectable bellies.

The late-night hush, restrained lighting and all that art on the walls, made the space feel like an extravagant loft, overlooking the wintering May streets of Melbourne's CBD. He'd helped Logan convert the upstairs show room into a poker den for the night, including the felt-topped table, centered under a wide rectangular light fitting, hung low for effect. Logan was useless on the tools, so Travis had extended the cord and lowered the light to make it just right.

*What a bunch of complete fuckwits...*Did he mutter it out loud, or just think it? This, when they all put on their funny little red fezzes, like party hats, and strung on their elasticated beards, making them all look like Freud or Charles Darwin.

Ridiculous! Did they think they were funny? Bohemian? Some kind of dumb secret society? Or were they taking the piss out of the rotund art academic – the only guest Travis recognised – who already had his own beard, and come to think of it, looked like he might think a fez was a fashion choice he could get away with? Douglas Blackthorn – head lecturer at the School of Fine Arts, where Travis had completed his training five years earlier – had been fastidiously ignoring him all night, like it was below his station to interact with the bartender. It was beginning to piss Travis off.

And Blackthorn had been fouling the air all night with his cigars, the smoke wafting over the other players and forming a nebulous haze trapped in the cube of light. No one seemed to notice. They were focused on the game.

Subdued murmurs, a nervous cough and a reckless chuckle, told Travis there was tension starting to build. But he didn't really care. He'd become pathologically bored... Shitless, actually. Bored and irritated. He took a discrete sip from the twelve-year old Scotch he'd liberated for himself and diluted with coke. *Sacrilege*, Logan would say, but fuck him.

As he slouched on the bar, his attention drifted to the rain-slicked city street below. Through the big front windows, he watched a late-night u-turner's headlights cut a swath through the pool of reflected street light coming off Lonsdale Street. The rain had stopped. He heard the tires squish as the wayward Corona went back the way it had come. The players were all very quiet. An expectant hush.

Suddenly an eruption of groans and expletives around the table. Cards were slapped down and someone laughed extravagantly.

'Fuck me, *the River*!'

'Lucky faggot!' This, in a degraded British accent, from his erstwhile art lecturer, Blackthorn, through a cloud of noxious smoke. There was a brief but tense pause, as if the other players feared their host's response.

'Skillful faggot, Dougy my dear, if you don't mind, and thanks for noticing.' Logan Tate didn't skip a beat and raked his winnings into a pile in front of him. A mess of fifties and a few grey *Mawsons*.

Logan had beaten the evil-tempered *Dougy's* three kings, by hitting a low straight on the river... Blind luck really. As the players completed their postmortem of the winning hand Travis examined Blackthorn and Logan from across the room. He had tried to ignore being ignored, but hot offence and indignation were brewing in him. Apparently Travis was good enough to drink beers with and listen to Blackthorn's self-serving bullshit down on the coast, but he was persona non-grata here... Was that it? *Dougy* – homophobic dinosaur that he was, would have no way of knowing what was going on between Travis and Logan – their little relationship – but Travis was puzzled; he'd once seen Logan verbally eviscerate a footy jock outside a busy city night club, for just such a comment. So had he not even noticed such crass bigotry coming from Doug, who was so out of place amongst the other players, like some kind of Edwardian Beelzebub? Surely the other players had picked up on his toxic energy, the moment Doug had entered the room.

The muttering and cursing died down. Someone was dealing a new hand.

'Travis! Travis? Where's my barmaid?' A smiling Logan half turned towards the kitchenette, but didn't even do his young protégé the courtesy of actually catching his eye. 'The spectators are thirsty! Another round, if you please.' To add insult to injury, he clicked his bloody fingers!

Travis delivered Logan's drink with professional aplomb, more or less confident it would be correctly perceived as surly indifference. He doled out the other drinks too. The *spectators*, he realised, were the three players now eliminated from the game. It was down to just Logan and a middle-aged bloke who looked like a businessman or a politician. He had the lion's share of the remaining money arrayed in front of him, and was looking at Logan like he was ready to eat him.

A young bloke Logan had identified as an 'up and coming artist' was dealing. The other two eliminated players looked on with varying interest. His gay-bashing, cigar-stinking ex-lecturer was still feigning contemptuous indifference and ignored Travis completely when he delivered his Scotch. That was okay by Travis... His was the drink he'd stirred with his finger, after ducking into the kitchen alcove and sticking said finger up his ass. 'Cheers,' he said brightly, thinking: *Nice to see you too, Dougy. Have ten more, old mate, until your savagely repressed homo-erotic urges are quelled... Or you die.*

Now that it was down to Logan and the bloke who looked like he didn't need, but urgently wanted the money, Travis had regained some interest in the game. He retreated to the kitchenette to watch.

One or both players passed for the next three hands, each waiting for the right cards. But this late in the game the re-doubled blind, at eighty bucks a pop, was going to bleed Logan dry, fast.

Finally he had to bet.

The suit called.... Both players checked on the turn. There were already three cards to a straight showing; the eight and nine of spades and the jack of hearts... and an off-suit two. From the bar, Travis could see Logan's cards as he lifted them slightly and fanned them out, the way real players did. But all he really saw was colour... Royalty. Pocket jacks? He couldn't be sure, but it looked like Logan might be sitting on three jacks, with the one in the middle.

The artist dealt the river. The jack of spades! A surprised murmur rippled around the table. It meant a flush was now a possibility, full house... Four of a kind. Everything was on.

Logan went all in.

The suit looked at him dubiously, as if trying to read him. He slowly pushed his whole pile into the center, with a cocky and contemptuous air. There had to be thousands of dollars. No playing chips for these guys. It was the real thing. And you couldn't go *all in* with just whatever you had in front of you. The bet had to be matched, and Logan knew it. Real money.

'Call,' Logan said evenly, fixing the suit with a steady eye.

The businessman leaned back in his chair and looked down his nose at Logan, tipping his head sideways. 'With what?'

'You know I'm good for it, Simon. Don't be a prat.'

'Well, you know what they say in the classics...' Suited Simon leaned forward and pushed his beard around to the side, smirking across the table. 'Show me the money.'

'Oh, for fuck's sake,' spat Blackthorn from behind a cloud of smoke. 'He's obviously bluffing... I'll fucken stake you, if that's what it takes... Jesus!'

'Don't worry.' Logan pushed back his chair. 'Count your money,' He flicked a disdainful finger at the businessman's pile of cash. 'I'll be right back.' He headed out the back, towards the storeroom, disposing of his silly fez and beard as he went.

He must have the jacks, thought Travis. *Four of a kind*! But Travis didn't think Logan was in the habit of keeping cash on the premises, at least that was what the sign in reception said. He was paranoid about being robbed.

By the time Logan got back, Travis had noticed the community cards had the makings of a straight flush – a ten and queen of spades would do it – beating even four of a kind. He reckoned everyone else had realised the same thing, staring at the three face-up cards, while they waited.

Returning with a package about three feet square, wrapped in brown paper, Logan nodded at the businessman's stash of money. 'How much is there?'

'Three and a half... give or take.' The fancy-suited roller looked curiously at the package and then at Logan.

'Right.' Theatrically, Logan ripped away the brown paper, revealing a painting – an aerial landscape in oils – all dotty trees and rocks. 'Fred Williams. Late sixties. Bloody priceless,' said Logan. He gave a sideways glance to the bearded Pom, Blackthorn, and winked, which struck Travis as a bit strange. 'Well, ten grand at the very least, if it were auctioned.'

Simon nodded appreciatively and massaged his chin, as if he were suddenly some kind of art critic. 'Really?' His meaning wasn't clear to Travis. *Really a Fred Williams? Really ten grand? Or really, you're offering a valuable painting as a poker stake?*

'He's dead, you know. Two years now. He'll go stratospheric in the next few years. Probably the best art deal you'll ever make. But in any case...' Logan reached down with his free hand and touched his two cards. 'I reckon I've got you covered... If not, you've just acquired yourself a Fred Williams. From his wonder years. Absolute bargain.'

'Alright.' Simon nodded. A smarmy smile. 'Show us what you've got then.'

'No. I called *you*.' Logan hoisted the painting and clunked it on the edge of the table.

Simon's smile broadened and he turned over his cards. The queen and ten of spades. 'Straight-flush!' There was more than a hint of triumph in his voice. A collective sigh emitted from the other players.

'Christ!' Logan snorted. He didn't seem that surprised. Maybe he thought the financier had been bluffing. But he wasn't, and neither was Logan. He reached down and threw his two cards face-up into the middle. Pocket jacks.

'Fucking hell,' breathed Travis from the bar. 'Shit luck, to lose with four-of-a-kind.'

Logan smiled and turned to Blackthorn and they exchanged a look, which for Travis' money, was the weirdest thing he'd seen all night. If you blinked you'd've missed it, and no one else seemed to notice. But Travis caught it – a kind of conspiratorial, knowing exchange, like they alone were in on some kind of joke.

In the end, the winning businessman left with the painting tucked under his arm, just like he was the cat that ended up with the lion's share of the cream.

Later, when Travis broached the subject of the painting, Logan tried to duck the question. But Travis didn't let him off the hook, and he'd said; 'Quite a nice little sideline you and Dougy've got going there,' which drew nothing but a hostile scowl from his lover and one-time agent.

'Okay Logan, I get it. Nothing to see here, eh? Don't worry, your secret's safe with me.'

Travis had winked, and Logan had only scowled even more.

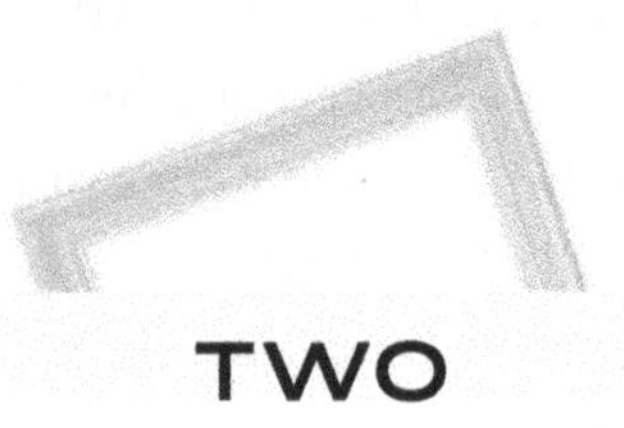

TWO

Saturday, May 17th, 1986

I pretended that I was an artist and was, therefore, harmless.
Angry Buddha, 2001

After showing the photographer out, Audrey stood for a time in the middle of the old squash court, just to take it all in. The vaulted space made for a perfect gallery; the high white walls, the recessed sky lights – shadowless light, soft and pure and perfect to paint by, Daniel often effused – and plenty of space to exhibit. She looked at her portrait – the one she'd just been photographed with – and marveled at the likeness; a wild, almost Cezannesque impression of her, penetrating and brutally honest. It wasn't easy for Audrey to see it hanging, as part of the show. It was stunning, breathtaking and disturbing. It gave her chills.

Hanging right next to *her* was the most spectacular of the Crayfish Point works. This one always made her feel like she was free-falling into its luminous depiction of the magical place Daniel had painted time and again. It was a location he believed was steeped in ancient transcendental energies; an intensely spiritual place for the long-ago murdered protectors of the coastal lands. A place for ceremony, she assumed, and a location to commune with the ancient ones and the spirits of the land and sea. He'd told her it was a vortex in the energy matrix of the land and he mused about its special meaning in the song lines of the indigenous people. Audrey knew it saddened him more than he would say, that many of the custodians of the ancient knowledge had been killed by his own colonialist ancestors.

And so he had painted it over and over again. This special place. At Crayfish Point, he said, *you could feel like you were on another planet. Isolated and inaccessible...* and yet, incredibly, only a ten minute drive and a thirty minute walk from his coastal home. *At Crayfish Point* – he'd told her, the first time he took her there – *you might end up doing weird shit; spontaneous behavior... Because the place has a strange effect on you.*

And sure enough it did, and they had.

In this particular painting he had truly captured it, in a way Audrey reckoned would make Van Gogh himself roll over in his Auvers grave and sit up to take a look. The starry night sky, splashed with the palette of intergalactic nebulae, all mirrored in the ominous still waters of the secret cove. The sinister shapes and ciphers of the ancient Ngangkari's broken headland, inky black against the transcendental splendor of the sea and the sky.

She shook her head, to break the spell and draw her attention away from the painting. She knew Daniel was already downstairs in the Artist's Bar; greeting the early-comers, getting them well lubricated and getting himself into character to work the room, before the official opening at eight. A slow turn allowed her to take in the rest of the exhibition; four large paintings meticulously spaced on each wall. Sixteen canvases in all, with the smaller works spaced out below them on the floor, just leaning up against the walls. Often these were the first to sell.

She stepped over the high threshold and out of the gallery – quite the maneuver in her tight black skirt, she was dressed for business – and hurried down the stairs and along the *rabbit run* leading from the squash courts to the main stairwell. At the open door of the waiter's change room she paused to examine herself in the full length mirror: Belted black pencil skirt and black three-quarter length coat over a white camisole. A bit of cleavage, minimal makeup, no flashy jewelry, just the bangles. Business, black tie, Bohemian all rolled into one. A good balance.

As she emerged onto the landing, Mietta's partner Tom – co-opted to play maître d' for the night – caught her eye as he herded some well-healed guests into the dining room. He gave her a wink and a smile over his shoulder, even as he launched into his practiced banter with the glammed-up restaurant patrons.

She paused for a breath at the top of the grand old staircase, and to compose herself, just in case she had to make some kind of entrance. They were expecting a good crowd and Audrey was buzzing.

*

She glided regally down the stairs, submerging herself into a raft of chatter coming up from the crowded foyer. A Friday night bottleneck. Restaurant patrons, thirsty city workers heading for the main bar, and punters making their way excitedly to the Artist's Bar for the latest *Private View.* As she reached the bottom of the stairs some eyes in the crowd came up to meet her. She gave them a beneficent smile, and it almost seemed as though the throng parted slightly to give her access to the cloistered entry to the cocktail bar, around behind the stairs. She chatted and gushed as needed, smiled naturally and warmly glad-handed those in her path, all the while moving towards the bar.

Mietta had renamed the cocktail bar the *Artists Bar*, and it had quickly become a favorite haunt for Melbourne's art scene parvenus and tuft hunters in search of a Bohemian refuge to flaunt their chic. The grand old Alfred Place building in the city had been the perfect new home for her lauded venture when she'd relocated two years prior. The first-floor ballroom was refurbished to house her award-winning restaurant: Formal French with nothing spared to create an authentically elegant, Gallic experience. The main bar near the front entrance soon became one of the trendiest nightspots for the city's business elite and fashionistas. But Mietta's love of the arts and long-standing desire to support and nurture authentic creative pursuits found its truest expression in the beautifully bespoke hidden spaces within the venue. The artist's bar and saloon, tucked around the back of the ground floor, became theatres for her enabling of the arts; from poetry and jazz to performance art, music gigs by some of the city's best emerging artists and – in Daniel's case – exhibition openings.

The Victorian-era building had once been home to an austere Naval and Military club. Few of Mietta's fine-dining patrons could have guessed that above their heads were two disused squash courts, now housing a young artist; home-grown but arguably cast in the old-school, European mold of genuine creative technicians. One of the courts now serving as his studio – with living quarters above it in the spectator's gallery – and doubling as a gallery on exhibition nights.

As usual Audrey felt she needed to pinch herself. A classic inner city artist's garret and gallery above what was fast becoming Melbourne's artistic heart. You couldn't make this stuff up – and likely no one would believe you if you did. *You wouldn't read about it*, her mother would say.

It had all been in the timing... Their fated meeting, and the ensuing fireworks; Daniel's artistic ascendency; Meitta's new tenancy, and most important of all, Audrey's Queenscliff connection with Mietta's sister. *Fate doesn't get any fatier than this,* Daniel had quipped.

And she knew Mietta secretly loved the idea of her restaurant guests being ambushed by a wild, paint-spattered artist in his jeans and black tee bounding down the stairs. She liked the authenticity of it, and she'd witnessed it herself on at least one occasion, Daniel claimed, when she'd vouchsafed him a classic Mietta raised brow and given her trademark guffaw, much to his amusement and the chagrin of the good diners.

Best of all, Mietta was happy for them to use the Artist's bar, from time to time, as their very own front of house. And so tonight for the third time, a Private View exhibition would start with cocktails and society down in the bar, before moving upstairs to the gallery for art appreciation and commerce.

Mietta's was quite the shop front, and the garret and gallery hidden in the upper reaches was pure Rive Gauche.

*

The charm offensive was in full swing, but he needed a drink. At times like these Daniel sometimes imagined himself an agile tree monkey, swinging effortlessly from branch to branch. Each guest or couple getting a quick-fire burst of candid charm and his full and focused attention, for a measured time... *Tick, tick, tick,* disarming smile and then off again. *Yes, absolutely, bourgie as hell,* to the Aussie actor and his wife; *Mietta is amazing, isn't she,* to the ABC executive and her entourage; *Yeah, fabulous turn out; who'd have thought,* to the advertising creative director and his partner.

He caught a glimpse of Audrey making her way towards him and used it as a way to break contact and get a signal off to James, behind the bar. He'd know what was needed. A Manhattan – just the one – to ground him a bit. He shimmied sideways towards the bar, and took a moment alone to survey the crowd. A wildly eclectic assortment of art scene hacks and pretenders; entertainment and media people; academics, artists, musicians and a mish mash of his and Audrey's friends, supporters and colleagues. He couldn't deny, a much better turn out than he was used to. A venue like this made it almost too easy. *Like inviting ants to a honey party.*

The cocktail bar was decorated in a kind of mid-century cabaret style. It really could have been Paris, or Vienna, with its muted hanging pendants and coloured glass lamps, strategic pedestals with statues or flowers, and a leather enfant gâté in the corner. The walls were hung with original paintings by Mietta's grandmother, and others by her two sisters. The antique bar itself looked like something out of New York in the 30s or 40s, and the bar staff were liveried to match. James slid his Manhattan across the bar to him, raised both eyebrows and mouthed the words *good crowd*. Daniel smiled gratefully and raised his glass. James was like his partner in crime. Later he would precede the punters upstairs and play drink waiter with the good champagne, already chilling up on the mezzanine. Working the crowd like the absolute bloody professional; always right on hand with a glass of the best bubbly at the psychological moment, when a deal was to be closed. He was worth way more than barman's wages and Daniel made a mental note to offer him one of the small paintings as a bonus after the show.

He made his way back through the crowd and met Audrey halfway. They kissed, and Audrey took his drink from him and had a sip.

'It's on,' he whispered in her ear.

She smiled brightly and nodded. 'It really is, isn't it?'

Without another word she pushed off into the crowd and he had a moment to watch her mingling and greeting, before he himself was collared by more punters. She would go one way; he'd do the opposite side of the room. He'd always considered himself pretty good at working a crowd... But he had to admit, Audrey was better.

*

Daniel peeled another sticky red dot from the dispenser and applied it to the frame of a landscape – one of the mesmerising and pretty ones, inspired by the fires that almost consumed his coastal home a few years earlier.

Someone at a show once asked him if it was hard letting go of paintings imbued with all that creative energy, all that *blood, sweat and tears.* Wasn't it like giving away a child? The question had struck him as both obvious and annoying, and he'd bristled at the time. *Yes, of course, there was a momentary tug of loss, but what the fuck was art for, if not to be appreciated? Paintings belong on walls, not in a vault or a storeroom. If someone connects with a piece of art, on whatever level, and if it has meaning to them – the acid-test being, meaningful enough for them to part with their hard-earned – then they should have it.*

Maybe it did feel strange to think of so many discreetly fragmented bits of his own consciousness, dispersed around the city, around the world, hanging in the hallways and living rooms of so many fleeting and ultimately anonymous art lovers. But it also felt good, and it satisfied in some way that deep-seated egoistic itch that artists seem compelled to scratch.

I mean, doesn't everybody want to be omnipresent?

He was starting to see red dots everywhere. The exhibition had developed a nice case of measles. If he'd learned anything from art dealers – and he couldn't say he'd learned much, other than, *stay away from art dealers* – perhaps it was some basic shop-keeping skills.

That's what art dealers are, after all; glorified shopkeepers, most of them alarmingly incompetent and ill-suited to even that task... Which was why he'd sacked his.

But the red dots were a beautifully simple sales catalyst. As the patrons fell more and more under the spell of the paintings – surrounded as they were on all sides by the squash court's high-walled diorama of imagery, and also under the spell of James's largess with the champagne – the multiplying dots, when they reached a certain critical mass, created a sense of urgency... Sometimes a kind of feeding frenzy would ensue, as that uniquely human emotion, FOMO, kicked in.

He checked himself. Cynicism was to be avoided. It was another thing that could too easily rub off on him from his past encounters with dealers.

In fact, tonight's crowd had been a very good one. The exhibition had started as they so often did, with a kind of reverent hush – almost church-like – as people acclimatised to the space and gradually opened up their mass media-dulled perceptive faculties to the unusual images surrounding them. At some shows there would be a little speech, usually by a self-appointed expert who considered themselves sufficiently informed and important to introduce his work. *For some participants in the carnival, the urge to be a middleman or arbiter of taste was sometimes just too hard to resist, even if they weren't an actual art dealer.*

Daniel had tolerated it in the past but lately he was adamant about dispensing with the preamble *and* the bullshit.

In the end it was enough that a 'Private View' gave patrons direct access to the artist and to his muse. As Audrey charmed them and put them at their ease, James kept the champagne coming at an even tempo, just enough to heighten artistic appreciation and loosen tongues and wallets.

For his part, Daniel just let it be known that he was open for interrogation. *Ask me anything; about art, painting, philosophy, religion... Whatever.* In any case, he reckoned the art pretty much sold itself.

You don't sell it, so much act as the agency by which ownership can be smoothly transferred to the new owner. A client will usually say they want to buy a painting within fifteen minutes of first contact. The trimmings are just that: polite and attentive service, location, reputation, refreshments, like-minded people, easy access to the artist(s) and their opinions, and a full consultative hanging and delivery service.

In truth, he was probably a much better salesman than he gave himself credit for, and it was because he believed in the product, and the process. The process as he saw it was to help the plebian art buyer overcome their post-modern cultural conditioning *not* to buy art... *After all, it isn't real estate, or fashion, is it?*

This too was all part of the service. It was his job to help them make the connection – to trust that small quiet voice – and allow themselves to step off into that transcendental space and experience something bigger than themselves, something timeless.

Christ, was he some kind of Shaman.... Or maybe just a 'snake oil salesman'? Just trust your gut, for God's sake... It's art.

But there *was* something more at stake than he and Audrey being able to pay the rent, and the customer taking home a commodity. With each sale he carried a gratifying image of the client and the canvas travelling through time together. This unique artifact, on a wall somewhere; a portal to another time – back to this moment, to a moment of liminal awareness – when something extraordinary, indefinable and personal had happened for them. Not only that, but like some kind of cosmic looking glass, it was also *his* portal, carrying himself *and his client*, back to Crayfish Point, back to the bleeding forest... Back to the point of inspiration, where ever and whenever.

If he were a purveyor of time travel, or shape-shifting fox magic… then quite likely the selling of it would *be pleasingly addictive, wouldn't it?*

*

And it seemed quite normal to Daniel that time stood still during his exhibitions. It was almost midnight when the last guests left, but it seemed like a blink of the eye since the first of them climbed the threshold into the gallery.

The show had almost sold out, the best result yet. He was still buzzing with adrenalin and probably so was Audrey, although she was looking much more relaxed than he felt; quite calm and content and obviously a bit relieved. He was still pretty jacked; wandering around the gallery, tidying up, and pacing up and down, counting the dots. He knew as soon as he slowed down, he'd be exhausted.

Audrey took his hand to stop him, and then put her arms around him. He relaxed then, and kissed her on the cheek.

'Success,' she declared.

'Fuck yeah.'

'Leave all this. We should go down and have a drink. Enjoy the moment.'

'We should. Evie and Rex'll probably still be down there, maybe some of the others.'

'You go. I'm going to get changed. I'll see you down there.'

Audrey went up to the mezzanine and he went the other way down the hall, but then doubled back for his jacket. He felt himself already starting to come down from the heightened state he'd been in for days leading up to the show. He needed sleep. A few drinks would help.

It was normal to be a bit deflated the day after a show, but he already felt an unexpected and unwelcome sense of unease creeping over him, even as he shrugged on his jacket and made his way back into the long dim hallway. He should be chuffed. The show had gone off.

Walking the ludicrously long hallway at night he often thought he could sense the ghosts of the old warriors whose club it had once been, watching him, mocking him. *The Goat*, he and Audrey had jokingly christened the resident entity they both sensed from time to time. But his unease tonight was different and it was incongruous. For some reason he thought of his old mate Casper, and in that moment half expected to see *him* materialise in the hallway.

It put him in mind of the old days, spotting in the bush. His other life.

That was it. The feeling of unease evoked one of the patrols back then; when everything is cool, but for some reason the bush just doesn't feel right; the noises, the birds or the wind, aren't quite right or maybe the light's a bit off. But everything's going according to plan and you're just about to turn around and head back to base....

Could that be it? Everything had been falling into place so remarkably well. A studio and gallery above the city's hippest restaurant and bar, sell-out shows, a shop front to die for.

If it seems too good to be true...

The hallway closed in around him and he bumped into the side, disoriented by a flash of memory so sharp and sudden that he caught his breath and grunted: *Him rushing back through the motionless bush, back past his advancing platoon; them momentarily frozen in shock at the sight of him going the wrong way.*

'Sorry dickheads, something's all wrong in our garden.'

THREE

Friday, May 23rd, 1986

Earth is an intergalactic prison for minor offenders... And we all do life.
Angry Buddha 2001

Doug Blackthorn left a couple of two dollar notes on the sodden bar mat and carried two pots back to the corner table, dodging a couple of young journos coming up the stairs.

Logan Tate drained the last of his beer from the previous round and clunked it down on the stained laminex table and belched. 'Bloody hell Dougy, better make this the last one. I'll be shit-faced.'

'Bullshit. Friday afternoon. Let y' hair down a bit, y'old twink.'

Tate wasn't entirely sure why Blackthorn insisted they meet in this place. He assumed irony was involved, or perhaps nostalgia. It can't have been discretion, the place was full of journalists. It was the traditional drinking hole for reporters from the Sun and the Herald down the road, and for a variety of other bottom feeders at the arse-end of the CBD.

Doug seemed to quite like it. Mingling with kindred spirits, perhaps. It had gradually dawned on Logan Tate that Blackthorn was a rather advanced alcoholic – amongst his other endearing qualities – and his love of beer in particular had intriguing, if somewhat disturbing, echoes of undergraduate enthusiasms long past.

'Anyway, I hope he doesn't try and sell it,' said Blackthorn, settling himself back at the table. He held his beer at eye level, like a toast, or perhaps he was critically assessing the paucity of head, before taking a large swig. 'We'll be fucked if he does.... I mean what the hell were you thinking?'

'I thought he was bluffing. So did you, if you remember.' Logan took a judicious sip, and eyed his drinking companion guardedly. 'But don't worry, he's wanted to get his hands on a Williams for years. Just too frigging tight to shell out for one. Anyway, I told him to hang on tight; that it'll go up ten-fold in twenty years. So he won't be looking to sell it any time soon.'

'Hmm. Good. Fucking wanker, probably wouldn't know a Monet from shit on the dunny wall anyway.' Using a fat thumb and forefinger Blackthorn tweezered a cigarette out of a largely squashed gold B&H pack and stuck it in the side of his mouth. 'And how's our baby-Fred going, anyway?' He flicked a plastic lighter and puffed vigorously, squinting at Logan through billowing smoke.

'Good. He's bloody talented, this one, and quick.... Getting a bit twitchy though.'

'What?'

'Well, you know. He's young, naïve, full of himself.' Logan shrugged out an ironical grunt. 'Look, he'll do whatever I tell him, as long as he thinks I might give him a show.'

'Hah! Fucking idiots, never seem to know they've gotta pay their dues, do they?' Blackthorn exhaled a cloud of smoke to mingle with the hazy smog in the crowded bar. 'He's not going to flip his shit or anything is he?'

'No, don't worry. If he starts getting scared, that's not such a bad thing. I've got him under control.'

Doug looked at him thoughtfully over the rim of his pot as he took a small swig, and then rolled a bit of ash into the amber glass ashtray in the middle of the table. 'How many more do you reckon we can do?'

'I dunno. We need to be careful.' Logan glanced around the room, thinking for a second time, it was a pretty weird place to meet. A pub full of reporters.

The upstairs bar, favoured by the newspaper people, was a seedy affair. Dingy and cramped with bugger all ventilation. Doug had told him about one veteran reporter who, according to myth or rumour, never left the pub; filed his stories from the payphone in the stairwell, interviewed sources over beers at the bar. Probably made the rest up. Looking around it was pretty clear the clientele was well focused on getting some Friday afternoon beers into themselves with utmost alacrity. No one was looking for a story. And it was starting to get pretty rowdy too.

He leaned in towards Blackthorn, more to make himself heard than out of discretion. 'The widow's pretty canny. She knows the body of work too damn well. We probably can't push it too much more, I mean she would spot a fake, if one made its way into an auction or something.'

Blackthorn's frown turned into a scowl and he sat forward too, and ground his butt truculently into an over-full ashtray. 'Maybe we need to expand our market, then. Start flogging them further afield.'

'Well... maybe.' Logan looked and sounded unconvinced. 'There's not that much of a market for him overseas. Not yet anyway.'

'True. So maybe we should think about diversifying into something more, ah... sort-after.' Blackthorn grinned a little menacingly.

'Oh... Are we talking about activating our, ah... Our well-placed emissary?'

'Why the fuck not? He's wheedled his way in there, hasn't he? Highest fucking echelons, thanks partly to my reference. He owes me big time, and you too... I mean you've taken him under your *wing*, as it were...' Doug screwed up his nose and dead-eyed him, to make sure Logan understood his disgust and distain for the relationship between him and his protégé, Travis.

'Well, maybe... But don't forget he's Quinn's godson.'

'Travis is?' Blackthorn blew a bit of smoke sideways and eyed Logan skeptically.

'Yeah, didn't you know that? That's the real reason he got the internship at the NGV. Friggin' director's his godfather – whatever the hell that really means.' Logan scoffed. 'Nepotism from on high. Nothing to do with your bloody reference.'

'Fuck me.' Blackthorn scratched his chin and took a large swig from his pot. 'Well it still makes him the ideal connection. I mean Quinn'll have him on a pretty long leash, and as long as *you've* got his dick in your hand.... Bloody perfect insider, I say.'

Tate cautioned his drinking buddy with a crinkled brow, and looked about the bar, as if satisfying himself that it really was crowded and noisy enough to cover their conversation. 'Well, we'll see... Meanwhile, I need the pissoir.' He pushed his chair back and looked around.

'Over there.' Blackthorn nodded toward the stairwell, then drained his beer and stood up, gathering up the empties from the table. 'You want another one?'

'No, I'm good.' Logan's beer from the last round was still two thirds full.

*

Coming back from the toilets, Logan caught Blackthorn leering at a young female journalist sitting up at the bar in a short skirt and sleeveless camisole. Doug was a regional art lecturer, head of the department. More letch than lecturer, Travis had told him. The kid had studied under him briefly, and said he was well known for molesting his young female art students. *You degenerate old bastard*, Logan thought as he took his seat and tried a sip from his almost flat beer. He was just about done drinking beer with Doug in this dive, but there was one other thing he wanted to ask him.

'Hey, teaching down south, you'd know this guy, this painter, who's set up shop at Mietta's in the city, wouldn't you? What's his name, Hardman, or something...?'

'What? No... I mean yeah, I know the name. Taught him a few years ago. Showed a bit of promise I thought, but then he disappeared. Thought he was down the coast having a nervous breakdown or something. Why... What's going on?'

'He's here in the city. Just round the corner.' Tate gestured with his thumb. 'Got a nice big studio right above Mietta's fancy new French restaurant. His own little artist's garret, like he thinks he's on the friggin' Left Bank or something.'

What? Really? How does *that* fuckin' work?

'You're not keeping up with current events Dougy, I thought you'd be all over this. You know Mietta don't you? Bloody legend in culinary circles, Michelin-starred Euro chefs and everything. A year or so back she moved her restaurant from Brunswick into the city, into this big old building in Alfred Place, off Collins Street. Used to be the Naval Club or something. The restaurant's in what used to be a ballroom – French, fancy, all the bells and whistles – and up above it, there's an old squash court or something. He's got his studio up there and he uses the space for art exhibitions, for fuck's sake, if it pleases the Lord.'

'Jesus...' mused Blackthorn. 'Who do you have to kill to get a gig like that?'

'Hmm... Must've known someone I suppose. Anyway Mietta sees herself as this patron of the arts. Apart from the restaurant, the place has all these bars and salons, and they have these nice little soirees; poetry readings, opera singers, jazz, intimate little plays, all kinds of stuff. Ground zero for hip bloody art scene believers.'

Logan was clearly getting a bit worked up. Blackthorn said nothing, just looked at him like he thought he might be losing his grip.

'And get this – There's a little cocktail bar downstairs they're calling *The Artists Bar.*' Logan laced the name with irony. 'Attracting all the hoi polloi, it is. And this bloody student of yours is having *private* little exhibitions. It all starts down in this Artists Bar, with kiss-kiss and cocktails, then upstairs for a friggin' art show.'

'Jesus... How do you know all this?' Blackthorn feigned a bit of incredulity for the sake of his colleague, and for emphasis, clunked his near empty pot onto the table and reached for his cigarettes.

'An acquaintance went to one of his shows last week-end. Packed house, she said, and here's the thing; seems like he's selling shitloads of art. Selling it direct to the public, if you don't mind. Mietta's letting him use it as his bloody shop front and... God knows if she's even charging him any rent... I mean what the hell!?'

Blackthorn started laughing. He couldn't help it, seeing his red-faced friend, all wild-eyed and breathing heavily. Clearly Tate had got himself into quite a state over this situation. He took a big drag of his ciggy and laughed again. It turned into a cough, which he quelled by draining his beer.

'Ouch...' He winced, as if sympathising with an injury. 'Selling direct to the public is he? That's setting a bit of a precedent, isn't it?' He suppressed a grin. He didn't know what kind of shape Logan's gallery was in. Dealing art could be a tough business at the best of times, although, right now business was supposed to be booming. But he knew Tate had a reputation for being a ruthless and manipulative dealer, particularly with young aspiring artists looking for a leg up... Probably an understatement, considering that right now he had one of them forging Fred Williams paintings for him...Well, for *them.*

But he still couldn't help be amused, seeing how personally Tate was taking this. Some enterprising young painter cutting out the middle man – stiffing the dealers for their fifty percent – going into business for himself and saying *fuck you*, to the industry. Pretty funny actually, and a little bit cool. 'From what I remember, he always was a bit of a loose cannon,' Doug ventured provocatively. 'Fair bit of raw talent though... from what I remember.'

'Loose cannon? That's a bloody understatement. And fuck raw talent! Thinks he can waltz into town and take a shit on the whole friggin' program? He needs to be taught some manners, I reckon. Needs to be told where to line up patiently to pay his respects.'

Blackthorn looked around the crowded smoky bar, concerned that Tate's raised voice might have been attracting attention. He needn't have worried, the general ruckus going on in the press bar at six o'clock on a Friday, made Tate's little tantrum pale by comparison. The juke box was blaring Dire Straits, it was two-deep at the bar and the decibels from competing conversations had ramped up ruinously in the last few minutes.

Time to go.

'Maybe we should go and check out one of these shows.' Blackthorn was intrigued by what actually sounded like a pretty interesting set up, and he also reckoned it behooved him to find out what his former student was actually up to.

'Yeah, we should do, shouldn't we? Go and see what's what.' Tate had to yell just to be heard. He looked around uncertainly at the swelling ranks of ragged reporters and suddenly felt out of place and distinctly uncomfortable. 'Let's get out of here!'

FOUR

Monday, May 26th, 1986

Being a spokesperson is an exacting display of diplomatic artistry, isn't it?
Angry Buddha, 2001

The woman from the paper was about Daniel's age, maybe younger. Was that young for a reporter, or old? He had no way of knowing. She stood in front of the unfinished painting on the easel for a moment or two, staring at it silently. Then she took a step backwards and sighed, before moving back in, right up close and peering at the lumps and furrows of oil paint on the canvas, the brushstrokes, she supposed you would say.

All around her was a surplus of paint of every colour, in blobs and streaks and stains; on the easel, on surrounding benches and structures, on rags and brushes, on the artist's jeans. A multitude of paint brushes of all sizes stood in jars or strewn about on various surfaces. There were tubes of paint, paint-stained jars of ominous dark fluids, and an assortment of receptacles and small implements impossible to classify. It was a very messy space. But on the canvas itself, the layers and streaks of paint resolved themselves into a precisely executed abstraction of some kind of magical-looking seascape. Was it just *her* seeing the curious and mesmerising play of light on the water and the waves? It occurred to her that her reaction to the painting was quite a personal thing, and slow-acting. It took some time to sink in.

She looked around sheepishly at Daniel. He was standing off to the side, his mug of steaming tea on the workbench, calmly rolling a cigarette, as if he was alone in his studio, just taking a break. He was actually trying to remember what the reporter had said her name was. *In one ear and out the other.*

'You know I'm not sure I could even begin to explain this.' She looked almost apologetic. 'And the ones out there,' she gestured towards the paintings on the opposite wall of the large gallery. 'They're almost indescribable... Affecting ... in some quite *visceral* way. Really. But not what I expected at all. Hard to categorise...' Her eyes went up as if searching a journalistic thesaurus in her head. 'Original,' she declared finally with an emphatic nod.

Daniel smiled broadly not without a little empathy for the struggling wordsmith. 'Original is a good word.' He delicately put a flame to the thin rollie he'd constructed and extinguished the match with a flick of his wrist. 'You see, even in fashion – and for the sake of argument, let's say art *is* mainly fashion, at least here and now, in our lovely post-modernist world – even fashion evolves and occasionally throws up something entirely new.' He paused to take a drag of his cigarette and directed a stream of exhaled smoke up towards the high skylight above them. The reporter looked interested but unsure, waiting for him to continue.

'And normally, art follows fashion.' He took a sip of tea and gave the young woman a probing stare over the top of his mug, just to see if she was paying attention. 'But *new* art – completely original art – that's another thing altogether. A much rarer beast, and usually it only arises from a cultural shift; from evolution of the collective consciousness in response to a changing world.'

The journalist nodded carefully. She had her notepad out and was writing something in it. Daniel pointed to his comfy armchair, offering it to her. 'Are you sure you don't want a cup of tea?' He dragged up the spare, a paint-spattered kitchen chair from near the door and sat down, carefully placing an old jar lid on the floor next to him, for an ashtray.

'No thanks, I'm fine.' His guest settled herself into the armchair. 'What do you mean when you say, *evolution of the collective consciousness?*'

'Well, look at art in the early twentieth century. Everything was changing fast and amongst other things, photography had been invented – changing forever the way people viewed the world. It changed the way we related to images. Literally changed our *frame* of reference.'

'Ah-huh.' The young scribe nodded, pen working.

'Then along come painters like Braque and Picasso and others; they were all influenced by this new technology, and their experimentation gave birth to cubism – something entirely new.'

'Cubism?'

'Yeah. Original, not necessarily decorative, but multi-perspectival and ground-breaking. Great art... Birthed from a world reinventing itself, a world constantly trying to transform its karmic history and thrust itself into the future.'

'Okay...' His young interrogator looked slightly pained and a little confused

'Not that it's ever recognised as such at the time... New art, I mean. *Actual originality.*'

'No?'

'No. Because in real time culture, the shopkeepers of the art world are usually caught with their pants down and their heads up their arses. If they can't deconstruct it and explain it condescendingly to the quivering masses – you know, put their commercial or academic stamp of approval on it – then they usually dismiss it, reject it and more often than not, tar and feather the offending artist for good measure.'

'Jesus. That sounds a bit brutal. Who exactly are we talking about, these shopkeepers?'

'You know, art dealers, critics, gallery directors, academics... Art *teachers*: they're often the worst offenders. I mean what can a teacher really know about something as subjective as art, other than what they believe themselves, or have been told to teach by the head of department? You can't educate somebody into adult artistry in a pathologically hierarchical institution, as though preparing them for a career in banking, or bloody arms dealing.' Daniel leaned forward and butted out his cigarette and looked up at the reporter. She'd stopped writing and was looking at him a bit wide-eyed.

'Tenured heads of university art departments in particular, should be rounded up en masse and shot,' he concluded matter-of-factly. The woman's eyes widened even more, and Daniel gave her one of his disarming and contagious smiles. She responded in kind.

'I'm joking of course –about shooting them – better leave that bit out.' They both laughed. The reporter looked a bit relieved.

'The point is, ultimately, originality prevails because – let's not forget – life imitates art, not just the other way around. Eventually the experts and the jackals and the shopkeepers catch up, with the mass media tagging along not far behind. Fifty years down the track...Bingo, the National Gallery's forking out one point six million for Picasso's girlfriend boo-hooing in multifractal splendor, for all of Melbourne's great unwashed to marvel at.'

'You mean the Weeping Woman? Purchased last year, wasn't it?'

'Yeah. And don't get me wrong. Great piece of art. But when it was painted, when old mate Pablo was tapping into that nascent techno-cultural shift, back in *his* times, the critics of the day were hysterical. Said he was insane, degenerate. Said his art was a product of a diseased mind, an affront to art.'

'Right. But it's always been that way, wouldn't you say? Isn't it the case that Van Gogh never sold a single painting, during his lifetime?'

'True. And you're absolutely right. History repeats... Nauseatingly. Particularly art history.' Daniel leaned back on the kitchen chair and put his hands behind his head. He realised that the young woman was not only quite charming, but very intelligent. Her dark curly hair hinted at some kind of Mediterranean heritage and her beguiling dark eyes had some mischief about them. She looked at him quizzically, waiting for more. She was not only smart, but professional, letting him do the talking. *Nothing worse than an interviewer who talks too much.* And Daniel was happy to oblige.

He threw his hands up above his head theatrically and said: 'So there we are, back in the here and now. Nineteen eighty-six. Serious artists here, in Melbourne, artists everywhere, struggling to tap into the next seismic shift that'll influence our species into the new millennium, and trying to distill *that* into some kind of new art. Something, as you say, *original*.'

'Damn! I think I might actually be starting to get it.' she proclaimed. She was beginning to feel more comfortable in the presence of this artist, who at first, seemed a bit larger than life; dynamic and passionate, with a powerful physicality to match. But now she'd discerned a gentle and compassionate nature in him and a sense of humour which acted as a foil to his obvious anger at an indifferent world. He was a good head taller than her, maybe close to six feet, with a shock of curly hair, cut fashionably short at the sides – red, but not really – on a girl, you'd say strawberry blond.

Most of all she'd noticed his kind eyes and a handsome, soulful face. 'I mean it really does make sense, the way you've explained it. It feels like I've actually understood something about art, and to be honest, I never really got it before.' She paused and looked at him a little mischievously. '*You'd* be a good art teacher yourself.'

Daniel frowned fleetingly, until he assessed she was joking. 'Bite your tongue,' he said with playful affront, and they both laughed.

'That man isn't bothering you, is he?' Audrey's voice reached them from the doorway. Her faux-serious tone was betrayed by an enigmatic smile and a playful glint in her eye. 'Has he recruited you into Artists for Anarchy yet?'

'I've been trying.' Daniel's face brightened when he saw Audrey. 'Been telling her what's wrong with art education.'

'Jesus wept, really? I'm sorry you had to hear that Kate.' *Kate... That was her name!* Behind Audrey, a middle aged man draped with camera equipment was struggling over the high threshold into the squash court. 'Your photographer's arrived,' she said as she offered him a hand with his equipment.

*

The photographer took a multitude of shots, in quick succession. Daniel, next to one of the big, striking pieces; Daniel and Audrey sitting in the gallery; Daniel working in his studio. They even got some shots of him at his typewriter in the study nook, up on the mezzanine, with Audrey looking on encouragingly. Downstairs they faked drinks in the cocktail bar, Audrey on the stairs, the two of them exiting out into Alfred Place. A thorough photographic exposition of the whole Mietta's experience.

All the while, Audrey used her image management expertise to smooth over the rough edges of the reporter's encounter with

Daniel, giving her a more urbane and business-like account of their endeavors in the art world: A bit of educational and work history, including the artist-in-residence stints back at the old school, some chat about how they met and a few insights into their domestic day-to-day in their unusual abode. She made sure to hand over the photocopies listing exhibitions and significant acquisitions. Downstairs it was more about the atmospherics and they talked about the routines at Mietta's and the running of do-it-yourself art exhibitions. And of course a bit of barely disguised invective about the Melbourne art scene; its art dealers and galleries, 'providing a support structure for successful artists', whereas their operation at Mietta's being 'a good example of what could be achieved outside the system'. It was all about Daniel of course, which was as it should be. Not so much about Audrey's qualifications and experience, and her key role in helping to keep the whole show running.

In the end the piece would appear the following Saturday in the weekend supplement of the Sun News-pictorial, the city's widely read tabloid; a two page spread with four photos, and a major feature article about a plucky young artist reviving old-school artistic traditions at the 'Paris end' of inner city Melbourne and thumbing his nose at the art establishment's gate-keepers.

If they had started out flying under the radar at Mietta's – with Daniel's hidden gallery and invitation-only Private Views – the cat was well-and-truly out of the bag now.

Daniel had been nervous at first about courting the media and attracting too much attention. He was leery of the mainstream art world in general. From what he'd seen of it in his youthful career, it had the appearance of some kind of cultural microcosm, all polished and self-conscious on the outside, but beneath the veneer, a hotbed of jealousy, manipulation and outright malevolence. But in the end he couldn't fault Audrey's logic: *Any publicity is good publicity. After all, what was the worst that could happen?*

FIVE

Saturday, June 7th, 1986

Stand still in the bush and it dances around you like a spherical miracle.
Angry Buddha, 2001

'So, why is it called St Arnaud?' Penny shifted her gaze from the main street and glanced at Jack behind the wheel. He was going nice and slow, letting her take in the sights – such as they were – of the country town where he'd grown up. It seemed to Penny there were pubs on almost every corner, all retaining their original colonial architecture; some with elaborate wrought-iron latticework encompassing long and wide verandahs; one called 'The Royal', of course, and all with the big round electric beer sign attached at the corner, for night-time illumination.

'He was some French guy, back in the day.' He looked at her over his sunnies and smiled, then re-focused on the road. 'Big military hero in the magnificent glory days of French colonialism. Made a name for himself murdering thousands of Algerian indigenous people and taking their land.' He darted another glance at his girlfriend, this time with a dubious pout. 'So he fitted right in here, back when *our* colonials were killing the aboriginal people so they could steal *their* land and plant wheat and run sheep – replacing forty thousand years of traditional land management with a dumb-arse monoculture.'

'Hmm...' Penny swallowed hard, and said, 'Gosh...' Sounding way too much like her own mother, but she was stuck for words. She loved Jack's irreverence and his passion. It was one of the things she found most attractive. But he sometimes made her feel ill-informed, a bit pedestrian, he knew so much about things she'd never really learned.

'In the early days, there were heaps of French settlers around here, and they thought he was such a stand-up guy, they named the town after him...

'Check this out.' Jack slowed the old Corona down to a crawl, which didn't really matter; there was no other traffic on the main street. 'This is the town hall,' he noted matter-of-factly, nodding to the left. 'Although, you'd be excused for thinking it might be some far-flung colonial fortress built to repel the heathen hordes.'

As they went slowly past, Penny saw that it was indeed a huge and imposing complex, clearly out of place in a small country town, with its towering edifices and battlements, all red brick and sandstone with narrow arch windows, and built solid like a palace. There were several entrances and porticos set out around a paved mall with plane trees struggling for life along the front. At the main entrance was the ubiquitous World War One memorial – the kind you see in every country town – two stone diggers standing guard, left and right.

'I see what you mean. Looks like they're worried about reprisals.'

Jack laughed appreciatively at this. Penny was funny and clever and gorgeous. He liked all those things about her. She was a dancer and an arts student, so she knew stuff about history and about art too. He sped up a little as they passed the town hall. 'Yeah, they should be.' They both laughed and then fell silent for a time, as they continued on towards the end of the main street.

The road narrowed and the plane trees grew thicker and there were some poplars and jacarandas too, and even some native eucalypts here and there. They started to see small renovated colonial cottages lining the road, which told Penny they'd left the main street and entered the old residential part of town. The short tour of Jack's small home town was evidently coming to an end.

Past the outskirts of the town, they traversed a sparse, arid forest of eucalypts, spindly and widely spaced in the dry sandy soil. Penny noticed the thin trunks were mainly black, either by nature, or blackened by fire, she had no way of knowing. Jack told her it was a *token* nature reserve around the outskirts of the town. Before long, they left the trees and passed a parched golf course, before entering an area of flat farmland that seemed unusually dry, considering it was mid-winter.

Beyond the Bull Mallees lining the roadside, flat paddocks of dry grass stretched to the horizon, broken only by the odd windbreak of trees delineating some distant boundary. The sun flared white hot in a clear blue sky, marred only by a few rainless white clouds scattered above like shredded rags.

'This is Dja Dja Wurrung country,' Jack stated after a while, making a vague sweeping gesture with his left hand as they sped along. 'They're the traditional owners of all these lands – everything from the upper Loddon to the Avoca, as far east as Bendigo and all the way south to Daylesford. Part of the Kulin nation.' He paused and looked at Penny. His eyes were intense and yet softened by something – something distant, or sad. Penny held her breath and nodded slightly, willing him to continue.

'Their people revered *Bunjil*, the ancestral creator – the wedge-tailed eagle. And *Waa*; he had a bit to do with it all too; in Kulin mythology he was the trickster. He's depicted in the old rock paintings as the Crow.'

Jack paused and surveyed the ancient landscape beyond the narrow straight of bitumen, and Penny did the same, suddenly feeling out-of-place, encapsulated in their speeding bubble of steel and glass.

'This was their land. All of it. For sixty thousand years, maybe more, they practiced their own form of biodynamic farming; grew crops, managed the rivers and fish stocks and the land animals. It was all done sustainably. They cared for the soil, the water, each other – everything was kept in balance for millennia and they integrated and cooperated across all the clans of the Kulin. There was an economy, and a culture, that was all about caring for and respecting country and the ancient ways, in order that the land in turn would sustain the people.'

'That's amazing,' declared Penny. 'I've never heard anyone explain it quite like that before.' In her mind's eye she had an image, from school days, of some European explorer gazing proprietorially from a hilltop, and then another awful image of beaten and moribund aboriginal people with chains around their necks. Listening to Jack talk about the countryside in this new and exciting way, she had a sharp flash of intuitive understanding, and all at once she knew that everything she'd been taught in school about Australia's history was quite probably bullshit. She had wondered what it would be like coming up to meet Jack's parents and see where he grew up. But she hadn't expected this. Jack kept on surprising her, and as she hung on his words, she felt happier than ever that they were together.

'Yeah... Well, we killed them all. Killed them with smallpox and state-sanctioned massacres in order to steal their land. But even before we did that, we killed them by ruining their land, degrading their soils, trampling their delicate system of agriculture with sheep and cattle and stupid bloody annual crops like wheat and barley. In just a matter of decades, the arrogant and senseless colonials turned most of the country from productive farmland – land which had been delicately managed by traditional practices for thousands of years – to a dust bowl.'

'Jesus... How do you know all this?' Penny demanded.

Jack gave her that look again, over the top of his sunglasses. A hint of mischief in his eyes. 'My uncle,' he said simply.

'Your uncle?'

Jack smiled. 'Hmm, I guess I should have warned you... the frontier wars are still happening, right here in St Arnaud, out here on the old Curren spread.' He nodded vaguely in the direction of the low hills ahead of them.

'Uncle Bill – rest his soul – was a Dja Dja Wurrung man. He didn't even know – not until he was in his forties. My mum too...' He paused for effect, keeping his eyes front. 'But my dad... not so much. Euro-bloody-centric colonial apologist through and through, I'm afraid.'

'Bloody hell,' breathed Penny.

'Indeed.' Jack decelerated and the car slowed almost to a stop as they approached a small side road on the right. As he turned down the track he said: 'Here we are then, home sweet home; the ancestral estates of the esteemed Curren family, and also home to a few Dja Dja Wurrung stragglers they didn't quite manage to exterminate.'

Jack was laughing now, Penny was pretty much speechless.

'And mark my words, it's all still happening even now, in the year of our lord, nineteen eighty-six.'

All what was still happening? Penny's mind went straight to massacres. 'What do you mean? What's still happening?'

Jack tossed his head and smiled at her. 'Growing wheat and other silly bloody white man bullshit.'

*

His mother gave Penny the grand tour of the veggie garden. It was her way of welcoming her. *Welcome to country*. Here were the broad beans, here was the endive. Spinach and silver beet everywhere, and the raggedly old asparagus patch down the back with the fruit trees either side, pared back to bare sticks. She paid careful attention to the beds containing the indigenous species her bother had planted, before his untimely departure. She seemed a little uncertain about the Midyim berries and the Illawarra plums, although the river mint was doing well – perhaps getting a bit out of control, actually.

Jack saw a sadness in her, a kind of reticence as she showed Penny the indigenous plants; almost as if the two aspects of her vegetable garden were as tricky to reconcile as the different aspects of own ancestral heritage. And it *was* complicated – Jack knew that – especially for his mother, being almost fifty when she learned of her indigenous roots, courtesy of her radically inquisitive younger brother. Married as she was to a pragmatic and conservative wheat farmer of Scottish and German stock, it had come as something of shock, to everyone, in different ways.

Jack had embraced it of course. Partly because of the special rapport he'd always had with his maternal uncle, but mostly because the revelation had made something click deep inside him; something that affected the way he painted, or more correctly, made sense of the way he'd always painted. In a way it had set him free, and it validated the intuitive sense he'd long had; that he was connected in some intimate way to the landscapes he depicted.

Suddenly he understood why he saw the land differently than others did; why he detected in it a vibrancy and an essence that he reckoned imbued his art with a special magic, whether or not anyone else could see it. But it was there – captured in the oils – and he knew by the way some people reacted to his work, they saw it too.

His uncle's revelation seven years prior, had come not a moment too soon, at a time when he had all but unraveled in the depths of a debilitating melancholia, brought on by an artistic crisis of confidence; in turn brought on by a despicable creative assassin who had masqueraded as a teacher. He had stopped painting. He might as well have stopped breathing, and at times in the darkness, he thought he soon would.

His uncle had rescued him, there was no doubt about that. The knowledge he'd brought, and the connection it implied, came as a glimmer of light beckoning him upwards, out of the sea of despair he'd wallowed in for more than a year. When he finally surfaced, he knew he had changed in some fundamental way; and when he picked up his brushes, he was sure of it. His transformation manifested as an unshakable faith in his artistic eye, and a new confidence in his path. He had enrolled in arts school at RMIT that same month.

Never again would he be swayed by the manipulative bullshit of others; least of all a toxic old failed artist like his former year twelve art teacher. The pretentious prick had taken an instant dislike to him and had gas-lighted him into doubting his ability all year, before finally failing him.... *Failing him*! With the clarity of hindsight he'd realised his teacher was jealous and probably racist too, and had abused his power to assuage his own deep-seated emotional problems in a way that was inexcusable. Jack had been not at all surprised years later, when he learned the man had left teaching and reinvented himself as a politician... *a politician, for fuck's sake!* The funny part – if tragic irony could be a source of amusement, and Jack was in no doubt that it could – was that the pompous bag of swamp gas, (that's what his uncle had called him) was now the Minister for the Arts in the state government. *Classic!*

*

After the obligatory tour of the veggie garden, they made their way inside for tea and banana bread. In the lounge room, the winter sun streamed in through the large north-facing window over-looking the vegetable garden and beyond it, the grassy slope interspersed with fruit trees, the weeping cherry at the gate, and the path down to the dam.

It wasn't so much a farm dam, as a small lake. One of the few concessions his mother and uncle had squeezed from his father, was to reestablish the natural flow of the runnel that had been blocked off to create the original dam. By restoring the flow of fresh water and re-introducing aquatic plants, the old dead farm dam had been transformed into a living aquatic environment, with several species of rushes and a dozen other aquatic plants. There were water birds and even eels and fish in the revitalised dam. You could wander down to the little jetty and throw a line in at dusk and, more often than not, catch a decent-sized trout.

An enduring memory from his youth was watching from the verandah as a hovering eagle had swooped down and grabbed a trout from the dam. He'd nearly jumped out of skin at the ungodly boom that followed. His father – having observed the drama unfolding on the dam – had come out of the machinery shed with his old four ten shotgun, and taken aim at the departing eagle. Even though this had happened years before his uncle had revealed their indigenous connection, it had lodged in Jack's memory with a prescient symbolism of the ever-widening gulf that would develop between himself and his father – the poignantly sad imagery of it – the white farmer trying to shoot *Bunjil* for 'stealing' his fish.

The north-facing garden sloping into the valley, was his mother's oasis – her little acre of paradise – spared the rigors of the remaining four hundred and fifty acres, where efforts were constantly underway to extract another crop of wheat or barley from the tortured land, or rotate sheep across the least degraded pastures. She drew much contentment from managing her own small allotment, and growing much of their household produce. But Jack still worried about her. She had never been quite the same after the death of her brother. And even before that, he had long sympathised with her own thwarted ambitions. She never complained, even though Jack knew the limitations of farm life hemmed her in. But there was never even a hint of complaint or dissatisfaction, and that, Jack sometimes thought – her unyielding stoicism – was the most worrisome thing of all.

His mother poured the tea and handed them both a cup on a saucer. She put the sugar bowl and a platter of sliced up banana bread on the coffee table between them, and bade them help themselves. 'So, Penny tells me you've gotten a couple of lucrative commissions through this new dealer of yours.' His mother settled herself into her armchair, deftly balancing her cup and saucer and eyeing him over her glasses.

'Not sure you'd call them lucrative,' he said, giving Penny a sideways glance, 'but yeah, managed to pay the rent for a month or two.'

'And didn't you say this art dealer might give you a show, in his gallery? That would be wonderful. Your father and I could come down and stay a few nights in the city. Make a trip of it.'

Jack knew this would never happen. His mother would have to

come alone. Urgent farming priorities would crop up at the last minute to preclude his father. Besides which, the elusive show didn't appear to be getting any closer to happening, and he had good reason to regret getting involved with the dealer in question.

He changed the subject and asked about his sisters. One of them was studying medicine at Monash University, another Commerce-Law at Melbourne Uni, and the other, Tracy, had married a local farmer's son – a son who *did* want to stay on the land. All three of his younger sisters, it seemed, were solid performers, in contrast to the eldest son, whose trajectory into fine arts and a life of dissolute bohemianism had been a bitter pill for his father to swallow.

And the farming son-in-law – the one married to his eldest sister – had, to some extent, filled the void left by a son who had willfully shirked his family legacy. But sadly it hadn't done much to heal the rift. It was no accident that he'd brought Penny up to visit when he knew his father and the golden-haired son-in-law were away delivering hay to drought-affected farms away in the West.

He sat and half-listened, watching Penny nod and smile and prompt his mother with polite questions, as she gave her chapter and verse of the sisters' exploits. He realised he hadn't really prepared Penny very well for the encounter, and he hoped it wasn't too awkward for her. They'd only really been seeing each other for just over six months and the trip had been spur-of-the-moment. Of course he'd mentioned his strained relationship with his father and he'd told her about how his mother had been a talented and somewhat successful artist herself in her youth, before opting for the life of a farmer's wife... And how she had always tacitly supported Jack's choice of career, even if she'd never really felt free to encourage him too explicitly.

Maybe he should have told her what had happened to his uncle, just in case it came up, or a bit about his sisters, or about his own melt-down, post-high school, before resurrecting himself and going off to art school... Well, when the time was right.

When they finished their tea and the conversation ebbed, Jack said; 'I thought I might take Penny down and show her some of my old work, down in the shed.'

'That's a good idea sweetheart. Why don't you do that, while I'll get on with dinner? Did I mention Tracy's coming over? Seeing your father and Jim are away, she's very keen to meet Penny.'

*

Halfway down to the dam, on a small flat bit of ground, with view of the dam and the paddocks to the West, there was an old wood shed. He and his uncle had restored it – pretty much re-built it – so Jack could use it as a studio.

As Jack and Penny strolled down towards the little shack, the sun was getting quite low, reflecting golden tones off the mirror-calm dam and making the well-watered homestead grass pop vibrant green all around them.

Bucolic, thought Jack, remembering a word he'd learned in art history to describe rural scenes painted by some old master or another. Thus inspired, he bent down and picked a flower – just a tiny thing really, sprouting from a weed, but delicate and orange and quite beautiful – and gave it to Penny. She laughed and leaned over and kissed him on the cheek, with one leg kicked back, like she was some sort of sprite herself, over-awed by the Arcadian setting.

As they approached the building she noticed the old stone wall on the lee side had been rebuilt and a long, high, timber-framed window added. Above the window was a strip of new corrugated iron, and more new tin and fresh cut timber rafters, where the roof had been replaced too.

On the flat grassy space at the front were two old deck chairs and an upended milk crate for a table. Jack unlocked the padlock and dragged open the big old barn door, and extended his arm, inviting her to enter.

'So, this is where the magic happens?' Penny smiled and looked around the interior as they entered. It was more like a comfortable little cabin than what she expected for a studio. To the left was a worn out but comfy-looking couch, and against the opposite wall, two funky looking armchairs, with carved timber armrests and red cushions, like they'd come straight out of the fifties. Between the chairs was a coffee table with a big chunky glass ashtray, emerald green, and next to it, a painted plaster statuette of Quan Yin.

The back of the shed was open and free of clutter, with a big timber easel centered on the back wall, and wide workbenches along both sides. On the left-hand side, above and below the workbench, deep and narrow timber shelves, which Penny noticed were almost all occupied by canvas stretchers slid in flat. The bench tops were cleared and clean, like the place had been packed up. All there was, up the sofa end, was a kettle and a toaster and a bar fridge underneath.

'Yep this is it. The alchemist's grotto. Check it out...' Jack indicated the long high window, running half the length of the south wall. We put that in when we rebuilt the old shed – me and my uncle – gives a nice light to paint by. It's a decent size too, a bit cozy, but big enough to work in. Gets a bit cold in the winter...'

He saw Penny had gone over to the rack shelving and was peering into the gaps and touching the frame of one of the stretchers. 'Can I see?'

Jack started with what he was willing to show her from his school days. He accompanied the showing with a self-deprecating commentary about how clunky and technically deficient they were.

Penny said she liked the way he used colour, and she seemed to genuinely like a couple of the early works with a middle-eastern theme, he'd briefly explored. He moved on quickly, and brushed over anything from his last year at school because, no matter what he said or thought about any of those pieces, he would always have the words of his year twelve teacher ringing in his years.

He pulled out some of the local landscapes and the tree studies, and then moved on to the ones with figures in the landscapes. She didn't like the ones with the spookily abstract farmer-like figures appearing menacingly from the shadows. He appreciated her honest reaction. They were meant to be scary.

She genuinely connected with the paintings where the figures were more ethereal, like spirits of native animals or even ghosts of native humans, moving through the landscape, but enmeshed in it, in tune with it. He loved that she got that, and he loved that her reaction to each piece seemed natural and organic.

Penny was oblivious to him watching her quite closely, watching her reaction to his art. He hated when people felt like there was some prescribed way they should react to art, like there was an instruction manual, written by the cultural gatekeepers. All visual data is subjective, Jack reckoned, and people should just let their brain and its contemplative mind do the talking, and react however they *felt* like reacting, in the moment – free of the expectations of others.

This was exactly what Penny was doing, and seeing this, he felt a sudden lightness in his chest – almost like breathlessness – and a crazy romantic notion blinked on in his brain, that maybe, just maybe, this girl really was the one for him.

He showed her some of the new landscapes, the ones that were more abstract, but somehow truer to country; colours more vibrant, but at the same time more genuine and earthy; and with a scope that was somehow broader and more holistic. A timeless quality.

Some of these ones looked almost like his brush strokes were evoking songlines, even though they were painted long before his uncle had even told him about his connection to country.

Penny seemed to hold her breath as he showed her three of the best ones, one after the other. Then she let out a long sigh. 'These are amazing,' she breathed, slowly shaking her head. 'I love these ones.'

Jack gave her a demure and tentative smile as he slid the last painting back onto its shelf. He had a kind prescience feeling, quite powerful, that he knew what was coming, and the lightness he'd felt a moment ago left him abruptly, and he felt a twinge of disappointment. *Don't say it, Penny.*

'Your landscapes are breath-taking. They're so good. They remind me of someone, a famous artist...'

Uh-oh, here it comes.

'An Australian painter, he's known for his landscapes.'

'Is it Fred Williams?' Jack enquired delicately.

'Yes! Yes, that's it. Your landscapes are incredible! You paint just like Fred Williams. It's crazy.'

Jack's crooked smile made her blink and she recoiled slightly, with a frown of puzzlement suddenly invading her pretty face. At that moment a bell rang. Penny looked up, her frown deepening.

'That's mum. The dinner bell. She just loves ringing that dinner bell. Shall we?' Jack held a hand out, in the direction of the shed door and as Penny squeezed past him, he declared in a quite solicitous and yet instructive tone; 'Actually, I always thought it was Fred Williams who painted just like me.'

SIX

Tuesday, June 10th, 1986

You are an aggressive primitive mammal, of no importance to anyone.
Angry Buddha, 2001

Blackthorn ground his cigarette butt into the saucer of his spent tea cup, and stared deadpan at the Vice-Chancellor's secretary, sitting behind her desk on the other side of the large anteroom. He gave her a fake smile, then deliberately dropped his gaze to the 'no smoking' sign sitting prominently on the end of her desk and popped up his eyebrows. Then he winked.

She gave him a cold stare, devoid of all humanity and the psychic thunderheads she'd been rolling across the room at him, went up to force ten. *Uh-uh! No,* she'd shrilled tersely and wagged a finger, then pointed at the sign, when he'd reached for his cigarettes. He'd lit up anyway, exaggerating his actions and flicking the dead match into a nearby pot plant. *Silly bitch.* Treating him like a school boy, called to the principal's office. *I'm head of department, Mary Poppins, for fuck's sake.*

And he hated being kept waiting. *What was Bragge up to? Friggin' megalomaniac in sheep's clothing.* Trying to make some kind of point by making him sit and wait?

The console on her desk buzzed. Mary Poppins jabbed a button on the panel with such vehement gusto, she might have been calling in an air strike. 'The Vice-Chancellor will see you now.' Her icy tone sounded like she was passing a particularly unpleasant and well-deserved sentence.

Doug got to his feet wearily as the upholstered door to Bragge's office swished open and the Vice-Chancellor, in a neat dark grey suit – made trendy with a tastefully understated psychedelic tie – stood before him with an arm outstretched towards his inner sanctum. His neatly mustached face wore a convincingly bright smile, even whilst his clear eyes were penetrating and perhaps a little wary.

'Thanks for coming Douglas. Do come in.'

As Blackthorn shuffled past him, the head man sniffed and looked around the anteroom as if examining the clarity of the air. He glanced at his secretary and sniffed again with an interrogatory frown. The incendiary glare she gave him sent him hurrying back into his office.

'Take a seat, Doug, make yourself comfortable.' Fred Bragge closed the door quietly on his still-smoldering secretary.

Blackthorn took a moment, looking around the generous office, resenting that it seemed ten times bigger than his poky cubby hole in the aging Fine Arts building down town. Through the long tinted window running along one side of the office, he could see students funneling beneath them, into the quadrangle. Bragge's office formed a bridge over the concourse below, so the Vice – like some medieval lord – could watch over his subjects from his throne room.

He sat himself down in one of two black cantilevered conference chairs in front of Fred's giant redwood desk, which looked like the office must've been built around it. It was a desk that belonged in the oval office, not a regional Australian university. The Vice settled into his big swivel chair, tomes of vicarious academic accomplishment arrayed behind him in an extravagantly large bookcase. 'So...' he ventured ambivalently, but didn't continue, just looked appraisingly at his head of Fine Arts.

'So...' Blackthorn echoed and deadpanned him with thinly veiled hostility. *So what the fuck am I doing here? I've got lessons to prepare.* In reality he was much more concerned about being late for his luncheon appointment.

Bragge sighed heavily. 'Look Doug, I'm going to get right to the point.'

'I was hoping you would.' Heavy sarcasm laced with venom.

'We've had another complaint.' The Vice paused and stared over his glasses. Blackthorn did the same and raised a brow, inviting his boss to continue. When he didn't, Blackthorn shrugged and said: 'Well, you can't always please everybody.'

'Did you even know one of your students has dropped out? Left the university? ... Another one, I should say.'

Blackthorn gave him a long, sullen stare and screwed up his nose. 'They're young people, Fred. Young creative people. Artistic. Emotionally friable. Some of them can't hack it.'

'That sounds a lot like what you said last time, Doug. It's starting to sound like an excuse. Do you even know who I'm talking about, the young woman in question?'

'No.' Belligerence in his tone.

'Well, I've had her mother on the phone three times in the last two days. She says you bullied her daughter, emotionally abused her. She says you sexually *assaulted* her.' Bragge was calm in the face of the antagonism brewing in his subordinate. He stared at him frankly, steadily.

Blackthorn smoldered... Then the explosion.

'Oh fuck off, Fred! Are you serious? For God's sake... She's mad!

Had some sort of breakdown or something. Probably been smoking too much pot...'

'Oh, so you *do* know who I'm talking about now, do you?'

'Look, you listen to me, Fred...' Blackthorn leant forward, an aggressive posture, angry grimace on his face. But Bragge cut him off, abruptly springing to his feet and leaning over his desk with both palms firmly planted on it. His urbane and cheerful demeanor was vanished.

'No! No, you listen to me, if you don't mind, Doug. This isn't the first complaint by any means, as you well know. It's starting to look like a pattern – a very, very disturbing pattern – and one which won't be tolerated in this university. So I suggest it would be in your best interests to sit quietly and listen to what I have to say. And I'll thank you to keep your foul language to yourself in my office.'

The two men glared at each other. A stand-off. In that moment Bragge was struck by a powerful and upsetting pang of culpable regret. Blackthorn's credentials had looked so good on paper. There was a lesson in that. The CV of an applicant from the UK, listing all those prizes, exhibitions and teaching appointments, really gave no clue to the character of the man, and Bragge was beginning to realise this one was deeply flawed. Not only was he a dinosaur from a bygone era of misogyny and imperialist arrogance, but it appeared – from the mounting damage he was doing to the university – that he was a bully, a homophobe and quite likely a sexual predator. Not to mention, by all accounts, a bad alcoholic, with a toxic and abusive personality. *Mental note; no more senior appointments from abroad, not without a personal interview.*

Bragge allowed the tense pause to run its course before continuing: 'And this comes just weeks after that article in the university newspaper... The mother told me, *that* was why her daughter wanted to come forward and make a formal complaint, because of the damning piece in the Planet. *That* made her realise she wasn't the only one.'

'Oh come on! Surely you don't believe what you read in an undergraduate-bloody-newspaper. It was garbage. Besides, it didn't mention anyone by name, and whoever wrote it didn't even have the gumption to put their name to it. Rubbish and anonymous rubbish at that!'

Bragge sat back down and gave his charge a cold stare. 'And yet everyone who read it – and unfortunately everyone did read it – everyone knew exactly what faculty it was describing and who was being implicated.'

'Bullshit! And defamatory bullshit by the way – if they'd had the guts to name me or to claim authorship.'

'Defamation. The last refuge of the scoundrel, isn't that what they say?'

'Have you finished Fred? Because I've just about had enough of your bloody character assassination.'

Blackthorn began to get up, but Bragge stopped him by leaning forward and snapping at him in a calm, but powerfully assertive tone. 'No! You sit! I'm not finished, not by a long shot. So no, perhaps no one would've or should've taken any notice of a provocative piece like that in a student newspaper; if not for the fact that it seemed to match, and make sense of, so many recent and troubling events. I mean it was only a year ago that the other complaint was made. Alarmingly similar story. You denied it of course. Same excuse, wasn't it? The young girl's unstable. Having a nervous breakdown. Couldn't cope with the stress of study...' Bragge was glaring at his aberrant art head, imagining his stare was a javelin, pinning him to his chair.

'And she did have a nervous breakdown, didn't she? *After* she left the university, *after* whatever did or didn't happen to her down in that art department of yours. And six months later she killed herself. You do know that, don't you Doug? A young, talented twenty year old woman, put into *our* care to be educated and nurtured. She suicided! Did you even know that?'

Blackthorn was silent. He shifted in his seat and glared at the Vice with undisguised malice; a manner about him like a dog who'd been kicked and was looking for a weak spot to attack.

'And it's not just these two terrible incidents. There's been rumours and talk for a long time. Questions. Troubling questions about what is actually going on down there. Like the boy whose earring was torn from his ear. An accident, you claimed. But he said to me, he *told* me – when I was finally able to get him to open up, which was difficult because I could see he was scared – he told me that *you* did it. *Stop being gay.* That's what he told me you said.'

'Questions? Rumours? For Christ's sake! Bloody innuendo is all. I don't have to listen to this bullshit.' Blackthorn rose up from his chair and shoved himself forward against Bragge's desk, as if the desk was naught but a frustrating barrier, preventing him from getting at the Vice-Chancellor. He pointed a finger close to Bragge's face and said: 'Slander is what this is. People need to be a lot more careful what they're saying about a tenured department head, and I'd say that includes you, Sonny-Jim.' His Scottish brogue had thickened notably with his anger and he glared fiercely at his adversary.

Bragge sat stone still, returning his stare with contemptuous indifference. A disconcertingly comical notion sprang into his mind, that Blackthorn in his riled state, with his bushy eyebrows and beard, resembled an angry Tolkien dwarf. But then he thought of his students, and how intimidating it might be to face a toxic and abusive authority figure like Blackthorn, and all sense of comedy abruptly evaporated.

Blackthorn was clearly peeved that his accuser was unfazed by his aggressive body language. He was used to people cowering from his rage, and it always gave him a warm glow of contempt for those weaklings who lacked the backbone to stand up to him. Like the kid with the earring. He remembered him alright; *the bloody little faggot; camping it up in his art room like he thought it was the friggin' Mardi Gras.* He hated Bragge for even mentioning him, *let alone those other bitches.* He realised now that he had always hated Bragge; *nothing but a trumped up Jew-boy, with his holier-than-thou attitude and bullshit everyman accessibility.*

Bragge just waited him out, staring past Blackthorn and his trembling finger, looking toward his office door. He waited with unruffled calm until Blackthorn's posturing became awkward. Then he dismissed him. 'You can go now Doug. You'll be receiving a written warning. You'll be getting two actually; one of them retrospectively addressing the similar complaint from last year, from the student who has since, tragically died.'

Blackthorn visibly paled and his eyes narrowed. He let out a puff of air, almost a grunt and turned around and shoved his chair out of the way, knocking it over. As he reached the door and flung it open he turned back to Bragge, to speak, but the Vice-Chancellor beat him to it.

'There won't be any further warnings,' he pronounced simply.

'Fuck you Bragge. If you don't watch yerself, you and this piss-ant little university of yours'll find yerselves in court.'

With that Blackthorn swept into the reception area, past the smugly smiling receptionist – back-handing her 'no smoking' sign off her desk as he went – and out he went, slamming the door so hard it was a wonder its etched glass panel stayed intact.

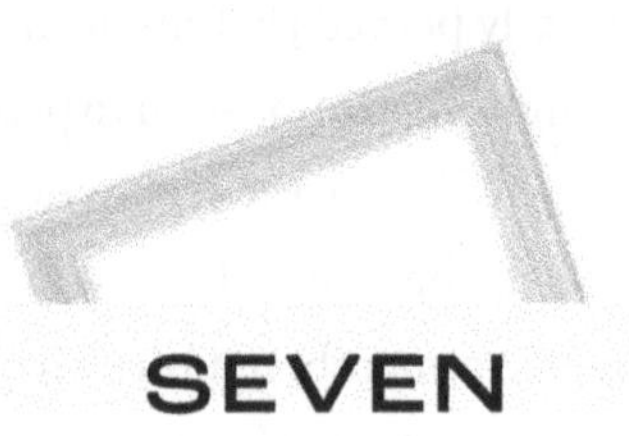

SEVEN

Thursday, June 19th, 1986

We were washed about in whirlpools by cruel, dizzy and unconscious gods.
Angry Buddha, 2001

Daniel tensed and launched himself like a hurdler, across a narrow surging channel and onto a large domed basalt slab, encrusted with tiny mussels and limpets. His free arm flailed about as he regained his balance and he watched the thick ribbons of kelp dragged away from the base of the rock as the wave receded. He swung his surfboard from under his right arm and got a good grip with both hands on the rails, while he focused his attention on the next wave, the last of the set.

Timing was the thing.

As the white-water surged towards him, he bent slightly at the knees, focusing all his energy into his thighs, then sprang up and over the wave, just before it swamped the rock. As he hit the rushing water behind the wave he paddled hard, digging his hands into the freezing water to take advantage of the surge, wary that the receding water could leave him stranded on the flat rocks and kelp surrounding the point. Many a surfboard fin had been lost getting in or out of the water at Crocodile Rock.

A flat rocky point, with nothing resembling a crocodile in sight, this much-favoured surf spot was 'down the coast', on a pristine stretch of the Great Ocean Road, where it descended from the high cliffs and hugged the beach, winding along just above the waves. Over the years – ever since he was a kid – he'd had his best and scariest surfs at *The Rock.*

He paddled hard for the channel, feeling the rip taking him now. The water was icy cold – mid-winter cold – and his hands and feet felt the shock of it, even as a few chilly trickles found the leaky seams in his old wetsuit. But he was oblivious to the cold, fully adrenalised as he stroked for the channel, and then turned to paddle up into the line-up.

Crocodile Rock was always like this; a massive adrenalin buzz from the moment you hit the water. There was something about the way those winter swells – made strong and straight by their long march across the Southern Ocean – hit the end of the point and rose up out of the deep water. On big days the scale of the rising swells – not just the height of them, but the thickness too – was awe-inspiring, and sometimes terrifying. You actually *needed* to be pumped on adrenalin to surf The Rock.

On smaller days it could be a fun wave, and a much shorter wave, breaking from the top of the point, only down as far as the shallow slabby section. But on big days, it would all link up. The bigger it got, the better it broke, with the *slab* becoming a super-hollow tube section down the line; stand-up barrels, for any who could hold their nerve.

Today was mid-size, nothing too challenging. But at any size, this place had a unique atmosphere, which seemed to evoke the thrills of bigger days. Memories of those classic gut-wrenching eight-foot surfs were somehow etched into the deepest recesses of his reptilian brain.

And there was no surf break quite like Crocodile Rock for its sneaky rogue sets. You'd be sitting there scanning for a set of waves and suddenly the horizon would just seem to jump a bit, almost Imperceptibly; and you'd know... *Just start paddling!* Heart in your mouth and guts trembling, you'd come up, over a smaller swell and then you'd see it, lining up way off the end of the point. An implacable emerald wall, devouring the flat water ahead of it, with its relentless rising, and threatening to pulverise the unwary in its maw. And most alarming of all, you'd know there was an even bigger one – or three – coming right behind it.

Daniel paddled parallel to the rocky shore now, gauging his position by the handful of surfers he could see congregated in the line-up off the end of the point. He strained against the resistance of the water, feeling the strength in muscles toned by twenty years of surfing. Nothing felt as good as surfing; the raw energy of it, the healthy exertion, and the bracing refreshment of the wild, cold, southern ocean. And it wasn't just riding the waves, it was the whole experience. Nothing got you as close to nature – so in touch with the primal essences of life – as immersing yourself in the vastness of the sea.

As a set approached the line-up, he adjusted his course, squarer to the shore, to get over it as it wrapped down the point towards him. The water was a misty turquoise colour, with a tinge of dirty green – a look unique to Crocodiles – which was due, he supposed, to the dark basalt bottom and the kelp. He paddled up and over the first wave, feeling the familiar roller-coaster thrill of rising and cresting. He veered back towards the line-up and paddled a bit harder, peering up the line towards the second wave of the set, a bit bigger than the last.

Someone was taking off, stroking hard and then springing to his feet just as the front of his board was sucked into the steepening wave. He dropped down the face and cranked a bottom turn, leaning over, his head close the face of the wave as he looked down the line. Then he slew off the bottom, carving a plume of spray and aimed his board at the vertical part of the wave a few meters down the line, jamming the tail in under the lip and pivoting hard, before free falling under the breaking lip.

Daniel recognised his brother's surfing style and let out a hoot – *Yeeeew-hooo!* His bother carved off the bottom again and went for another re-entry. But this time, his rail dug into the sucking steep face of the wave, and as Daniel paddled up and over the shoulder, the last thing he saw was his brother and his board get caught in the pitching lip and *rag-dolled* over the falls.

As the rain of offshore spray eased, he stopped paddling and turned around to view the boiling white water, behind the wave. His brother's board speared up out of the turbulence and a few moments later his brother's head popped up and he shook the water from his eyes. He slid his board under him and paddled hard towards Daniel, who was sitting astride his board, laughing and smiling appreciatively at the spectacle provided for him.

'Fuck me, did you see that? I got absolutely flogged.'

'Nice take-off though.'

'Yeah, Hey, it's going off, isn't it? Bloody pumping!'

'Fuck yeah,' Daniel agreed and they turned and paddled together towards the line-up, their shared excitement doubling the anticipation of a banging good surf.

*

As they approached the line-up, Daniel counted just three other surfers. *Pumping Crocodiles and only five surfers on it...* It could only happen on a weekday in mid-winter. Two of them he knew well;

Mark was a friend of his brother's and the other one, Will – a young GP and anti-nuclear activist – was an old and close friend of the family. They'd all surfed together since they were kids.

The other surfer, sitting way deep, about ten meters up on the inside, looked familiar and it took Daniel just a moment to recognise it was Travis McRae, a fellow painter, several years his junior; brought up in Torquay and trying to make a name for himself as an artist in Melbourne, just as Daniel was. They'd surfed the same breaks for years, and been to the same art school, although not at the same time. For a long time he'd been uncertain whether Travis admired him as some kind of mentor, or whether he was jealous, or perhaps – he sometimes mused – Travis reckoned he was a better painter than Daniel. One thing for sure, he was one of the hottest surfers on the coast and as far as Daniel was concerned, an arrogant son-of-a-bitch in both those constituencies; art and surf.

The four friends exchanged greetings and enthused excitedly about the surf, and the classic winter morning, and the lack of a crowd.

'That's that guy, Travis, isn't it? Will said to Daniel, as he paddled past, nodding in the direction of the lone surfer further up the break.

'Yep. That's him.'

Fuck, he's way deep. He can't make any waves from up there can he?'

'Hmm...' Daniel pursed his lips in consternation and he raised a brow. 'You might be surprised.'

Pretty soon they settled into a routine hard-wired into every surfer who sits in a line-up; the watchful waiting, lined up like ducks astride their boards, rising and falling with the motion of the sea, necks craned to scan the ocean for any sign of the next set of waves. The order they lined up in was defined by an unwritten law; first was Will and Mark, then Daniel, because he'd only just paddled out, then his brother, because he'd caught the last wave.

A set loomed. They all paddled. Mark took the first one, turning into it early and taking a high line, zooming past, as the rest of them scratched for the bigger wave behind it. Will looked like he was struggling to reach the next, much larger wave. Caught too far inside. But then, at the last minute he wrenched his board around, and even as the wave started sucking him up the face, he took two massive strokes and launched himself in a classic kamikaze-Will take-off. Daniel watched him free-fall, the thundering eye of the barrel exploding behind him, before losing sight of him, as he himself surged up the face of the giant and paddled over it. He had a moment of weightlessness as he crested the wave and in that brief instant he wondered whether Will could possibly have made the drop.

He hit the flat water behind, and it knocked an *'oomph'* out of him as the spray rained down. The sight of the third wave sent a jolt of extra adrenalin through him, and he suddenly seemed to be paddling with almost superhuman strength. It was one of those Crocodiles rogues – lining up way out, and deep inside. If he paddled hard enough, he might still position himself perfectly to take off. But Travis was paddling for it too. Paddling furiously. He was on the wrong side of the peak, but also further out to sea. He could take it early and still make it through the section... *Fuck!* He had priority. Daniel had to let him go. *Probably be the wave of the day!*

All he could do was let his paddling momentum take him up the face of the huge beast, like an elevator, giving him a prime view of Travis stroking into the huge wave in perfect position... But for being almost impossibly deep. Travis skimmed down the face, executed a beautiful, fluid bottom turn and then casually stalled, positioning himself seamlessly inside the magnificent monster as the lip pitched right over him. He was completely barreled, trimming expertly along the sucking face in perfect sync with the tubing wave. *He was going to make it!* Just before Daniel crested the wave's shoulder he had time to see Travis's face light up in a manic grin. Even in that brief instant, Daniel detected a hint of malice in the grin, an arrogance in his lurid eyes, which said, *Yeah, I'll take any damn wave I want.*

*

Daniel scanned the ocean, and then turned and peered down the line, seeing the three surfers strung out in a row, paddling steadily back towards the line-up. It would take them a while, they'd all had good long rides. He looked out to sea again, willing another set to come before they returned. It was his turn now, and nothing was going to stop him getting the next wave.

He sensed, more than saw, a set coming, and paddled a few strokes towards the inside. His brother was right beside him, also hunting his next wave. Daniel gave him a cautionary 'big brother' look, just in case he'd forgotten who was next in line. The first wave of the set was too small and they both let it go. The next one was bigger, lining up for Daniel. He paddled hard.

'Go, go, go!' His brother yelled encouragingly. Daniel knew there was an ulterior motive; his brother was hoping for a bigger wave behind it. But Daniel was committed, paddling towards the steepening face. He felt the wave lifting him, as if it would go right under him, but then, the reassuring surge as the powerful cresting top of the wave grabbed his board. He sprang up and trimmed, without going to the bottom, because he could see the wave standing up ahead of him. He stayed high to gather speed and flew down the line, letting his board gather momentum as he did shallow carving turns – top to bottom – just enough to maximise his speed.

He saw the shoulder fattening up ahead of him and threw his arms up and leaned back, transferring some weight onto his back foot to execute a massive snap on the diminishing shoulder. He allowed himself a fleeting, wry smile, when he saw the huge plume of spray he created swamp Travis, as he paddled out. Pivoting back around, he lined up the next section – the slab section. He pumped to regain some speed, just as the wall in front of him went vertical and then threw up and out. He shortened his last turn and stalled, feeling his board hover and then slot gratifyingly into perfect position.

He crouched low and trailed his right hand in the face of the wave, to steady his line, peering ahead as the lip arched over him. In that instant, he was inside the wave, crouched in an almost fetal position, completely enclosed in the fluid embrace of the wave's vortex. His field of vision filled with spiraling green around the bright ellipse of the outside world. *Barrel vision*, they liked to call it; that fleeting moment of dynamic inception, when the tangible world vanishes and time stands still. The surfer's Holy Grail.

*

Up in the carpark the four of them caroused like teenagers, high on the endorphins of a remarkable surf. This was one they'd all remember and talk about for some time to come. As they strained to pull off wetsuits and toweled themselves against the winter chill, they regaled each other with details of their exploits, sometimes complimenting, sometimes boasting; laughing about their wipeouts and marveling at the barrels they'd seen each other get.

There was something unique about the post-surf euphoria

– thawing out, and rugging up in the winter sunshine after a memorable surf – the camaraderie it generated. Daniel sometimes thought it was one of the best things about surfing. They all knew Daniel was the alpha dog of their surfing pack, arguably the best surfer amongst them, and the oldest. He was certainly the most enthusiastic. He pretty much always got the most waves, and also told the best stories about his surfing deeds; but no one begrudged him, because his enthusiasm and animation was infectious and really quite endearing.

As he sat on the tailgate of Will's car, struggling to insert a numb foot into his sock, Daniel posed the question: 'Did you see that first wave Travis got out there? Kind of snaked me for it... I thought he was gonna be way too deep.'

'That was fucked up – he got so barreled,' enthused Will.

'I thought there was no way he was gonna make that,' claimed Mark.

'But he bloody did,' said Daniel's brother, 'Got the wave of the day, the fucking little prick.'

They all laughed at this. Then for a moment the talk turned to how many waves they'd each lost to Travis, who, they had to admit, was an exceptional surfer, but was also the most annoying hassler of all time.

As their chatter subsided, Travis's head popped up out of the bushes just behind them, coming up the steps from the beach track.

'Shh, here he comes,' said Mark in a fake conspiratorial voice, just for a laugh... because everyone could hear.

Travis gave him a wry grin and looked the rest of them over coolly. 'Morning ladies... How'd we all go?'

'It was fucking insane, wasn't it?' This rhetorically from Mark, followed quickly by expletives and affirmations all around, with everyone agreeing to the exceptional nature of the morning's surf.

'You got some good ones,' Will said to Travis as he made for his car, parked next to theirs, and retrieved his keys from on top of the wheel.

'Yeah, we all did. Fuckin' banging, wasn't it? I saw you get one real good barrel out there, Dan.'

Daniel deferred with a chuckle and the conversation paused while Travis wrestled off his wetsuit and the rest of them started packing their stuff into their cars. As Daniel was loading his board into the back of Will's station-wagon, Travis came over in just his jeans and barefoot, towel in hand, drying his long hair. 'How's it going up in the big smoke Dan? I hear you've got a pretty good gig up there... Mietta's, or something?'

'Yeah, Audrey's a friend of Mietta's sister, and they're letting us use a space above the restaurant as a studio. It's pretty cool. Right in the city.' Daniel didn't want to elaborate too much.

'How is Audrey? She still making trouble?'

'What do you mean, trouble?' Daniel gave him a questioning frown.

'Well, I ran into one of your old mates the other day, and he wasn't a happy chap.' Travis had moved up close to Daniel, just close enough to invade his personal space a bit. He was one of those people who could seem antagonistic, even just discussing the weather... He could be asking after your mum, and still seem like he wanted to fight you.

'You mean Blackthorn?' Daniel knew exactly who he was talking about. He and Travis had both been taught painting by him back at art school. 'No particular mate of mine. And hey, art school's just a distant memory for me now. Anyway, why would you want to have anything to do with that fucking Svengali?'

'Pheeew! ... Svengali? What the hell's a Svengali? Just saying... I only crossed paths with him at a *social* event. A card game actually.

Purely incidental. I was just an observer. But he did have a bit to say about that anonymous article in the uni paper. Caused quite the shit-storm apparently. And he did seem pretty certain who'd written it.'

Travis was difficult to deal with in and out of the water. A complicated and probably a damaged individual. He seemed to have a finger in every pie, and he was pretty sure he had more than just a passing acquaintance with Blackthorn. Daniel knew Travis pretty well, but not really by choice. He was one of those people you get to know not so much through affinity, but more as a result of proximity. All those years surfing the same breaks around the Surf Coast, and then both of them ending up artists and attending the same art school. Travis started there the year after he left, but still... Their paths crossed quite a bit.

And Daniel knew things about Travis that he probably shouldn't. For example, he knew he was secretly gay, something that seemed at odds with his aggressive, blokey surf persona, but was quite obvious when he was moving around the art scene in Melbourne. Weirdly, their surfing solidarity, and the conservatism of mainstream society, made him feel like he was obliged to keep this in confidence.

And then there was his relationship with Blackthorn. *What was that all about?* After all Blackthorn was known to be rampantly homophobic, as well as being manipulative and abusive. But in the years after art school, Travis seemed to have stayed in contact with him, almost as if he was one of the acolytes Blackthorn loved to manipulate and use. None of it gelled with Travis's assertive personality, down here, in his natural coastal habitat.

Maybe it had to do with Travis's developing art career, about which Daniel knew little. But Daniel had heard a rumour that Travis had buddied up with a dealer in Melbourne, and some said it was more than just business. If Daniel knew anything about the art world he assumed it was a mutually manipulative liaison, in which both were in it for what they could get.

One thing Daniel didn't know about Travis, was that he was actually well-connected in the art world through his mother. He would have been very surprised to know that Travis was actually the godson of the director of Melbourne's NGV.

Daniel didn't want to take the bait regarding Audrey's journalistic exploits, so he asked Travis about the card game. 'What sort of card game?'

'Well, it was a pretty bloody interesting one, actually Dan.' Travis raised his eyebrows in mock wonder, and then looked around at the other surfers, who were gathered around listening, inviting them into the conspiracy.

'Poker it was. Texas Hold'em, of course. Blackthorn was there. He was being his usual charming self, and did his dough, like a dickhead. He really can be an obnoxious arse-hole, can't he? Anyway, the interesting thing was that someone – who shall remain nameless – couldn't cover his losses and paid the winner with a painting.'

'What sort of painting?'

'Well you might ask, Dan. It was a fucking Fred Williams – or so they would have us believe.'

'What do you mean?'

'Bogus as a three-dollar note, I reckon. It was a bloody fake, mate.'

*

Back at the house, Daniel poured three cups of tea from the stove-top ceramic teapot; one for himself, one for Audrey and one for

Will, who'd decided to come in for a quick cuppa and to say hello to Audrey.

While the tea brewed, they'd been telling Audrey about the surf, and then their encounter with Travis in the carpark. She was intrigued. She'd only met him a couple of times, but Daniel had told her some pretty interesting things about him. Her impression was that he was a bit of a fuckwit.

They all sat down at the old kitchen table and Will stirred a teaspoon of clumpy brown sugar into his tea. 'What is this stuff?' He asked curiously digging the spoon back into a mound the colour and texture of dirt, housed in a wonky hand-made pottery bowl.

'Unprocessed brown sugar,' explained Daniel. 'Better for you.'

'Right,' Will scoffed. 'Like wholemeal sugar, is it?' He chuckled at his own joke and looked around the kitchen. The old Anglesea house was to him, very much like an ancestral home, just as it was to Daniel. It had belonged to Daniel's grandparents; but as a child, Will had spent countless Christmas holidays staying there with Daniel's family. During his teenage years, when he and Daniel's younger brother had started surfing – trying to emulate Daniel and his older surfing mates – they'd come down on weekends and school holidays, obsessively chasing waves, hitch-hiking along the coast, and, occasionally being allowed to tag along with Daniel and his mates, some of whom even had cars.

Daniel's grandparents were long gone, but still – up until his recent move to Melbourne – Daniel had been living in the big old four-bedroom Anglesea house, with his studio in the back shed. So it had remained the staging post for surfing, and a place to crash on weekends. The layout and the smell of the place, the unchanged furnishings and even the kitchen utensils, together with the sprawling bush garden were all redolent of memories of growing up.

Teaspoons tinkled and they started sipping their tea. 'So what did he say?' Audrey demanded.

'He asked if you were still causing trouble,' Will blurted out with a mischievous grin.

Audrey responded with a look of mock surprise and innocence. *Who me?* Then she laughed out loud and looked at Daniel, who nodded and smiled.

'What did he mean by that, anyway?' Will persisted.

Daniel and Audrey gave each other a *do-you-want-to-explain-or-shall-I* look.

They took it in turns telling recent events, in which Audrey had felt compelled to write, anonymously, a piece for the university newspaper after she had dropped out of her Arts course. It was a largely allegorical piece which none-the-less implied pretty clearly that the head of the art department was a sexual predator who was known for molesting and abusing his young female students. Audrey said after deciding to leave, she didn't feel she could remain silent about it.

'I mean I was out of there, so I had nothing to lose. I was safe. You see, he'd demand sexual favours, in exchange for not failing the course. Or if he'd been touching you up, or some other form of abuse – you know not just physical but emotional too – you knew you'd better bloody well stay silent, or you'd fail the course. An absolute piece of shit... A real nasty piece of work.'

'A Svengi... a Sfango... What did you call him Dan?'

Daniel smiled at Will and shook his head. 'A Svengali.'

'Exactly,' said Audrey.

'What the fuck's a Svengali?'

'Someone who exercises a controlling or mesmerising influence over another – usually for a sinister purpose.' This sounded like a dictionary definition to Will. He was increasingly impressed with

Audrey. She was highly educated, an intellectual, but also kind and funny and mischievous.

'And so Travis is mates with this guy? They're friends?' Will sounded doubtful.

'I don't know. Travis was taught by him, same as me… It's complicated, they're both pretty strange individuals…'

'Put it this way,' interjected Audrey, showing none of Daniel's equivocation. 'If Blackthorn's the Wicked Witch of the West, then Travis is one of his flying monkeys.'

They all laughed hard at this for a few moments and then fell silent, sipping their cups of tea.

'He said something else pretty interesting though…' Daniel began.

'Hmm?'

'Said he reckons someone's been faking Fred Williams paintings.'

'What?'

'Yeah. Reckons he was at a card game and someone used a painting to pay off a poker debt. Travis said he reckoned it was a fake.'

'Really?'

Daniel shrugged.

'He's full of shit.'

'Yeah, probably.'

EIGHT

Friday, July 11th, 1986

One need not be a revolutionary in an age of awakening, just become the holder of your beliefs, and the author of your life.
Angry Buddha, 2001

Jack wiped the spatula he'd been using with a piece of rag and gathered up the two brushes he had going and plonked them into a jar of turpentine.

There... Louder this time, definitely someone knocking on the front door. He gave both hands a good wipe on his work jeans – already well and truly encrusted with paint – and headed down the gloomy hallway. The front entry was bright by contrast, with a ruby, golden light spilling through the leadlight window next to the door.

The afternoon sun hitting the porch showed him a broken silhouette, someone standing on the other side of the glass. He wondered why Penny hadn't heard the knocking, but then he remembered she had a dance assessment at Uni that afternoon. She wouldn't be home until late.

He worked the latch of the old box lock and hoisted the door, so it wouldn't scrape the sill as it opened, and there he was – Logan Tate – standing on his porch, wearing his habitual shit-eating grin. His dapper suit and tie told Jack he'd come straight from the gallery. He had a paper bag in his left hand which he held out to Jack and said: 'Hey man. I got you some cheese and quince paste from the market.'

Reluctantly Jack reached for the package – an image, unbidden and fleeting, of Tate as mischievous child leaving paper bags of dog shit on people's doorsteps; the bag set alight, so the occupant opens the door and instinctively stomps out the flames.

Tate brushed past him without being asked, taking a few steps down the hallway before turning to watch Jack close the front door. 'So, how's it all going? Just on my way home; thought I'd drop in for a look, see if you need anything.'

Need anything.... A fair-dinkum art dealer would be a start. Jack pointed down the hallway. 'I'm just finishing up down the back. You want a cup of tea or something?'

'Nah, all good.' Logan continued down the hall towards the studio. Jack peeled off into the kitchen and threw the package of cheese on the bench. He watched Logan enter the bright living area, which had been re-purposed as a studio. Tate stopped in the middle of the room, to examine the unfinished painting resting on Jack's easel.

Jack watched him from the kitchen. A long-past renovation had turned the back of the house into an open-plan kitchen, dining and living area, with sliding doors and big windows bringing light in from the small tree-lined backyard. Except for the early morning sun, it created a good light to paint.

The rental was a pretty typical two-bedroom Fitzroy terrace. His studio had taken over most of the living area, and Penny had colonised the dining area, with her desk, standing lamp, reading chair and big tallboy bookcase creating a cozy study space. They usually ate their meals at the kitchen bench, or sometimes in front of the TV in the second bedroom, which had a comfy op-shop sofa bed, so it could double as a spare room.

Jack opened the old Kelvinator and found two cold stubbies in there. 'How about a beer then?'

'Yeah, I'd go a beer, thanks.'

Logan took the long-neck from him without taking his eyes off the half-done painting. 'Cheers.' He had his head tilted at an odd angle and was leaning in towards the canvas. 'This is looking good, real good.'

'Yeah, well I'm not so sure. It's got a long way to go yet.'

'No, no, it's great!' Logan stepped forward to look more closely at the top part of the canvas, where Jack had started on the sky. 'I like what you're doing here, this scumbling... That's working. And I like the curved horizon too. Gives it a kind of *viewed from space*, feel.'

Jack took a long swig on his beer whilst surveying the unfinished canvas. 'Yeah, well I don't know. I'm just not sure this one's going to fly.' He knew saying this would bait Logan, but he couldn't resist. There was something about his so-called art dealer that just didn't sit right. Nine months since he'd first gotten him to look at his work, and still his career didn't seem to have gathered any forward momentum.

At first, it was all; *gee-whiz, holy fuck, stop the presses... A new star is born*. Logan wasn't the first to make the comparison with the great Fred Williams, but he was certainly the most enthusiastic, and his advice had been unequivocal; keep doing what you're doing, the more *Williamsesque* the better. And, *no, no, it's not imitative, not if the technique is your own, and you have the landscaper's eye, and the gift of execution, like you do.* We all have our influencers, he'd said, and nothing occurs in a vacuum. Art history was a progression, he said, and maybe you're going to take it to the next level. Maybe you're the *next* Fred Williams... Looking back now, with the wisdom of just a little bit of hindsight, he could almost feel the nice warm, cozy feeling of Logan Tate pissing in his pocket.

Logan took the bait. 'What are you talking about? This is looking really bloody good, maybe one of your best...'

'I dunno man, I was thinking maybe I need a change. Maybe do some still life, paint some bowls of fruit or something for a while. Getting kinda bored with landscapes...'

'What? Are you nuts?' Logan spun around with a look of dismay and alarm distorting his normally calm features. One look at Jack told him he was taking the piss. 'Don't be bloody silly. Look, I've said it before and I'll say it again; you need to *trust* me. I know what I'm doing.'

'Really? Seems like you've got me hidden away, doing these Fred Williams look-alikes for your clients, who presumably can't afford a real one... Where is that getting me exactly?'

'It's getting you well paid, for a start.' Logan's tone was suddenly snappy and malicious. Jack was instantly annoyed.

'Well paid?... Well-fucking-paid?' Jack matched Logan's shitty tone and raised the ante a few notches. Something about the whole deal with Tate had disturbed him deeply from the start. He'd repressed it, because Tate was an established dealer – potentially his ticket to the mainstream. But now it was bubbling precipitously to the surface, beyond his control. 'Well paid compared to what? The cleaner, the gardener... Your friggin' house maid?'

Tate looked at him like he was a teacher disappointed with his pupil, and let out a sigh. But Jack wasn't finished.

'Maybe I'm in the wrong profession. I should've studied law, or stock-broking, or maybe learned how to kick an inflated pig's skin around in a paddock, because Christ knows in this brain-dead, half-arsed, post-colonial shit show, there is bugger all support or appreciation for anyone silly enough to try to actually create something – anyone actually trying to contribute something to the artistic growth of this fucking cultural abattoir we're living in'

'Alright, I know...' Logan had heard it before... Maybe not quite so spirited as today. He put his beer on the workbench and held up both palms, trying for a placating gesture, but it didn't work; the dam wall was well and truly breached.

'No support, no funding, no god-damned recognition of the artist's role in enriching the fabric of society – any decent society that is – one that's not obsessed with football and gambling and friggin' cars... *and* with oppressing women and minorities *and* totally fucking it's indigenous population.'

Jack gave his dealer a piercingly interrogative look. Tate took an involuntary half step backwards. 'Do you know how many arts grants I've applied for? Pissy little grants, mind you; barely enough to pay the power bill, so you don't freeze your tits off in your fucking studio...' With this last rhetorical question Jack kind of ran out of steam and breathe too. He drank down what was left of his beer and tossed it into his studio rubbish bin.

'Anyway, fuck it.' He seemed suddenly deflated. 'If my dealer, says, just keep pumping out those pretty little derivative landscapes, then I suppose I don't have much choice... But I *would* like to know what the plan is... If there is one.'

'The plan's the same, like it's always been. We have to seed the market.' Tate's tone was calm, advisory, a touch condescending. 'Each of those landscapes is being carefully placed, with regular buyers, collectors, even other small-time dealers... And some regional galleries. When the time is right, you'll be presented to the art world. But only when the time is right, because it's all about the timing. Then it'll be a bloody triumph.'

Logan held up his stubby like he was making a toast. 'An Aussie landscape virtuoso for the new millennium, with a fresh, progressive eye *and* an indigenous lineage; which puts us way ahead in the cultural stakes. *Better* than Williams! We're gonna make history son, but you've got to trust me. I've been doing this for a while, and I know what I'm doing.'

Jack had his arms folded across his midriff. His bottom lip was giving his top lip a real good massage and he peered at Logan with a skeptical eye. *The new fucking millennium? That's fifteen years away.* 'So, any clues about just when the *debutants ball* is going to take place? When am I getting my own exhibition?'

'Soon. Very soon.'

'Soon...' Jack failed to hide his cynicism. 'And until then, just stay cool, and keep doing what you say.'

'Right.'

Jack felt a rebellious and righteous passion brewing, so far deep down inside himself, it felt like magma looking for a vent. It was a feeling of hurt, and there was pride too. Whatever it was, churning inside him, it felt deeply aggrieved. He knew it had to do with his anger at a crass world that failed to value creativity; it was also about personal insult and injury from family and teachers; but increasingly, he recognised that the affront he felt was broader and deeper; something generational and old. It was about dispossession. He knew he should keep a lid on it. He knew Tate wasn't to blame, not really. In fact he was ostensibly his ticket to acceptance. But a deeper instinct told him that Tate was all wrong; he wasn't sure why, but he'd be fooling himself if he thought he could contain his exasperation.

'Nah, fuck that. I'm thinking I might turn this one into a portrait of Penny.' Abruptly Jack pushed past Tate and grabbed a spatula and dipped in some brown paint. 'I think I'm moving into figures in landscape.' Before Tate even realised what he was doing, Jack had slathered two big semi-circles of dark paint in the middle of the canvas and then started on the hair with two more broad wavy strokes.

'What are you doing?' Tate recoiled in horror. 'You fucking idiot...'

'What's going on?' Both men turned with a start, to see Penny standing in the opening of the hallway, a puzzled frown on her face, as she looked from one to the other, wondering what the fuss was about.

'Hi Penny.' Logan gave her an uncertain smile.

Penny switched her focus to Jack, a questioning crinkle on her brow.

'Logan was just leaving,' he stated matter-of-factly. 'He did bring us some cheese though.' Jack's tone was scornful and short, and he looked at Logan like he was an over-sized rat.

*

Jack retreated from the impossibly crowded dance floor and headed to the bar, for one last beer before closing. He was knackered. He could barely keep up with Penny; she'd dance all night if she could. He took a swig from the pot he'd procured, just to quench his thirst, then found a spot on the corner of the bar where he could lean and watch the band.

The Painters and Dockers were doing an encore number. The drunken Rainbow Hotel patrons had screamed and screamed for it until finally lead singer, Paulie Stewart had relented, telling the crowd: 'Just one more... But only because you're the best audience in the whole fucking universe!'

Die Yuppie Die was reaching its frenetic climax with Stewart tearing around the small pub stage as if it was ten times its actual size, strutting and pouting like a punk hybrid of Jagger and Peter

Garrett. The thumping bass and drums rocked the foundations of the old pub and the lead guitar vied with the tenor sax and trumpet, creating an irresistible rhythmic rock/punk beat that had the entire room jumping.

The milling crowd on the dance floor bounced in time with the bass line as a row of lights above the stage pulsated rhythmically, painting the revelers in alternating primary colours. He watched Penny swaying and grooving, her long hair swirling around as she wagged her head, in unwitting parody of her idol Paulie, whose own long auburn hair swirled about him as he punched out the lyrics and swayed and jagged in time with the beat. Jack knew Penny was a little bit in love with the charismatic lead singer of the Dockers, but he didn't mind. He was pretty impressed with the Dockers himself, they were one of his favorite bands, because they were punk and they were fun and they would take the piss out of anything and everything. Irreverent. And he liked that they didn't take themselves too seriously. He'd once met the lead singer Paulie, and he'd found him to be kind and empathic and seemingly free of the ego and pretense you'd expect from a rock singer.

The encore number finished with Stewart, now shirtless, writhing around on the stage as if under attack from his mic stand, giving his all to the last of the lyrics *and* his signature theatrics. As the last guitar cord reverberated through the covered beer garden, and the horn and sax pumped out the staccato finishing notes, the crowd erupted in beery rapture. They gave an enthusiastic, if distracted ovation to the band as they filed off the stage, waving their hands above their heads in acknowledgement of their loyal pub audience. The silence was quickly filled with confused and rowdy unrest, as the pub patrons in various stages of intoxication gradually realised it was over, the bar was closed, and it was time to go home.

*

Jack and Penny paused outside, as the exiting patrons flowed around them. The pub was only a couple of minutes-walk from their George Street terrace, but they quickly decided to go via Brunswick Street and hit the kebab shop on the way home.

As they stepped onto the footpath someone bumped right into Jack, hard enough to push him into Penny. The bloke ricocheted off him and grunted a half apology and raised one hand, without looking back and then staggered on towards the corner.

'Excuse us,' said Penny ironically. As they watched him disappear around the corner; a lanky character with his long blond hair tied up in a ponytail. Jack thought he looked a bit familiar, but then again, so did a lot of people in this, their local neighborhood.

They wandered slowly towards Brunswick Street, enjoying the freshness of the chill night air, after the heat of the crowded pub. Penny was on a high, like always after a solid night's dancing. She was humming one of the Docker's songs and half dancing, half walking along the footpath, every now and then doing a little swoop or a twirl.

Their talk naturally turned to what they been discussing before their night out, and Penny continued the conversation where they'd left off a few hours earlier: 'Is Logan really so bad though? I'm thinking any dealer is better than no dealer, right?'

'You're absolutely right.' Jack let Penny take his hand and joined her momentarily, awkwardly, in her footpath boogie. 'But yes, he really is that bad, at least I think he is... I dunno, he just seems dodgy. Doesn't he seem dodgy to you?'

'I can't tell. He's the only art dealer I've ever met. Seems okay. Maybe a bit slick and smarmy. But least he's not a sleaze. I don't get any creepy vibe from him or anything.'

'I think he's gay.'

'Oh, cool. So anyway what's the problem with these commissions he's been getting for you? It's good to sell some paintings, isn't it? ... Get them out there, get some recognition.'

'Well, yeah, but if he likes them so much and he's able to sell them to his clients, why won't he give me an exhibition? I mean, it's been nine months.'

'Hmm... Well, maybe you just need to be patient a while longer.'

'I've been pretty bloody patient...' They were coming up on the kebab shop, and Penny hooked her arm through his and gave him a squeeze.

'I know you have.'

'There's something else too,' Jack confided as they stopped at the door of the take-away. He looked at her sheepishly and lowered his voice. 'He told me not to bother signing them.'

'Really? That's a bit strange, isn't it?' Penny pushed open the swing door of the shop and they caught a delightful whiff of roasting lamb and garlic.

Two other people were already at the counter and some others sitting waiting for their orders. As they approached the counter, Jack realised one of them was the guy who'd bumped into them outside the pub. He looked at Jack and squinted, his head wobbling a bit, as if he was trying to focus. He looked quite drunk. Then he gave kind of a contorted smile and tipped his head sideways. 'Don't I know you?' His tone was questioning but somehow quarrelsome at the same time.'

'I dunno... Maybe.' Jack shrugged. He had a growing sense he did know this person, but from where? Pony-tail guy shifted his attention back to the kebab vendor. The middle-aged Greek-looking man took his order, and then Penny and Jack's too.

'Wait a minute,' he protested in voice too loud for the shop, and stood up straighter – half a head taller than Jack – pointing an unsteady finger at Jack's nose. 'You're that landscape guy, aren't you?'

Jack was bewildered, but after a moment, the penny dropped. He'd seen this guy at Tate's gallery! Jack himself had only been there three times in the whole nine months, but this guy was there, on at least one of those occasions. Logan hadn't introduced him, but pony-tail guy had been there for sure, in the background. Maybe he was an employee, maybe another artist; a family member perhaps.

'You've been doing those landscapes for Logan, haven't you? The ones that look like bloody Fred Williams-es.' He slurred a bit at the end, and his finger, which was still pointed at Jack, sagged.

Jack was speechless. He had no answer for this guy, this drunk in a kebab shop, who was looking at him weirdly, like he wanted to fight him. Jack wondered desperately who pony-tail guy actually was – this reproachful stranger, who seemed to know something about him – and what did he have to do with Logan Tate?

Travis McRae looked offended when Jack didn't respond and he frowned. Then, as if distracted by another thought, he started patting himself down, first his shirt pocket, then the hip pockets of his jeans. 'You got a cigarette?' He tilted his head back and poked his chin at Jack, giving his demand a hint of coercion.

'Mate, I don't smoke.' Jack felt his hackles rise, involuntarily reacting to the belligerent manner of the stranger.

'Fuck.' Travis licked his lips, and then switched his attention to Penny. 'How 'bout you, sweetheart?'

'No.' Penny took Jack's arm. He responded by sliding along the counter a bit, away from the tall drunk, and putting himself more squarely between Penny and the stranger.

'Huh...' Travis blew out a long puff of air as if exhaling smoke from a make-believe cigarette. Then he smiled a manic and unfriendly smile, exposing a missing tooth, one back from the right incisor. 'Well, anyway... Probably only get five or ten years,' he said thoughtfully scratching his cheek.'

'What?'

'For art forgery. You'll probably only get five to ten years.'

'What the fuck are you talking about?' Jack squared his shoulders and instinctively shifted his weight forward. Just as quickly, Penny pulled him back.

'Art forgery.' He said loudly and conclusively as if giving an answer in a quiz. A dubious smirk at Jack. 'I mean don't tell me you don't know what Logan's been doing with those lovely little landscapes you been painting.' Travis was having a bit of fun now. Now he had the guy's attention. *It really was the landscape guy – how 'bout that!*

'Been flogging them off left and right as the genuine article. Work of the great man himself.' Travis had seen several of this young bloke's landscapes – even though Logan had tried to keep them under wraps – and he'd certainly seen the one he'd used to pay his poker debt. It was no Fred Williams – it was one of this guy's look-alikes, he was sure of it. *Well, pretty sure anyway.* He didn't really know what had happened to any of the others, but it wasn't hard to join the dots. Logan was up to some nefarious shit. *Anyway, what the fuck?* He was feeling pretty loose... *Why not have some fun, with this little prick?* Besides, as far as Travis was concerned, the paintings were just a little bit too good... And that pissed him off.

'Who the fuck are you?' Jack squinted at the stranger and shook his head slowly. His tone conveyed skepticism and hostility in roughly equal measure.

'My friends call me Crayman,' said Travis. The shop owner plonked his neatly wrapped take-away in front of him. Travis grunted gratefully and grabbed his kebab and turned towards the door. 'Just sayin', he said, then he baulked strangely and did a weird little feint, and thrust his kebab towards Jack as if it was a sword... A little thrust and parry. 'Heads up fuckwad, that's all... Just sayin'.'

Penny and Jack turned in unison, tracking the crazy drunk guy as he veered towards the door. Penny's mouth was agape.

'You're fucking insane,' Jack advised him coolly.

Travis McRae turned back as he opened the door. 'Well at least I'm not a fucking art criminal!' Travis chuckled to himself as he staggered out onto the footpath thinking, in his drunken state, how funny it was that he'd randomly run into Tate's tame forger.

'*Not a fucking art criminal,*' he muttered again to himself. '*Ha!*'

Deeply amused he was, in his clouded state, because an art criminal was exactly what *he* was, now that those two reprobates, Tate and Blackthorn had brought Travis into the fold, to help them with their audacious little plan.

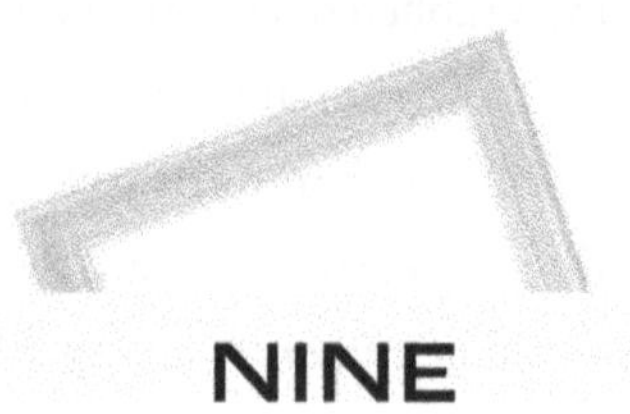

NINE

Wednesday, July 16th, 1986

Our expert has written plenty on the subject of art, about which he knows a bit. Alas our composite character knows little from an experiential point of view – he doesn't do it. He's far too busy in his field.
Angry Buddha, 2001

Ellery Quinn positioned himself proudly alongside the small green painting, framed in dark timber, and glanced side-ways at the swarthy, rotund man standing on the other side of the artwork. Then he squared himself up and puffed out his chest, head up, and faced the photographer, fixing the lens with his most inscrutable smile. If he could, he would've given his bow tie a spin, just for the amusement of Wendy and her entourage of international guests.

After the photos they gathered around the painting and Quinn gave them the informal lowdown; how he, as Director of the National Gallery of Victoria, had acquired Picasso's Weeping Woman. He skipped over the donors and the foundation altogether and didn't even mention the Cohens – who'd stumped up more than half the cash – because, as Wendy knew perfectly well, acquiring a priceless artwork was an art in itself, and a very delicate one at that. And, whether she cared to admit it or not, he was the grand master of it – and he knew she knew it.

'And so there she is – nothing short of a coup of Napoleonic proportions for the NGV.' He glanced at Wendy to gauge her reaction to his hyperbole. 'The most valuable acquisition ever by an Australian gallery, and one of Picasso's most striking pieces from the emotive and tragic Guernica series of works.'

Wendy de Flores, Chair of the NGV's Board of Directors, was giving him one of her looks, like she was trying to tell him not to over-egg it... *Like she would have a clue.* He returned her gaze and trumped it, signaling that he might just trot out his most clichéd quote... *Because what the hell* – this delegation was from the Middle East – *they wouldn't have heard it before.* 'It's the face that will haunt Melbourne for the next hundred years,' he enthused and gave Wendy an impudent grin, and a barely perceptible wink.

She rolled her eyes.

He wondered if she was thinking about the collateral damage along the way; like the Swiss dealer, Serge, who was still baying for his blood after *that* deal had turned sour. But Wendy of all people should understand, engineering a feat like this required a great deal of international diplomacy, and even some intrigue. People had agendas and people were looking to make out. It required nous, and sometimes there were casualties.

The important thing was; they had her now, and as he returned his attention to the painting, and continued his discourse for their guests, it was with a warm and satisfied proprietorial feeling. *The Weeping Woman was finally his.*

He gave them chapter and verse on the background of the painting, and its relationship to the famous Guernica in Madrid – painted by Picasso in 1937 in response to the bombing of a Basque village of the same name by the fascists. He explained that Picasso had tried to capture the horror of death and destruction reigning down on the village without warning.

'Around this time, he created several smaller works depicting the terrible grief of a woman, whose child was killed in the attack. His mistress and muse, Dora Maar was his model for the Weeping Woman, and this painting is, I believe one of the most emotive of that series, and therefore one of Picasso's most significant works.'

He went on to explain the use of colour; the ghastly acid greens and purples to convey dread, the handkerchief motif in contrasting white; the abstraction of the eyes, popping with fear and grief, distorted and up-ended to emit a torrent of tears, and the shadow on the wall behind her, evoking a sense of claustrophobic foreboding. He left out the stuff about La Llorona, the curse of the weeping woman, because he had no time for that superstitious claptrap.

He was still unclear as to just who these people were – this delegation from a national gallery in Dubai or somewhere – but Wendy had assured him it was important enough for her to book him for lunch and so, he supposed he would find out. *Hmm... no such thing as a free lunch*, he mused dubiously as Wendy rounded them up and issued instructions for rendezvousing at some French place in Collingwood.

*

The owner made a fuss over them briefly and then left them alone to peruse the hand-written menu. They were seated at a table for six, in its own little nook by a window, overlooking a leafy inner city street. The restaurant occupied an old-fashioned corner hotel, re-modelled to convey a kind of casual, Provençale chic. The chef was one of Melbourne's most highly rated practitioners of a new wave of Aussie-French fusion cuisine sweeping the city.

Wendy did the introductions and by the time he had all the

names straight Quinn had gathered that her guest was someone important in the government of the UAE; cultural advisor to the President, no less. Zaid al Benghazi was also high up in one of the region's biggest Universities, and a fellow art historian of considerable note. He had with him some kind of embassy minder, who doubled as an interpreter, when needed, and another guy who looked for all the world like a bodyguard.

So, it was a diplomatic visit. He suspected Ross Maynard, the Victorian Minister for the Arts had probably had a hand in it, and that made him wonder, with a vague sense of foreboding, what role Wendy wanted him to play.

They ordered drinks, mineral water all around, which prompted Ellery to ask Wendy about the sixth place setting. Were they expecting someone else? Her response was to raise her eyes and look past Quinn towards the door. A smile and a wave.

He turned to see who she was beckoning, the sixth lunch guest: *What the hell... Why him?* Quinn gave the late-comer an involuntary, vexed smile then tried, belatedly, to force some bonhomie into it.

'Good of you to come Douglas,' said Wendy and put out a hand. Douglas Blackthorn took her hand and leaned over and kissed it. *Jesus! Such a ponce.*

Blackthorn smiled at Ellery and gave his bushy brows an ironical jiggle.

'Douglas, you know Ellery. And of course Zaid, and this is Qadir from the embassy in Canberra. She didn't bother with the bodyguard.

Blackthorn put his hand to his chest, in the Arab way of greeting. Zaid, the cultural attaché, stood up and shook his hand warmly, like they were old mates. Blackthorn then gave a small bow to the other two men and put a familiar hand on Quinn's shoulder, as he took his place at the table.

Once the pleasantries were over and the waiter had been back for their food order, Wendy decided it was time to get down to business. 'So, Ellery,' she sighed slightly and straightened the knife and fork in front of her; 'our friends up at Spring Street have been approached by their federal counterparts, with a view to strengthening cultural ties between Australia and the UAE. As you may be aware, they're already Australia's biggest trading partner in the Middle-East, and Canberra's quite keen to extend cooperation into other areas; not only the arts, but sport, tourism, education – the whole gamut. So Zaid's here at the invitation of the federal Arts Minister and of course he's had a word in Ross's ear and asked that we show him a good time here in Melbourne. Quite the honour really, he's only visiting the National Gallery in Canberra, and us down here.

'He was quite keen to have a look at our new acquisition, of course...' She paused and smiled at Zaid.

'Picasso – such an interesting artist, don't you think, Mr Quinn?'

'Yes, yes, absolutely. One of the century's most important, at least, in our Western tradition. Please, call me Ellery, by the way.' Quinn smiled at the guest of honour and then at Blackthorn, before giving the chairwoman a subtle interrogatory squint.

'And of course Douglas is here because Southern University and Zaid's University in Dubai – they've already established an exchange program of sorts... Sister institutions I suppose you'd say?'

'Well early days yet,' said Blackthorn, 'but yes, we've already started a student exchange program... In its second year now.'

Zaid smiled. 'Indeed. Douglas has been very helpful. He is a true friend to the University of the United Arab Emirates.' He opened his hands, palms upwards in what looked like a gesture of gratitude.

With perfect timing, a waiter appeared and put Zaid's meal in front of him.

Once they all had their meals, they concentrated on eating, with a little small talk, mainly about the food. Quinn and Zaid both had the lamb loin, served with a rustic tomato and garlic gravy. It was very good, they agreed. Wendy and the minder had the fish, topped with some kind of cheese soufflé and Blackthorn had the duck, with which he was enjoying a nice Pinot, he'd acquired somehow. Everyone else was on mineral water.

The body guard, it seemed, was getting by on water and nothing else. He was starting to make Quinn a little nervous by his acute level of vigilance, which seemed enhanced by his having not much to do, whilst everyone else ate. He seemed comically out of place in a little neighborhood lunch spot in Collingwood.

After the meal, Wendy started up again: 'So, then, our bureaucratic brethren – the ones in Canberra, that is – they want someone to go to Dubai, a goodwill visit if you like. A bit of fact-finding, you know, see how it's done over there, and of course be treated to some reciprocal hospitality.' She looked directly at Ellery. He gave her his best Easter Island head imitation in return. *Sweet Jesus... Here it comes. So this is what lunch was about.*

'The federal minister had a word to Ross, and of course he thought you'd be the perfect man for the job. You know, show them how much we care; send them our celebrity gallery director, someone who really knows his stuff.'

Quinn tried to keep his face neutral as he glared at Wendy, meanwhile his eyes transmitted intense and incensed alarm.

'Of course Doug has been over there already to visit the university and set up the exchange program, but this would be different; more of a diplomatic mission, more a meeting of minds between the state-run national galleries.' Sensing Quinn was about to erupt, Wendy went on, quickly: 'And you've already got this trip to London next month, and you'll be stopping in Dubai anyway, and – apologies Ellery, for poking into your affairs – I did check with your secretary, and she said it would be a simple matter to change the flight to give you a layover of a day... or two.'

For the sake of decorum and with some considerable effort, he contained himself and took a deep breath. As he exhaled it was with a sinking sensation, as he realised it was a *fait accompli*. She had him cornered. 'I'll check my calendar and get back to you, Wendy.' This he said through gritted teeth, giving her a neutral, but quite disappointed look.

Sensing some tension, Zaid chose the moment for a bathroom break. He gave a questioning nod to his bodyguard and he, his bodyguard, and the embassy minder headed for the toilets.

Wendy fidgeted nervously with her dessert cutlery, but Quinn ignored her. Clearly she had duded him. He focused his attention on Blackthorn instead. He had plenty of reasons not to trust Blackthorn, and now he was wondering just how he was mixed up in this. He knew enough to know it wasn't because of an altruist interest in education and cultural exchange. There would have to be something in it for him. Blackthorn sipped the last of his Pinot, his eyes darting back and forth between Quinn and Wendy.

Yes, you are a shifty bastard.

Blackthorn was looking for a waiter, fingering his empty glass; obviously uncomfortable with Quinn's attention.

'So, you know this guy Doug? This cultural advisor to the Emir? Lecturer at the university?'

Blackthorn gave up his search for the drink waiter. He looked sheepishly at Quinn and then at Wendy, for support. He didn't reply, just gave a kind of half-shrug and twisted the corner of his mouth.

'And, he's the Assistant Director of their national gallery as well?' This question to Wendy.

She nodded.

'Anything else?'

No answer.

'Anything else Doug? ... Is he a *dealer* by any chance?'

Blackthorn leaned sideways a bit and turned the palms of both hands to the ceiling. 'Well, you know... It's the Middle East. Things are done differently over there.'

'Really? So, he runs the National Gallery, heads up the university, all chummy with the Emir and he's an art dealer to boot. Probably got a nice commercial gallery of his own in downtown Dubai. Nice little private collection too, I bet.' He switched his focus from Blackthorn to Wendy and back again, then slapped on an extra layer of sarcasm. 'Oh, this is just marvelous!'

'It's the President, not the Emir' Blackthorn corrected him. 'Actually Zaid's his cousin, and his gallery's in Abu Dahbi, not Dubai. It's like I said, there are cultural differences. They're all one big happy family. Lots of fingers in lots of different pies, all over the place. It's not a big deal. Don't worry, you'll have a ball.'

'Really?'

Blackthorn shrugged.

Quinn turned to Wendy and repeated the question with even thicker irony: '*Really*?

Wendy smiled wanly and pursed her lips.

'Oh, wait...Here they come.' He gave Wendy a sardonically spiteful on-and-off smile. 'Well I suppose I better pack my Fedora and sandals – Looks like I'm off to Dubai.' With that, the germ of an idea occurred to him, and Quinn wondered distractedly whether it might be possible to palm the Arabs off to his godson, Travis, as part of his internship at the gallery. *Give him some international experience... Something for his resume.*

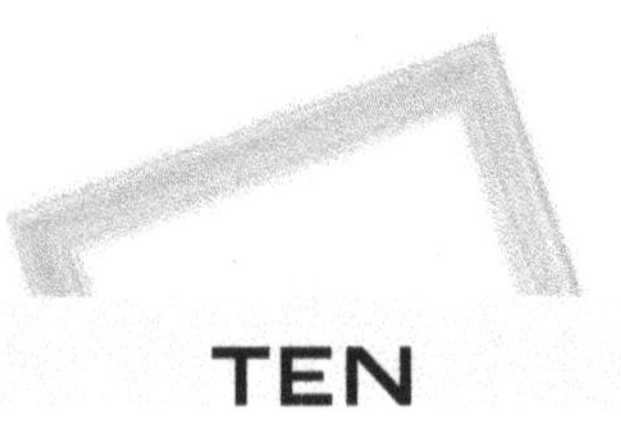

TEN

Friday, July 18th, 1986

They ... flounder about in the art sandpit, stepping on children and toys – killing our future visuality with thuggish bureaucracy.
Angry Buddha 2001

By eight o'clock the atmosphere in the Artist's Bar was getting frantic, even a bit manic. Excited anticipation and alcohol-fueled merriment was ramping up steadily, with the raucous dissonance of dozens of competing conversations. Daniel wondered briefly, if the Manhattans had been a good idea. It seemed the cocktail had become synonymous with his Private View exhibitions at Mietta's. A friend had even told Audrey they'd heard someone in their circle of art industry friends refer to Daniel and Audrey as *The Manhattans.*

If anyone had told him six months ago that one day soon he'd be stumping up for cocktails for sixty exhibition guests – all financed by the proceeds of selling his paintings – he would've pronounced them mad. But here they were, *Private View V* – the third to be held at Mietta's – and the bar was packed with willing punters and the usual assortment of the city's art-scene socialites and dilettantes.

James behind the bar gave him a nod and a smile as he passed. They were two-deep at the bar, but James looked cool and calm, his movements precise and unhurried. James once told him the secret to working a big crowd was to slow down: *When it feels like it's getting out of control, take a breath and take it down a notch. You gotta consciously slow it down; efficiency automatically goes up. It's like a meditation. If you panic, you're dead.*

Daniel moved on, resolutely working his way through the crowd, greeting and smiling; a quick chat here, a handshake there... *Thanks for coming...* He kept going, making for the side door. It was time to get upstairs, so Audrey could make the announcement and start shepherding them up to the gallery.

He spotted Audrey at the bottom of the staircase. She was surrounded. A middle aged woman with big hair and a kaftan had her attention – an administrator at the Arts Centre, he thought. *What was her name?* And a young couple, one of them a musician... He knew he should know that name. *Damn. Think!*

Audrey saw him come around the corner and gave him a strange look – *not just rescue me from this lot* – something else was wrong, an edge of panic in her quick glance.

'Hi. Great to see you. Thanks for coming.' He grabbed the musician's hand and gave it a pump and kissed the arts administrator on the cheek, but none of it jogged a name from his frazzled brain. 'Mind if I steal Audrey for a moment? We're about to start moving everyone upstairs for the show.'

The three of them drifted away, possibly a bit miffed. Daniel gestured at the stairs with a thumb, one foot already on the first step. 'We good to go?'

Audrey grabbed his hand and pulled him towards her, frowning; her eyes oddly intense.

'What's up?'

She put her lips close to his ear: 'I just saw Blackthorn. He's in the front bar, drinking with one of his mates.'

'Fuck! What the hell's he doing here?'

'I *know*. What the *fuck!?*' Audrey was clearly rattled. Her eyes transmitted a combination of anger and fear. She looked around uncertainly and then shook her head and shrugged, letting out an exaggerated sigh.

'Well, fuck him. Let's not worry about it now.' Daniel looked warily down the hallway towards the front entrance, as if searching for a target.

'Exactly.' Audrey straightened herself and looked up at him with a confident and aloof expression. 'On with the show. You get upstairs. I'll start rounding them up.'

*

He'd put the exhibition together almost like a retrospective; maybe because the paintings themselves had retrospective references all through them. Some were a progression of the Crayfish Point paintings; an incendiary red dawn and the black, bleak headland framing a primordial sea, calm as a mirror, a window to the boundless stars; and Crayfish Point by moonlight – the endless ocean rippling like quicksilver under its icy bright orb. And then there were the totems and figures invading the sacred seascapes from somewhere deep in the collective psyche – threatening, or so they might seem to some observers – hovering over the outlandish shore... Watching. Transforming.

Quietly he observed the reaction as people stepped over the threshold into the gallery, like they were being sucked through a portal in to a new dimension. He supposed they were in a way. It was one of the things Daniel loved about showing his art; watching for the effect. It made him wonder; did the shaman hunters of the deep past hold exhibition openings or salons in the caves of

Lascaux? At first, the expectant hush – almost reverent, then sometimes a muffled gasp, or a quick intake of breathe – every now-and-then a burst of excited chatter, and then repeat, as new customers stepped in and followed the circular path which was, strangely, always clockwise, never counter.

Daniel watched them discreetly.

He had time to, because they were distracted. In this moment they didn't seek out the artist for attention, they were consumed by the art. Only rarely did someone, in the initial throes of observing the work approach him. The display of creativity seemed to make some people nervous at first, and they shied away from the artist in a way that amused him and annoyed him in equal measure. Nonetheless he reckoned he had a sixth sense for spotting a viewer who was ready to buy. Even whilst he gave them space, he was alert to the signs that someone had made that fateful connection with a piece.

Observing the spectators, he saw that the intrusion of figures into the land and seascapes was having its effect. There was some disquiet. *Where had they come from?* The tortured Christ-like figure rising up from the ocean horizon was actually a *Billy* figure – transported forward in time from his early days lost in the Otways – painting the phantoms of the forest. The totems were enigmatic, timeless humanoid giants, flamboyant and spooky; and on the dawn-lit beach, a Saigon execution, referencing his long obsession with the horrors of war. The rest of the exhibition was composed of the remaining bushfire landscapes – some of the best ones, vibrant with colour and chaos – the dark apocalyptic skies above, making the trees and rocks below glow with a prescient vitality at the approaching inferno.

He found himself up on the mezzanine – helping Audrey and one of the bar staff organise more champagne – when he saw them at the doorway to the squash court. Blackthorn first, lurching in over the threshold, then swearing about it, because he'd spilled his drink. Even from above he could see his face, petulant and ruddy with alcohol, like he was spoiling for trouble, as was his wont. Another man came in behind him and for a moment Daniel was stumped, even though he knew the face, he couldn't quite place him.

Blackthorn surprised him by abruptly looking up at the mezzanine, and catching his eye. Daniel froze and then forced out a halting smile. Instinctively he looked to where Audrey and the waiter were going down the stairs with the champagne. Blackthorn's eyes followed his, to Audrey, and stayed there. He tracked her all the way down the stairs; then looked back up at Daniel, his close-set eyes small and piercing under the electric light. A menacing scowl told Daniel he was making the connection; Daniel, he knew from art school, years ago and they'd crossed paths since, and he sure as hell knew who Audrey was. But he was just now, putting it all together – *they were a couple.*

Audrey caught sight of the intruder near the bottom of the stairs and fluidly veered in the opposite direction, merging with the crowd, offering top-ups from her bottle of Fleur de Lys. She shot Daniel a *holy shit* glance between customers, and he swore under his breath and headed for the stairs himself. Blackthorn appearing at a crowded exhibition, made his gut clench – a paralysing, dread panic – like someone had rolled a grenade into a crowded cellar.

At the bottom of the stairs he could already hear Blackthorn's voice drowning out the collective chatter; the strong accent and bombastic tone drawing the crowd's attention in the small gallery. He surveyed the scene with a creeping sense of horror: Blackthorn was standing in front of the Crayfish Point aerial, a few paces back, giving himself room, whilst his companion looked on. A snap of sudden recognition and Daniel knew who the other man was: Logan Tate, big-time dealer; from Helicon – one of the city's leading galleries. *Fuck!*

'...And what *is* this? Something half-finished? Some sort of attempt at post-modern dog's breakfastism, if you'd ask me.' Blackthorn was drunk. He gestured towards the painting with his glass and some liquid slopped onto the floor. He turned to his friend. 'Wait – don't tell me Logan – you've been modelling for the artist, haven't you?' He leaned forward and waved his hand in a circular arc in front of the painting, imitating brushstrokes. 'Here... Right here, I think the *artist* has perfectly captured your flaccid dick after a night on the piss... Fucking brilliant!'

Blackthorn roared with laughter and staggered backwards a couple of steps and then poked his head forward and squinted. He tipped his head sideways and back again, then turned to Tate, a look of mild consternation on his face: 'You know Logan, I think they might have hung it upside-down.' He guffawed again and slurped his drink.

Tate gave him a humorless sneer, embarrassed by his companion's uncouth behaviour, and surmising that Blackthorn must've been drinking well before they'd arrived at Mietta's. He said nothing, but looked past Blackthorn as the artist approached them.

Daniel put himself squarely between Blackthorn and his painting. 'This event is invitation only, and *you*, weren't on the list.' Daniel had on his boots with the heels; it gave him a good head-and-a-half on Blackthorn and he realised in that instant, that his old teacher was actually quite short, and stouter than he remembered. He leaned in and looked down at the interloper in a deliberate attempt to intimidate. It occurred to him that Blackthorn, for all his barrel-chested bombast and posturing, might actually have a touch of small-man syndrome, and maybe that was partly to blame for his psychopathy.

Blackthorn swayed back and forth, and a little side-to-side. His mouth formed a grimace, amongst the foliage of his bushy beard. 'Awh-shit, Logan, I think he wants to see your credentials.' His beady black eyes slide away from Daniel, trying to maintain focus. 'Tried to teach this young punk how to paint, y'know. Tried to. But I don't remember saying he could stick his fingers down his nappy and smear it all over the bloody canvas.'

'Get the *fuck* out!' Daniel leaned right into Blackthorn's face, his voice low and vehement, hoping no one else would hear. 'Get out, or I'll throw you out myself.'

'Think you're bloody clever don't you, you fucking upstart!' Blackthorn seemed suddenly sober, focused. He glared at Daniel with a kind of hateful fury, made all the more worrying because of his drunken state. 'You and that lying bitch girlfriend of yours? How long do you think you're going to last, once I've finished with you, huh?' His lip trembled and he subdued it by chewing on it. His eyes narrowed into a squint and he jutted his chin menacingly. 'You've got no idea who you're dealing with, do you?'

'I know exactly who we're dealing with... A fucking predator.' Daniel dead-eyed him with the coldest of stares. 'A molester. Not only that but a failed painter whose tried to reinvent himself as a teacher and can't even do *that* right, because he can't keep his dick in his pants. You're a fucking disgrace!'

Blackthorn snorted, as if the abuse hadn't fazed him at all, and raised his glass to drain it. But Daniel – on an instinctive and crazy whim – snatched it out of his hand; wanting to rattle him with some kind of physical intimidation, a show of force, or at least of reflexes. He looked at the glass in his hand and couldn't believe he'd succeeded, without breaking it.

Blackthorn rocked back, uncertainly, looking at his own empty hand. Daniel switched his attention to Tate. 'I suggest you get your toxic mate the hell out of my exhibition.' He wagged his head in the direction of the door and stared at the dealer with what he hoped was the mien of someone on the edge, just barely holding back their rage.

Tate grabbed Blackthorn by the elbow, saying 'come on' and moved toward the entry, where Audrey's drinks waiter was directing traffic; getting new arrivals to turn right, away from the altercation. This had disrupted the usual clockwise motion of the crowd and everyone had stopped. Most were now looking at the confrontation instead of at the art.

Blackthorn had let himself be shepherded by Tate towards the door, but then, he wrenched his arm free and turned to face Daniel, then looked pointedly around the squash court until his eyes alighted on Audrey. She glared back at him, a stare fit to turn a lesser sinner to a pillar of salt.

Seeing this, Daniel raised his arm and pointed at the exit. 'Out!' He commanded. He didn't care who heard, everyone was watching now anyway.

Blackthorn paused at the door as if uncertain of how to negotiate the threshold then looked back at him: 'You'll get yours, y' bloody piss-ant pretender... You and that slanderous tart of yours. You mark my words.' With that he was gone, ducking through the portal, leaving Tate, looking awkwardly from Daniel to the circle of faces all now watching him. His face was hard to read; something between outrage and embarrassment. Despite the awkwardness of the moment he took a few moments to scan the paintings hanging on the wall nearest to him, with an appraising eye. When he looked at Daniel again his expression had shifted, to something like affront or even resentment; then he was gone too, following his friend out of the makeshift gallery.

There was dead silence in the room. All eyes were on Daniel. He smiled professionally, feeling a bit like an actor who'd lost the script. He looked to Audrey as if she might play theatre prompt – remind him of his lines – but all she gave him was an ironical grimace and a little shrug.

'Well...' He put his hands together in front of his chin, in his best imitation of a master of ceremonies. 'I hope everyone enjoyed this evening's entertainment... A little piece of improvised performance art for you.' He chanced another glance at Audrey and saw her breaking into a smile, her eyes bright. 'Thank you, to our two, ah... *performers...*' He raised a hand vaguely towards the exit. 'A marvelous performance, I think we'd all agree. Very convincing.' Daniel put his arms out as if embracing the crowd, or inviting them to resume looking at the art. 'And so... On with the show. Please, enjoy!' To his relief, he got quite a few knowing laughs, from those who appreciated his little gag, and even a smattering of applause from some who may have actually thought it *was* part of the show. In any case, a hum of chatter quickly started up again and the show did simply go on.

*

In the end it was one of their most successful. It almost seemed that the drama at the beginning of the night had created an edge of excitement which carried though the whole evening. Everything hanging had sold, and he and Audrey went on working late into the night; selling three more large works from the storeroom, to customers who'd missed out on getting what they wanted in the exhibition.

Downstairs, James was cleaning up in the Artist's Bar. When

they told him about the disturbance in the gallery, James responded with his own story of a ruckus he'd had to sort out in the bar.

'It wasn't that drunken Scotsman, was it?' Audrey asked. 'Loud and obnoxious with a beard and a very bad attitude?'

'That sounds like him...' James gave the counter one last swipe and threw his towel into the corner. 'Buy you guys a drink? I'll tell you all about it.' James lined up three tumblers, added some ice, then retrieved a jug from the fridge, with a couple of inches of amber fluid in it.... The remains of the Manhattan mix.

'Him and his mate were sitting up here at the bar.' He nodded towards the end of the counter as he poured the mix over the ice cubes. 'The stocky one with the accent seemed a bit agitated, right from the start. Mouthing off to his friend about something, I wasn't sure what, at first.' James unscrewed a large jar and extracted three Maraschino cherries by the stems and put one into each drink. He came around through the bar hatch and picked up one of the drinks and held it up to Audrey and Daniel. They each did the same, and clinked glasses.

'Cheers!' James took sip and smacked his lips. 'Fuck yeah, I needed that'.

'So, did you hear any of what they were saying?' Audrey was intrigued. She took a sniff of her cocktail and swirled the ice cubes around.

'Bits and pieces, yeah. Mainly swearing and cursing, every bloody expletive under the sun. Like someone had really gotten up this prick's nose. Extremely pissed off, he was. Then I heard him taking *your* name in vain...' James looked at Audrey. 'So I kind of hovered in a bit closer and opened up my ears a bit – you know, took a bit more notice – and then I hear him saying...Well I can't really say what I heard.' He frowned and sipped his drink. 'I can't really repeat it; that's how bad it was. I was shocked, and you know, it takes a bit to shock me.'

He held Audrey's gaze for a moment, then switched attention to Daniel. 'So, I'm starting to get a bit annoyed myself, naturally. But anyway, next thing, the *other* guy starts up, and he's getting stuck right into *you* Dan; saying your exhibitions are a scam, and that you're a shit painter and something about you not paying your dues.' He swirled his drink and watched the ice cubes rotate. 'I'm thinking fuck me, these guys are absolute scum bags; but you know, the bar's still pretty busy, so I just take it under advisement and think, okay, I'm gonna ignore them – for now.'

James looked thoughtfully at the rows of bottles behind the bar for a moment or two, while Daniel and Audrey watched him silently, waiting for him to continue. 'Anyway, then the nasty one – the real drunk one – he starts up again, but this time even louder and more aggressive; and it's all about *you* Audrey, like you've rained on his parade, fucked him right up in some way. And the language...' He flicked a glance from Audrey to Daniel and back again. 'Even worse than before...'

'So what happened?' Daniel asked, watching James, with a look of mild horror, tinged with bemusement.

'Well I've gone up to them – I'm thinking, *fuck you idiots* – and I tell them that in their humble bartender's opinion, they've both had enough to drink, and they might want to consider fucking along off.'

'Bloody hell, *No*....' Audrey breathed and took a tentative sip of her drink. 'I can just imagine what happened next.'

'Yeah, so then, he just turns on me ...'

'Blackthorn.' said Daniel, with a worried frown.

James nodded. His eyes held a look of amazement, almost awe. 'I've never heard anything like it. Just the most extraordinary stream of abuse! He's just attacked me – verbally – like no one's ever done before. Ever. And it just went on and on, every expletive in the book. It was like this guy *invented* swearing. There were words *I* didn't even know...' James paused and looked at the mirrored bar shelves again, then back at Daniel. 'It was really fucked up.'

They both looked at James with concern, breath bated.

'What did you do?'

'Threw the mother-fucker out, of course.' James' deadpan reply came with a cheeky half-smile.

'What?' Daniel and Audrey exclaimed in unison.

'Fuck yeah. Came out from behind the bar – that shut him up pretty quick, he fairly shat himself then – got him by the scruff of the neck, and frog-marched him right down the hall and out the front door.'

'Jesus!' Audrey couldn't hide her admiration.

'What about the other guy... Tate?' Daniel wondered out loud.

'Went out, under his own steam... Meek as a lamb.' James grinned and crinkled his nose, then reached for his drink.

'Well, I'll drink to that,' said Audrey. 'Well done you, James!'

They all raised their glasses together and clinked them ... Just like musketeers.

*

At the traffic lights, the driver craned his neck to look at his two back-seat passengers, by way of his rear-view mirror. He was anxious, but still chose to say nothing. Despite being feral drunk, Blackthorn was strangely alert and watchful, like a wounded beast might be. He caught the driver's worried glance and growled: 'What the fuck are you looking at?'

The driver tweaked his mirror to bring the other passenger into view, the sober one, who had hailed him. 'Is he going to be alright?'

'Just drive the fucking taxi, Gilgamesh...' Blackthorn slurred the derogatory epithet and it degenerated into a guttural belch.

'Don't worry he's fine,' said Tate.

'If he vomits in my taxi, you'll be paying to have it cleaned – and for the time it's off the road.' The driver re-adjusted his mirror as the traffic light changed, and accelerated across the intersection.

'You just keep your eyes on the road boy-oh, and mind your fucking business, you little bastard, or we might have to drop you off – back in Delhi.'

Tate looked at Blackthorn sternly and shook his head. 'Leave him alone.... Christ's sake Dougy, haven't you caused enough trouble tonight? That was bloody embarrassing, back there.'

'Embarrassing? Fuckin oath it was embarrassing! Those two trumped up shysters, with their Private-fucking-View.' Blackthorn glared at him and blew an involuntary belch in his direction. Tate recoiled and wound down the window on his side.

'What? You don't reckon they deserved to be brought down a notch or two? I mean did you see 'em? Two friggin' nobodies, pouncing about like bloody royalty.' Blackthorn conjured a cigarette and a lighter from somewhere and tried, unsuccessfully, to light it; unable to coordinate flame and cigarette, in either space or time.

'No, no! No smoking in the vehicle.' Their driver decelerated sharply and veered towards the curb, letting them know he was serious. 'It's not allowed at all. I'll have to ask you to get out here...'

Tate leaned in and deftly snatched the cigarette from Doug's hand and threw it out his open window, then wound it back up. 'Sorry. Just keep going.'

The driver frowned and slowly accelerated.

Blackthorn pouted and sulked for a moment before continuing. 'Well I know *you* didn't enjoy seeing that, I mean Christ... You saw those paintings, didn't you? Fucking brilliant. Paradigmatic shit, that was...' He gave Tate a long hard stare across the back seat, and all of a sudden, he didn't seem drunk at all. 'Don't quote me, but just between you and me...' He flicked a glance at the back of the driver's head. 'I mean... fuckin' hell, have you ever seen anyone can paint like that?'

Tate held his eye for several moments and sighed. 'I don't know, I mean where did he even come from? And selling direct to the public... Who *does* that? It's a... It's...'

'Game-changer?' Blackthorn ventured. 'And selling it by the shit-load. Three sell-out shows already, apparently.'

'*Game-changer*... It's a bloody catastrophe is what it is. Does he know what he's doing?' Tate looked suddenly exasperated and perplexed. 'I mean did he ever even *have* a dealer?'

'I don't l know. Like I told you, I knew him a bit as a student. Thinking back, maybe he *was* a bit of a loose cannon, maybe a bit impatient. Maybe he just thought fuck those guys for their cut, I'll go it alone. Pretty gutsy move, if you think about it.'

'Don't shit me Doug. You know how fucked up this is. It's the sort of thing can set a real bad precedent... Who knows where it could lead.'

'Yeah, I know.' Blackthorn leaned his head against the seat back and closed his eyes, as if he'd suddenly decided to take a nap – but only for a moment – then he said: 'You know who I think the real problem is? It's that bloody girlfriend of his. It was probably *her* idea. Probably fancies herself as some kind of entrepreneur. She's landed herself this fuck-off talented artist and she's looking to make a big score.'

'Really?'

'Yeah.' Blackthorn gave him another hard stare, loaded with malice. 'I know her, and take my word for it, she's trouble....

Lady-fucking-Macbeth!'

Tate looked at his companion for a long time, as if giving careful consideration to his hyperbole, before saying thoughtfully: 'Well, maybe someone needs to sort the two of them out then...'

Blackthorn snorted out a grunty little laugh and closed his eyes again, still leaning back against the seat back. A reflective silence, Tate thought, or maybe he really was going to sleep.

Abruptly, he sat forward and changed the subject: 'How about our boy? How's he going? Any more joy there?'

'Well, like I said, he's prone to getting a bit twitchy, but don't worry, he'll keep doing the job. There's another real good one almost ready to go.' He thought briefly about how Jack had defaced the latest landscape, but dismissed it as a bit of flighty artistic passion that would soon pass.

'He's pretty good isn't he? I can hardly tell the difference myself. Are we sure our mate Freddy wasn't slinging about more than just his paints and brushes, out there in the outback all those years ago? It's almost like you've bloody *cloned* the old bugger...' Blackthorn chuckled into his beard. 'Where did you get him anyway?'

'I dunno, somewhere in country Victoria; up north I think. Studied at RMIT. He's a natural. Could have quite the career if he plays his cards right...' Tate trailed off pensively. He had a fleetingly remorseful notion that his patronage of Jack wasn't necessarily going to help his career; in fact more likely, it would put an end to it before it started. He shrugged it off.

'So, he can do a nice little abstract expressionist landscape, a la Fred, but do you think he's up to knocking out a bit of cubism? I mean, doing a bloody Picasso is a whole different ball of wax.'

Tate frowned in alarm at Blackthorn's mention of Picasso and tipped his head towards the taxi driver. Blackthorn dismissed his concern with a derisive puff of breath and a smirk, but Tate frowned and answered him in a theatrically lowered voice: 'Piece of cake for him; he could do a bloody Caravaggio...'

He watched Blackthorn nodding his head slowly, the alcohol starting to wear off and simultaneously take its toll on him. 'Hmm... And how's our inside man going – that little bastard Travis? He's a bit of a fucken loose cannon too, isn't he?'

'Well, let me tell you, Travis has got himself ensconced at the NGV like a bloody finger in a bum, thanks to the patronage of his dear, old God-daddy.' Tate smiled and raised a brow. 'Hey, tell me, what was all that palaver with the delegation from Dubai? You went to lunch with them, didn't you?'

'Yeah, it was crazy.' Blackthorn visibly sparked up and his eyes brightened. 'Zaid brought a little posse out here for a visit. Wendy asked me along because of all the University exchange bullshit.

'She'd arranged a visit to the gallery; like a sort of a *good will* thing, and then we all went out for lunch... It was fucking brilliant.' He gave himself a little self-congratulatory chuckle. 'I reckon he made the whole trip out here, just to have a look at it. Don't think he really believed we had it; I mean who would know – a *real* Weeping Woman, hanging in some gallery in the outer-Antipodes – certainly no one in fuckin' Dubai would know, that's for sure...' Blackthorn nodded sleepily for a moment, before continuing. 'And the best part is, now Quinn's gonna drop in and see Zaid in Dubai on his way to London next week.'

'No, no... mate, you don't know the best part...' Tate stifled a chuckle, and Blackthorn gave him a quizzical frown.

'What the fuck are you talking about?' Blackthorn belched and lowered a brow suspiciously.

'Quinn's taking Travis with him to Dubai!' Tate exclaimed happily. 'He was so pissed off about Wendy railroading him into the visit, he's delegated dealing with the Arabs to Travis. Give him some international experience... Says it'll look good on his resume.'

'You have to be fucking shitting me!' Blackthorn suddenly seemed quite sober, wide eyed, excited even.

'I kid you not.'

'That is absolutely bloody brilliant.' Tate watched the pieces slowly falling into place in Blackthorn's addled mind, behind his bleary eyes. 'Does he know? Did you tell him Zaid's our potential buyer?'

Tate nodded like an excited child. 'He loved it. And you know the best part about Travis? ... He's a fucking sociopath. No moral compass whatsoever. He laughed like a drain, when I told him.'

'No compunctions about fucking Quinn behind his back?'

'You know, Travis would do it just for shits and giggles, he's such a friggin' narcissist. He reckons god-daddy has a massive ego... Thinks he practically owns the bloody thing. And he says Quinn's been banging on forever about the rubbish security at the gallery. He's very pissed off that no one will stump up to fund a decent security system, or even to *insure* the bloody thing.'

'Wait, you mean it's not insured?'

'Nup. State government can't afford it.' Tate grinned. 'Travis reckons Quinn's probably got half a mind to disappear it himself, just to make a point... Stick it up Maynard, the Arts Minister, for his penny-pinching. Anyway, when they get back, Travis has already softened him up to give him another project to work on.'

'Like what?'

Tate's grin widened. 'Sending the Picasso on loan up to the National Gallery in Canberra.'

'You have to be shitting me...That is too bloody perfect. He's a fucken legend, this Travis of yours.' Blackthorn grinned a little demonically. 'You sure you can keep him under control?'

'Don't worry. He's cool. Doesn't give a rat's arse about anything.'

'How long would your lad need to make a copy?'

'Only a few days... A week, maybe. Off she goes up to Canberra,' said Tate jauntily. 'Little bit of a delay in transit, and then before anyone starts to shit themselves too badly... Voila! There she is, safe and sound in Canberra.'

With that, Tate glanced up and caught the taxi driver watching them in the mirror. The driver averted his eyes. 'I think this is your stop,' he said quickly, and with a hint of apprehension in his voice.

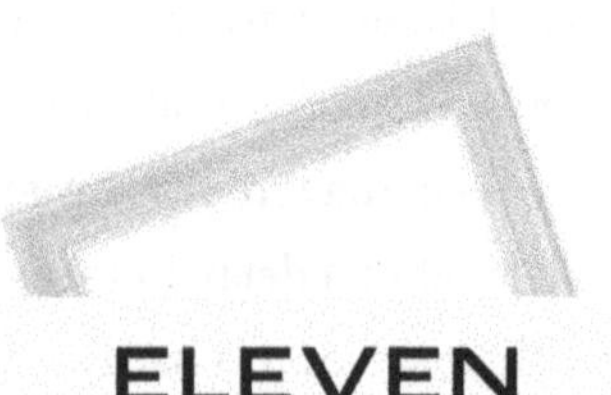

ELEVEN

Friday, August 1st, 1986 (two weeks later)

You do realise that global society is based on the concept of a street gang, don't you – it's really just levels of sophistication and dress code that could confuse the individual observer.
Angry Buddha, 2001

Weeks had passed since Jack had seen or heard from his so-called dealer; weeks since the drunk in the kebab shop told him Tate had been passing off his paintings as the work of Fred Williams.

Since then his work had tanked. He'd had something of a meltdown that very night, and Penny had had to talk him down. By the following morning he'd been ready to go to Tate's gallery and have it out with him; tell him he knew what he was doing, and where to stick his bullshit commissions.

Penny had talked him out of that too, making the point that drunk, pony-tail guy wasn't exactly the most reliable source. Maybe it was all bullshit. *Best to bide your time and see what happens next...*

But he hadn't been able to paint. His creative wheel had seized up. There were uncomfortable echoes of the year he left school, after his teacher had undermined his confidence. It felt like a post-traumatic re-boot.

In the end – after staring blankly for days at the landscape he'd defaced – he did what he'd threatened to do, in the spur of the moment, when Logan had visited him last. He turned it into a portrait of Penny; her head and shoulders slightly off-centre in the foreground, with the not-quite-finished landscape in the background. And it was pretty good, he'd been unexpectedly pleased with the result in the end... Penny, not so much.

But at least it had got the juices flowing again, and when he wondered what to do next, the answer came to him quite naturally and fully formed. A self-portrait. But no ordinary self-portrait, this was going to be something special; a Vermeerian interior – a study of daily life, *the artist at his easel* – with all the emotional intensity and light and detail of an old master, if only he could pull it off.

It was ridiculously ambitious, and it was exactly what he needed to focus his attention, and take his mind off Tate and his bullshit landscapes. *And what would the artist in the picture be painting?* He wasn't sure yet, but it sure as hell wouldn't be an expressionist landscape.... A still life perhaps, or a nude, or maybe just their cat, Dim Sim. Whatever was depicted on the artist's easel in the painting, it would be an eloquent *fuck you* to Tate.

*

Jack was jolted back to reality as the tram jerked and rattled into a hard right-hand turn, adjusting its course for Port Melbourne. The wheels screeched and he looked out at the stationary traffic as they left Clarendon Street behind, and shuddered along beside an old red-brick factory on the corner. It was in the process of being converted into apartments or shops, or maybe both... Gentrification.

He wondered why Logan Tate had gone off the air for three

weeks, and why the hell he now wanted to meet him in a café down at Port Melbourne, of all places.

The call had come early that morning, when Jack was already at his easel. He was ten days into the grand project – *the artist in his studio* – and it had absorbed his attention so much that he'd almost forgotten about Tate. *Almost.* Part of him just wanted to move on; forget about his misadventure with the shady city dealer; overlook his own gullibility and shame, and just get back to work. His latest project felt like a new beginning.

But part of him knew damn well there was unfinished business. If it was true – what the guy in the kebab shop had said – then he was going to have a chunk of Tate's hide; have his say, loud and clear, at the very least. It was hard to believe anyone could be so brazen, so exploitative, so downright criminal... A respected metropolitan art dealer, no less. And yet sometimes, as he repeatedly turned it over in his head, it was the only thing that did make sense. All the bullshit about him being the next Fred Williams. *Don't worry about being imitative. For fuck's sake*! How could he have been so naïve?

What burned him most was that Tate had played to his weakness, and exploited him without a second thought. Because the truth of it was, he *did* paint a lot like Fred Williams, he always had. He knew it, and plenty of other people had said so along the way. This rotten prick had found his Achilles' heel; his own creative conceit, that shadowy and pernicious motivator of the aspiring artist. In his secret heart, Jack reckoned he *was* better than Williams, or at least that he could be one day. *Should he be ashamed to admit it, even if only to himself?*

How else is a young aspiring artist, with no reputation or support, supposed to motivate himself, other than by having unshakable confidence in his own ability and sometimes; overblown expectations of success? And only a hopeful artist knows how fragile that confidence can be, in the absence of validation.

This was why, Tate's bullshit validation was so hurtful. In so many ways a worse betrayal than his gas-lighting art teacher from so many years ago. Did Logan Tate know that he was playing with fire? This crooked dealer with no moral compass, picking him out as some kind of easy mark to misuse, just to make a quick buck? Did he not know that in his haste to exploit; in his abrogation of all decency, he had accidently set upon somebody whose past experiences had made him hypersensitive to such betrayal?

As Jack watched the urban landscape change outside the lumbering rattler, he sensed rather than knew that they were approaching the water, and when they turned down Bay Street, he was sure. By the time he saw the steel blue strip of ocean bisecting the windscreen of the old tram, he had an uncanny sense that a fuse had been lit and was smoldering away somewhere deep inside him.

He would see what Logan Tate had to say for himself, at this improbable rendezvous at the Blue Lotus café, down by the bay. But if he didn't have a good explanation, Logan Tate might just find that he'd bitten off more than he could chew.

*

The young waiter reminded him of Penny. She smiled at Jack and carefully put their coffees on the table with a demure nod. Jack thanked her, while Logan sat back with his hands clasped in front of his chin and the tip of his thumb gripped between his teeth, watching Jack carefully.

Jack lifted his cup and took a tentative sip, returning Logan's gaze with calculated calm. A bland stare.

'You still haven't said how you're progressing with that next landscape.' Logan ignored his coffee and continued to interrogate Jack with his eyes. 'It was looking very bloody good before you cracked the shits and scribbled on it. Did you fix it?'

'I told you, I've been working on something else. Something important.'

'Important!?' Tate made no attempt to hide his scorn.

Jack gave him a cool, hard stare for a moment longer than was comfortable, for either of them, then deliberately shifted his gaze to the front window of the café and the bright seascape beyond the esplanade. 'And you haven't told me why you dragged me all the way down here to drink shit coffee in a bloody ice-cream shop.' Jack looked again at his dealer and then darted a glance around the little bayside café.'

'Thought you might appreciate a bit of sea air. Get you out of the studio for a bit.' He fingered the handle of his cappuccino cup, turning it slowly around on the saucer.

Jack responded with a sardonic scowl.

'Well, if you must know, my mother lives down here. I was visiting her this morning, and like I said, I thought you might enjoy an outing.'

'Penny's away for a long weekend, and she's taken the car. I had to catch the friggin' tram all the way down here.'

Tate shifted his weight in his chair and sighed impatiently. 'Let's just cut to the chase, shall we? When will it be finished? I've already got a buyer lined up for this next one.'

'When? Maybe when you tell me what the fuck's really going on.'

'What are you talking about?'

Jack took a sip of his coffee and eyed Tate over the rim of the cup, but didn't answer until he'd carefully replaced the cup on the saucer. 'Who's Crayman?'

'Who's what?'

'Tall guy, blond hair, ponytail. Smart-arse. I've seen him before, at your gallery.'

'Do you mean Travis?'

'I don't know, do I? Is he the one seems to think you've been passing off my paintings as *real* Fred Williams landscapes?'

'What!? That's ridiculous. What are you talking about?'

Jack looked dispassionately at his nemesis. It was an empty and dismissive stare, held for long enough that Logan eventually dropped his eyes. Jack enjoyed making him feel uncomfortable; this conniving bloody dealer with his smarmy attitude and his white privilege. He decided right then and there, there wasn't going to be any debate. He could already read it plainly in Logan's body language and on his face; the guilt.

When their eyes met again, Jack laid his palms on the table and leaned in and said flatly: 'I'm done.' He stood up.

'Wait. Wait. Listen.' You don't know what you're talking about. Travis's a ratbag. You can't listen to anything he says.'

Jack paused and picked up his coffee cup and drained the last of his cappuccino. 'I don't believe you. I reckon you're a bloody liar. Thanks for the coffee... and the memories.' He turned to go.

'Alright, *wait...*' Tate got up and pulled a five dollar note out of his wallet and flung it down on the table. 'Let me explain.'

Jack put a hand up next to his head in a *no thanks* gesture, and made for the door. Tate followed him. Outside on the footpath, Tate blocked his path to the tram stop. 'Okay, listen to me... Listen! Maybe it *is* true. What if it is?'

Jack gave him a contemptuous stare of disbelief, momentarily lost for words.

'There's no harm done. They've all been private collectors. They don't know, and they never will... It's lucrative. Look, I can organise a bigger cut for you. You could make some real money. Trust me...'

Jack turned on him abruptly, making him flinch. 'What?' He frowned like he was looking at some inexplicable anomaly. 'Trust *you*? Fuck off!'

As he strode towards the tram stop, Tate called after him. 'You're making a big mistake.' Jack kept walking. 'You could be in a lot of trouble, Jack.' An unmistakable undertone of menace had crept into Tate's voice.

Jack slowed down and stopped, still with his back to his defunct dealer. When he turned around his face was set like stone and there was a dark and turbulent fury brewing in him. His eyes shone with an unsettling intensity as he retraced his step to where Logan stood firm; watching him with an uncanny and plucky kind of belligerence, considering the anger clearly emanating from the young artist.

Tate's back straightened and he lifted his chin slightly, conveying a hint of arrogance. 'If someone's been forging Fred Willams artworks, who do *you* think has been doing that exactly? I mean, not to belabour the point, but whose brushstrokes are all over those canvases? Kind of like a smoking gun really...'

'Fuck you...They're not copies of actual Fred Williams paintings, they're just landscapes in his style – you said it yourself – just like his paintings, but different; maybe better, maybe worse, but they're not his. And anyway, they can't be traced back to me, because I didn't even ...' He stopped as if the words had literally jammed in his throat and a chill descended over him. A peculiar intuitive rush made his legs feel weak, and for a brief moment he thought he would piss his pants.

'Sign them...?' Tate finished his sentence for him.

Jack felt the oxygen leaving his lungs without replenishment;

the weight of a singular idea, bearing down on him. How, *How?* ... *How could he have been so stupid?*

'Are you sure about that, Jack?'

Separated by no more than two yards, they stared at each other like predator and prey, each uncertain which was which. Jack had a sickeningly vivid recollection of Tate suggesting he not bother signing the paintings... And a galling memory of his own mind going blank: *Oh gosh... Okay, don't sign them... A bit strange, but okay.*

Fuck, fuck. Fuck!... Stupid!

'Maybe you did sign them after all.' Tate's eyes narrowed to grey apertures; his tone and expression, that of a parent chastising a toddler. '*Maybe* even with Fred's signature?'

Jack lunged at Tate and pushed him in the chest. 'You fucking cunt!' The dealer staggered backwards, arms flailing, eyes wide. He barely kept his feet.

Blinded by rage Jack charged at him again, but Logan side-stepped and batted him away. Jack turned and lunged again. He couldn't see properly; tears of anger blurred his vision, but somehow he managed to get hold of Tate and wrestle him to the ground. His boots scuffled a semi-circle on the gritty footpath as he tried to get purchase; tried to immobilise the struggling dealer. His elbow scrapped across the concrete, taking off skin, but he didn't care. He was grunting and swearing; raging inside, part of him enjoying that this fuck-head dealer was on the ground in his fancy suit, getting himself mugged for his shit-fuckery.

Jack was vaguely aware of people passing by them, taking a wide berth – looking on aghast, no doubt, at the bizarre spectacle – on the mid-morning bayside esplanade. Tate, wide-eyed in shock and panic, struggled intermittently, realising with sinking fear that Jack was much stronger than him. Jack had him in a head-lock, trying to pull his lying head right off his shoulders. 'I'm gonna kill you,' he whispered raggedly into his ear. 'You didn't expect *that*, did you?'

A shadow fell over them, blocking the morning sun, and Jack realised someone was standing over them. 'What's going on here?' The voice of the passer-by was loud and resonant; an authoritative tone. Despite himself, Jack responded instinctively; loosening his grip on his victim, and giving him one last contemptuous shove, in order to get himself to his feet, leaving Tate on his back on the concrete.

A large stocky man, casually dressed, with a thick overcoat on top, was staring at him reproachfully. He had square features, rounded out by age; short-cropped dark hair, greying around his temples. Jack thought he looked like a retired policeman.

'Well?' He demanded, glaring at Jack, then shifting his attention to Tate, who was getting to his feet, brushing himself off and straightening his suit.

'It's okay,' said Tate obligingly. 'A family matter.... Something quite upsetting. We'll be fine. But thanks for your concern.'

The man looked at Jack, who was still scowling at Tate, then back at Tate. 'Hmm... Okay...' he nodded but seemed unconvinced. Then he straightened his back, as if called to attention, cleared his throat, said 'righto, then,' and strode off along the footpath.

'What do you think you're doing? Are you mad?' Tate hissed at him through gritted teeth, a weather-eye on the stranger, to make sure he was out of earshot. 'Do you want to get us both arrested?'

'No. Just you.' Jack snapped back, aggressively. 'You fucking criminal.'

'What the hell's the matter with you?' Tate made exaggerated work of brushing himself down, checking for damage to clothing and skin. He eyed Jack warily, who was still breathing heavily, still looking angry. It occurred to him that he should cut the crazy kid adrift right here and now; he was clearly unstable and apparently even dangerous. Probably uncontrollable. But he still needed him. Where else was he going to find someone with his extraordinary skills at such short notice; someone who could be *persuaded* to cooperate in their new project?

But *could* he still be persuaded? That seemed to be in doubt, now.

Shaken by the unexpected attack, maybe even in shock, Tate wondered if he'd seriously misjudged this young artist. Maybe threats and coercion wouldn't cut it with Jack.... Maybe he was just too damned willful.

'Tell me why I shouldn't put you into the police for art forgery right now? And for bloody assault?' Tate found a hole in the knee of his suit pants. 'Shit. Look at this.'

'I'm sorry...'

He hadn't expected that. The kid appeared to be calming down. All of a sudden, he looked more contrite than angry.

Jack felt the adrenalin draining out of him, and he took a deep breath and brushed himself down. How had he let *that* happen? It wasn't his habit to resort to violence, not since the school yard, at least. But no one had gotten under his skin quite like this dealer, and to have all of his worst fears confirmed; to know he'd been played for a sucker... Betrayed, again. The tension had been building for some time, whilst all along, his intuition had been telling him, correctly, that something was amiss. There really *had* been a fuse burning inside him... And he'd just exploded. *Fucking hell. He could be in a world of trouble.*

'Why would you do something like that? Jesus!' said Tate, re-gaining the initiative. He examined Jack closely for signs of remorse. Maybe all wasn't lost after all. 'Alright never mind, I think we'll both live. But listen... you've got to *listen* to me alright? It's not a big deal, okay? This is how the art world works. I've been doing this for a long time, you know, and it's not always beer and skittles. It's actually a bloody jungle and sometimes you have to get a bit creative. Sit around staring at your bloody navel and some apex predator's gonna come up behind you and rip your guts out.' He stared at his young charge, looking for some sign of understanding or agreement. Jack looked back with a worried expression and chewed his bottom lip.

'It's dog eat dog, right. There aren't any rules...not really. Just survival of the fittest. I mean this kind of shit is going on *all the time*. No one cares. Everyone's scamming each other left and right. Well... There *is* just one rule; don't get caught... Alright?

'Anyway, we've got this under control. Everything's going to be okay, just trust me...Yes?'

Jack wondered who 'we' was, all of a sudden. He was a bit taken aback that even after he'd wrestled Logan to the ground and threatened to kill him, the strangely resilient entrepreneur had bounced back so quickly, and was apparently assuming, that somehow Jack was already back in his camp... All was forgiven.

Jack gave a non-committable *ah-ha* and squeezed out a pained smile.

A ripple of doubt crossed Logan's face, which he dispersed with one of his synthetic grins. 'Come on, let's cross over and walk along the beach. Blow the stink off us. I'll tell you about our new project. It's something big...' Tate checked the traffic both ways on the esplanade. 'I know you're gonna love it,' he yelled over his shoulder with thinly veiled sarcasm.

Jack checked the traffic himself and followed his dealer across the road and up onto a wide footpath flanked by a bluestone and cement sea wall. Away from the meager protection of the shopfronts, a bracing westerly blew at their backs and Jack wished he'd dressed more warmly. The sea was the color of slate and the wind-swept beach was deserted, as they made their way along the promenade with hardly a soul in sight. Even the footpath was empty of pedestrians.

In more favorable conditions Jack liked the bayside beaches in winter. The open expanse of the bay and the wild, ever-changing procession of weather rolling in from the Southwest; it gave relief from the hustle and bustle of inner-city life. But this day, the grey skies reflected his mood and the buffeting wind matched the turmoil in his mind.

Raising his voice to make himself heard over the wind, Tate sounded ostentatious and full of himself, as he continued on with some platitudes about the art world and his esteemed place in it. Meanwhile Jack racked his brain, trying to think up a better strategy. Obviously losing his shit wasn't going to achieve much. He was rueful and embarrassed at what he'd done. The best course of action was to hear Tate out – gather some intelligence as it were – and give the appearance of going along... Buy time to think of a way out of the mess he was in.

Where was Penny when he needed her? She would have some ideas; she always did. She was practical and smart when the shit was hitting the fan. He suddenly felt bitterly disappointed that she was away for the whole weekend.

'Anyway, that's enough of all that palaver,' Tate stopped quite suddenly, causing Jack to skid to a halt on the sandy path. The dealer scanned the beach and the ocean beyond, and patted the rounded top of the sea wall conspiratorially, suggesting Jack join him gazing at the ocean, so they could talk. 'Best we just get down to business.'

Business? ... Jack thought ominously. He rested his forearms on the wall next to Tate, and stared glumly out to sea. It was a grey world, colours all muted by the heavy overcast. A bit of brightness to the sandy beach, but then an endless expanse of grey; the ocean quite flat with a dusky tinge of green, and the sky the same, with just a hint of distant blue and some bright white clouds, fringing the western horizon. Looking past Tate, he could see the Abel Tasman moored at Station Pier, one splash of colour against the dark ocean and the aging façade of the old Federation wharf buildings.

'Do you know anything about aging canvases?' Tate began thoughtfully.

'Huh?'

'You know, distressing the canvas, various techniques to cause yellowing; make it appear older than it is.'

'No.' Jack screwed up is nose, deliberately giving a Tate a look which said; *are you mad?*

'Hmm, that's okay. I've got a guy knows all about it, and he's quite the whizz with historical pigments too. He can show you. You'll be amazed, there's quite a science to it.'

'Quite a science to what?' Jack's expression was vexed and quizzical.

'Oh...and then there's the glazing, to finish it off with just the right surface finish. It's important how the glazes have aged... Or appeared to, anyway.'

'Exactly what the hell are we talking about?' Jack narrowed his eyes and leaned slightly in toward the dealer. In that moment, the wind gusted, and a seagull suddenly appeared, hovering unstably, not far above Tate's head. It cawed raucously, as if empathising with Jack's incredulity and then dipped a wing, and both men watched as it wheeled away down the beach.

After tracking the gull, Tate turned back and looked winningly at Jack. A genial smile. 'We're talking about art forgery, my dear boy. Real, fair-dinkum art forgery...for fun and profit, very big profit.'

Tate seemed amused by the expression on Jack's face. *You can't be serious.*

'Don't look so shocked. My guy can help you with all the technical stuff – the science – but it's your technique we need, your mastery of the brushes. With you on the job we can make it perfect. So yes, we're as serious as we can be – serious to the tune of twenty thousand dollars, that'll be your cut. Set you and Penny up for life, just about.' Tate watched Jack, carefully, gauging his reaction.

Jack's heart sank; it may have even stopped beating for a time. He dead-panned Tate with what felt like a completely blank expression. It wasn't deliberate, it was more like his face couldn't find an appropriate expression. He forced out a smile, and said 'Wow.' The mention of the twenty thousand dollars only meant one thing to him: Tate was talking about serious crime. The term *jail time* reared up in his mind, and he wondered for the second time who Tate meant by *we*. It seemed more important than ever to let Tate think he was going along with the idea. Somehow, that had become his strategy. A strategy to buy time. But how much time was there to buy? He wanted desperately to tell Penny, to unburden himself. She would have a shit fit. But she would also have ideas.

He swallowed hard.

'Tell me more... when's all this happening?'

Don't you worry about that, I'll keep you posted. Just be ready... Soon,' he added raising his eyebrows. 'Maybe even next week.'

Jack's gut twisted inside him and he forced out another smile, relatively sure it would have transmitted more as a grimace.

Tate laughed sympathetically.

'And what is it, exactly... that we're talking about... *copying*?'

'Can't say too much.' Tate touched a finger to his nose in a way that irked Jack to his core. 'But you might want to brush up on your early century European expressionism; maybe focus on a bit of cubism.'

*

Somehow Jack had contained himself until he got back to the city and inside his front door. Then, as he kicked off his shoes – a frenzy of kicking that sent one arcing off into the bedroom and the other soaring down the hallway, narrowly missing the pendant light fitting – he swore repeatedly and loudly.

'Fuck, fuck, fuck, FUCK!' He muttered, in time with his paces, as he stomped down the hallway.

He found himself in the kitchen, casting around as if lost in an unfamiliar house. He ran his fingers hard, up through his hair, like he was trying to keep his head from exploding, and then slammed his hands down onto the island benchtop, looking blindly through into the living room – his studio – breathing heavily. His mind was in turmoil, confused. Blind rage barely contained. He had a sudden urge to sweep his arms across the counter and dash everything on it to the floor. Probably the only thing that stopped him was seeing Penny's big fancy video camera – borrowed from the dance academy – sitting amongst the benchtop paraphernalia.

He sighed heavily and turned to the refrigerator, glaring at it for a moment as if he were uncertain of its function. 'Fucking bastard!' He spat, admonishing the innocent appliance as he wrenched open its door, and extracted a beer.

He took a deep breath and summoned sufficient Zen to calm himself enough to search for the bottle opener. He hoofed the fridge door shut and located the opener in the kitchen draw, right where it should be. The satisfying *fitzz* of the cap coming off elicited an odd wave of relief and for a moment he felt like he was going to cry. Swirling emotions were clearly doing whatever-the-fuck they wanted with him, and it made him feel uncomfortably out of control.

He retreated to the studio and plonked himself down in the old armchair opposite his easel, where he would normally sit to contemplate and appraise. He sat and drank his beer, staring blindly ahead not even seeing his half-finished portrait, muttering occasionally, things like; *fucking cunts, assholes, shit-heads* – not even knowing who *they* were... Tate and his shadowy partners in crime.

When he did focus on his current piece standing on the easel, a new wave of pious anger welled up in him, because he realised that Tate had killed the project with his interference; his criminal bloody coercion; his devastating insinuation into Jack's life and career.

It took some restraint not to fling his empty bottle at the canvass, but instead the rage channeled itself into another tirade of aimless invective: 'Fuck me! Cubism? Fucking hell... Cubism! For fuck's sake...' Finding himself on his feet, he realised he was going to need something stronger than beer and went looking for Penny's gin.

Three gins in, he called Penny's mother's number, hoping he wouldn't sound too pissed. She sounded concerned and motherly. Jack assured her nothing was wrong. She told him Penny was out having lunch with some of her old school friends, and there was no telling what time she'd be home.

His disappointment was tempered by the fact that he was starting to feel pretty loose. The more relaxed he got the more his anger subsided, and along with it, the fear. And just enough alcohol had inspired a bit of creative, imaginative thinking. He was starting to have plenty of ideas. Some of them involved dismembering a certain art dealer and consigning him to a lonely, shallow grave; but others were interesting and possibly even helpful to the situation he was in. Halfway through his third gin – just before he'd tried to call Penny – he'd had one of those fleeting moments of lucidity, recognising that if he had one more drink, all that inspired thinking would most likely be lost to the fog and stupor of the morning after.

But one idea would stick – because it had hit him like an epiphany, half-way through gin number two –the realisation of the significance of Tate's Cubism reference.

I mean cubism for fuck's sake – what has cubism got to do with anything?... Only that the most valuable artwork in the entire country, is a work of Cubism; Picasso's Weeping Woman, right down the road in Melbourne's NGV, purchased just last year – if memory served – for about two million dollars.

Holy fuck. They were going to make him paint a copy of the Picasso!

Jack had drained that second gin in a single huge gulp, and proceeded directly to a third. *Surely not. This can't be real. They can't be serious, I mean, how? How would they get their hands on the painting? And why? What would be the use of a copy? Surely everyone would know it was forgery. What could they be planning to do with it?*

And how the fuck did Tate think he was capable of painting a convincing copy anyway? He knew bugger-all about cubism, and cared even less.

Disbelief gave way to a resurgent wave of anxiety and panic as the implications of Tate's plan came crashing down on him. *This was fucked. It was a disaster. He was going to end up in jail. He had to find a way out.*

After hanging up the phone from Penny's mum, he could feel the merciful sedative effect of the strong alcohol starting to kick in, calming this new wave of panic.

But he had an overwhelming urge to share the disastrous scenario with someone. He couldn't wait for Penny... And he couldn't go on drinking alone, not like this; he needed a drinking buddy and a sympathetic ear he could trust.

He picked up the phone and dialed his mate, Genghis (aka Miles). When he heard the line connect and the reassuring voice of his old friend, he immediately felt better... more grounded, like maybe the whole scene wasn't as fucked up as he thought. Maybe he'd blown it out of proportion. Miles would have a different take on it all, a fresh eye and probably some advice. But one thing for sure; at least he would make him laugh.

'Hey Jack, what's goin' on?'

'Let's get fucked up... I've got some crazy shit going on, shit you wouldn't believe.'

'Aliens?' Miles suggested.

Jack snorted a truncated laugh into the phone. 'Nah, worse mate...Art dealers.'

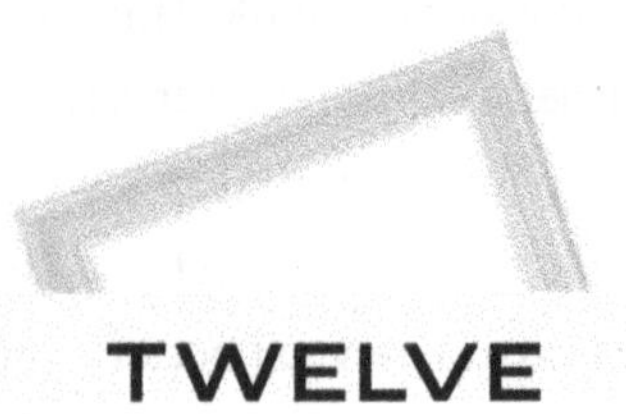

TWELVE

Saturday, August 2nd, 1986

'If you believe television, then baited hooks await us all beyond the safety of the living room hypnosis bunker. Are they training us to be hooked, or warning us about the dudes in the boat?'
Angry Buddha, 2001

One million days after the foundation of Rome in 753 BC, Daniel Hardman sat cross-legged on his large blue mediation cushion, watching television and drinking a coke straight from the can.

In addition to the curious anniversary of the Romans, the luminous, blue, shimmering screen had advised him that Clint Eastwood was mayor-elect of Carmel, California, and the remains of the seven Challenger astronauts had been found on the ocean floor, off the coast of Florida.

Yet another day of blood-spattered horror, and/or celebrity banality, was clearly lurking just outside his bunker. Thank goodness for the marvels of modern media, otherwise he'd be unaware.

Under the influence of mild doses of psychotropic recreational substances, he liked to sit up close to the TV and channel surf, as if doing so might help him to penetrate its realm; this infernal box, which had become integral to the recent evolution of his degenerating species. The device itself, he had long thought, was quite stupid, although the delivery system and advertising was impressively clever. But what fascinated him most were those two dimensional life forms who inhabited that flatland of moving imagery and sound. Their stories were simple and yet, cunningly manipulative.

Televisual Valium for the tired worker.

Another thing that intrigued him no end, was the multi-locational, time-travelling, shape-shifting format of television.

Gently and mindfully, with just a squeeze of his thumb, he activated the god-like channel changer... *Wooosh – He is transported instantaneously to a substitute reality: Now in a boat; the frame of his containment vessel convincingly bobbing from side to side with the surges of the virtual ocean within.*

The fishing channel. One of his favourites... Well, perhaps it was a love/hate thing. The expansive vista of a wild and unknown seascape, but always with some old duffer catching fish after fish, groaning on about how excited he is, and what tackle is the most efficient for mass piscocide. Then cut to the televised fish-bully graciously letting one go, with smug piety and sometimes even a kiss.

Lucky fish – that's your fifteen minutes.

He heard Audrey's gentle footsteps swishing around him and she plonked herself down on the couch behind him. 'So, what's happening out in the *real* world?'

Daniel answered without taking his eyes off the fishing. 'Well the Roman empire is a million days old today, Halley's comet is waving bye-bye for another seventy-five years, and Saddam Hussein says he wants to kiss and make up with Iran, if you can believe it... Oh, and all the workers from Chernobyl have been shipped off to some Siberian Gulag; for incompetence and anti-revolutionary distractedness.'

Audrey scoffed gently. 'I don't know whether any of that actually happened, or if you're just making it up.'

'I know,' he agreed sympathetically. 'Neither do I'.

She let out a quiet little laugh and then said: 'Didn't your mother ever tell you'd get square eyes if you sit too close to the television?'

'She told me a lot of things that weren't necessarily true: Spinach'll give you muscles; there's no monsters hiding in the closet; your elders deserve your respect...' He got up from his cushion and came over and sat next to Audrey, put an arm around her and kissed her on the cheek. 'Pretty fucked up world we're living in, eh?'

'Only if you watch late-night television.' She yawned and snuggled into him. 'Every civilization thinks it's going to see the end of days, it's all very human – it's in our DNA.'

'Maybe... But only since we got all *civilised*. I mean, when we were hunter gatherers, we just did our shit – hunted and gathered, let the days pass, living in the moment. Just *being*. Didn't try to have careers, or wars. Didn't sweat about the mortgage.'

'Didn't have to organise art exhibitions.'

'Eh?' Daniel looked up with mock surprise and offence. 'Yeah, we had exhibitions alright... The caves, of Lascaux... All across the Arnhem Land plateau, Kakadu. They were big time artists, the first Australians. Just didn't have to try and sell any of it.'

'Well, speaking of selling; I've got a busy day tomorrow – having the surplus value of my labour exploited by Max – so I'm off to bed. You coming?'

'I'm not really tired, in fact, I'm still a bit jacked. Probably shouldn't have had that Coke,' he confessed. He worked the remote and the display on the box shifted through various scenes in quick succession. It time-travelled back to 1944: A column of German prisoners marching down a road, through a broken streetscape, their hands on their heads. Just the sort of documentary to suck him in, keep him up too late – feeding his old appetite for images of horror from his parent's generation – images he'd painted often, but still hadn't exorcised from his consciousness.

Audrey got up and kissed him on the forehead, looked at the TV and then back at Daniel, giving him a dubious frown. He smiled meekly, and dispatched the captive Nazi's with a flick of his magical controller.

'I actually think I need some fresh air. I might just roam the empty streets, like a lost and lonely soul for a bit before bed.'

Audrey smiled appreciatively at his hyperbole. 'Okay, just don't bring back any hungry ghosts. We've got enough up here already.'

*

Daniel grabbed his coat off the hook by the door and looked around at the squash court studio, configured as it was with their demountable living area in one corner. The Chesterfield lounge doubled nicely as a gallery centerpiece, the television got a table cloth over it and flowers, on exhibition nights. He reckoned it wouldn't be a moment too soon when they moved into their own rented terrace in Brunswick, in a few days' time – a real house, with a garden. He was definitely going to plant veggies.

The squash court had served them well as gallery and residence, but the multi-purpose studio and living area, together with the mezzanine sleeping area and barely functional kitchen nook, could only go on for so long. The bathroom – downstairs, out the door and along at the far end of the spooky hallway – had been a bridge too far for them both, in the end.

He could hear Audrey rummaging around upstairs, getting

ready for bed. 'I'll be back,' he intoned in his best *Schwarzenegger* accent, and stepped over the threshold.

Her faint response reached him as he ventured along the dim tunnel toward the stairs: 'Watch out for cyborgs.'

At the landing he skulked around the corner and past the restaurant's double doors. He was in stealth mode, and disinclined to explain himself to the maître d' or engage in idle chit chat this late at night, especially in his somewhat altered state. He caught some murmurs and glimpsed a stalwart table of two, delaying the inevitable. You could almost taste the end-of-service ennui emanating from the room as he snuck past and down the main stairs.

The lights were still on in the Artist's bar, but it looked like it was all done, but for the clean-up; and at the front, the cocktail bar had only a few stragglers, and a bored barman polishing glasses with a thousand-yard stare.

Out the front door, he paused for a moment on the pavement. As much as he liked being in nature, he also loved the inner city – especially late at night. The latent energy of the slumbering city had a curious, and enlivening effect on him. He imagined himself in New York, the sleepless metropolis.

He took his time strolling down the narrow laneway, which narrowed even more as he approached the corner. A pedestrian striding down Collins Street could blink and miss Alfred Place altogether. He liked that about it, the anonymity of their mysterious address, hidden in the heart of the city. It made him feel mercurial and a little clever, like a magician hiding an elephant in plain sight. It was a fitting setting to practice his fox magic.

At the corner, he headed west, toward the heart of things.

The *Paris end* of Collins Street was devoid of people in the midnight chill, leaving just the skeletal winter remains of the elms and the looming architecture. A crazy hotchpotch of Victorian, neo-Baroque, Venetian gothic – just about anything the nineteenth century city fathers could poke a stick at – scattered randomly amongst the modern; where-ever the grand old structures had escaped the attentions of Whelan the Wrecker, back in the barbarous Thirties.

He wandered past Saint Michaels, neat and spooky in the gloom, and further along he was surprised by the theatre lights of the Regent across the road, blinking off coincidentally with his passing. The bluestone flagging of the town hall was his cue to turn south, down Swanston Street and before long he was outside Saint Paul's, with the iconic Melbourne pub across the road, the famous clocks diagonally opposite, and the wide empty cardinal intersection of Melbourne spread out before him.

A last tram lumbered towards him from across the river, followed by a lone car, and then nothing. The heart of the town was deserted. He thought about turning left along the mean streets of the city's underbelly, opposite the station, but it would limit his walk to just a block or two. He needed to expend some energy, get some air. He would cross the river, go down as far as the gallery.

He crossed the empty intersection against a red 'don't walk' and headed for the bridge, in the shadow of the towering Gas and Fuel offices, blighting the southern riverbank like some dystopian apartment block, dropped in by Stalinists. The wind off the Yarra chilled him and made him appreciate the warm glow from the Victorian street lamps lining the bridge. He crossed on the east side, where the palm trees reached up to the bridge from the southern bank, and continued on – opposite the Arts Centre, with the heavily treed Alexandra Gardens on his left, and the wide expanse of St Kilda Road to his right – until he was directly opposite the National Gallery. There he stopped and looked across the deserted thoroughfare at the great grey rectangular edifice; a building he'd heard the new director – with his contrived schoolboy wit – describe as the Kremlin of St Kilda Road. *Ha ha, you fucking silk-stocking Brahman.*

The very sight of the gallery always filled him with a confounding fusion of feelings and thoughts. Here was the repository of all art deemed worthy to commend to the great un-washed masses of Melbourne.

'Is there any real art in that place, Dan?'

Daniel wasn't particularly startled by Casper's voice. He'd been half expecting his old mate to turn up again, and he'd had that prickly sensation all the way along past the gardens – that sense of being watched. Just like Casper, his old instructor, to want to show him up ... The master spotting the spotter.

'Who can say? Real art is pure magic, isn't it? ... Like indigenous art,' he mused gently to his old friend. 'And teachers of real art are the shamans of the current epoch – they've got the job of instructing the next generation in the power of creation.'

'It's a big job, protecting the source,' Casper whispered.

'Hmm...But how did art become nothing but a cultural commodity?' he asked his old friend, rhetorically. 'A sad bit of history – a bad patch perhaps, and a fucking blot on the cultural landscape.' Casper listened and nodded. 'Certainly an insult to the true purpose of artistic activity.'

'Still, what'ya gonna do? It's the gnomes, as usual...'

'Yeah, the fucking gnomes. So... We just watch as decreased funding and dictated exclusivity pulls the wagon train-junket tour of self-justifying cultural commentary into an increasingly tight, compressed and desperate circle.'

'Until it disappears up its own arse,' said Casper thoughtfully. *'How did it come to this, do you reckon, Dan?'*

'Could be a failure of courage and vision... Insists art is nothing more than realist décor, with the occasional reductionist finesse into farcical, rhetorical, self-reflective, technically bereft, prancing, fashion-riddled role-playing...'

'Maybe tell us what you really think Dan... Although I reckon you're absolutely right.'

They fell silent for a time, watching the cascading water wall under the wide Syriac arch of the gallery front, from across the wide boulevard. Eventually Casper said: *'There's more trouble coming you know, but don't worry, I'm here to help.'*

He looked at Casper and noticed he was dressed like a garbo – filthy overalls and a city council logo. Casper started laughing. Daniel laughed with him.

'Just give me the nod, don't listen to anyone else. It's just more gnome stuff, OK? Who's the girl, by the way? Don't you think she looks like trouble?'

He started laughing again.

Daniel whispered, 'Casper, you're dead.'

Casper looked up and replied, *'So are you, stupid. Have you forgotten everything we learned out in the bush? This place is a jungle too, you know, full of bugs and very dangerous. See you later.'*

Casper peeled away, back into the park and disappeared.

When Daniel looked across the road again, he saw someone standing behind the water wall... Or in it. It was a woman, in a white dress, her hands held out in front of her as if to catch the falling water. He stared dumbly across the road, unsure whether to trust his eyes. He crossed over the service road, not taking his eyes of the white figure, for fear she would vanish if he looked away. The White Lady seemed to look back at him, earnestly, through the gallery's veil of tears. He started to cross St Kilda Road, wanting a closer look.

Abruptly, the vacant night was rent by an eardrum-splitting screech and a dissonant bell rang in his head. As he jammed to a stop in the middle of the road, the side of a tram flashed past him, seemingly just inches from his face. His heart jump-started itself and skipped all over the place, as he gasped and then swore. By the time he gathered his wits and looked up, the White Lady was gone, and when he looked to his left to spy the offending tram, it was gone too.

A ghost tram – that's what he would call it, when he got home and told a bleary-eyed Audrey about his strange encounter – a ghost tram and The White Lady, entrapped in the water wall of the NGV.

Fuck! Maybe Casper was right...Trouble really could be brewing.

*

Travis laid down the carefully constructed plywood box and opened the lid to reveal a lining of tissue paper and bubble wrap, which he patted and smoothed across the inside of the case.

From the top drawer of Quinn's antique redwood desk he extracted a small screwdriver which he held under the light of his desk lamp and rotated, examining the curious, tiny twin prongs, specially designed for removing the 'snake-eyes' security screws. He pocketed the screwdriver and sat himself down behind his godfather's desk and surveyed his realm for a moment or two, indulging himself briefly in a fantasy of himself as director of the NGV, and imagining how much fun it would be to *fuck shit up* in the rarified atmosphere of Ellery's elite arts administration constituency.

Well, let's not get ahead of ourselves, he thought. It would be amusing enough to pull this little sleight of hand with Ellery's precious Picasso. Vanish her for a few days en route to Canberra – just long enough for Logan and Dougy's clever little forger to work his magic – and then back before anyone gets too excited. He would have to admit, he was looking forward to seeing Ellery's face when he first realised she's gone missing in transit. Be beside himself for a few days, and – he was supremely confident – Quinn's first instinct would be to cover it up, until the two of them could sought it out.... Easily long enough to get the job done and the painting back, he and Logan had surmised.

He also indulged himself with a chuckle about his chance encounter with Tate's tame painter, down at the kebab shop. Doubtless he shouldn't have said anything, but he had been pretty loose that night, and he couldn't resist. The look on the kid's face had been just priceless... Like a rabbit in a spotlight, the poor little bugger.

In the desk draw, he spotted Quinn's fancy gold Peerless ballpoint – a parting gift from Harvard, apparently, and a prized possession – and so he took it and uncapped it and examined it in the dim light. *Yes, not a bad idea, just in case something goes wrong, and someone pulls some kind of forensic shit... Ellery's own pen, and in his own hand.* Travis had spent some time perfecting his godfather's hand writing – during the many idle hours of his internship – and so, he gently bit his lip and concentrated quite hard, as he bent over the blank conservator's card he'd brought with him. After a moment he carefully inscribed five words on the card and then sat back and examined his handiwork, giving himself a small nod and a murmur of satisfaction. He glanced at his watch.

Time to get moving.

He pocketed the card and went across the room to the under-bar fridge and extracted a six pack he'd brought in earlier. The beers were good and cold.

Over the last week or two, he'd established a *modus operandi* for himself of working late some nights, in his pokey little office, just down the hall from the director's. In the process, he'd cultivated a relationship with the security guards, especially, Ben and Dave, who did the weekends. He'd established a habit of having a few beers with them some nights, before he went home. Travis had also become their reliable and discreet purveyor of high quality cannabis.

Travis enjoyed moving through the cloisters at night, with the lights down low; complete darkness in some areas, but for the faint illumination of the odd exit sign. Distant spot-lit artworks in other sections, giving an impression of apparitions inhabiting the place with him. It gave him the creeps a bit, but also a perverse sense of belonging, that he knew his way through the maze of darkened gallerias.

It had been his idea to bring the whole thing forward to Saturday night, instead of waiting until the following Tuesday. For the one thing, there were only two weekend guards, and he knew Ben and Dave were on this Saturday. And he knew they liked a beer, and he knew they liked a good *choof* even better.

But best of all, the weekend would buy them extra time. With weekend staff on deck all day Sunday, and then the gallery closed for cleaning on Monday, no none would even start to think about following up the arrival of the painting in Canberra until well into the week; Wednesday or Thursday at least. They'd have almost a full week to get the job done... *Brilliant.*

With the six pack under his arm, he made for the tea room near the back stairwell. Ben and Dave would be just clocking onto the graveyard shift.

'Hey men, is it beer o'clock yet?'

The two middle aged guards, each gave Travis a wry smile, and they all settled down around the laminex kitchen table and cracked open their beers. True to form, before they were even onto the second beer, Ben asked Travis with utmost discretion, about the possibility of another of his special *deals.*

'Well, I'm waiting on a delivery from up north, but y'know I always look after you guys...' With a magician's flourish he extracted a sizable joint from his jacket pocket and gave it to Ben, whose eyes lit up. Dave just shook his head.

'Have a good night.' Travis drained his beer and stood up. 'Gotta get going... Enjoy!'

Outside the tea room door, instead of turning left towards the exit, he went right, towards the European galleries. As he went, he chuckled to himself, thinking about how he'd packed that joint with so much sticky, resinous Noosa buds, Ben and Dave would be practically paralyzed and talking to each other in ancient Egyptian hieroglyphics, for hours to come.

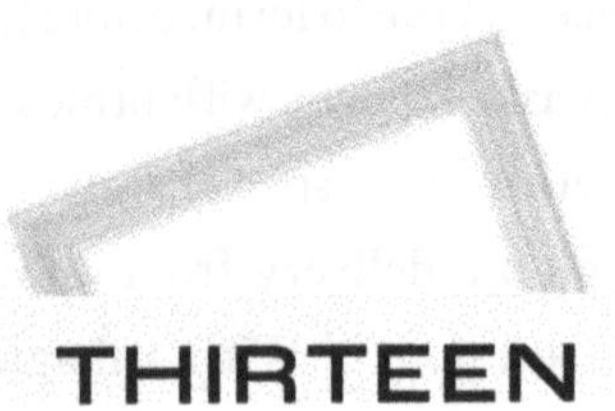

THIRTEEN

Sunday, August 3rd, 1986

What's waiting for us out there might just as well be invented by us, as dictated to us. What's it to be, peace or terror, illumination or illusion, choice or slavery?
Angry Buddha, 2001

Jack woke to the rancid piss-stink of old carpet and a taste in his mouth like something scraped from the bottom of a birdcage. His head was wedged between the timber foot of a sofa and a beanbag. Then, still barely conscious, he found himself on his feet, like he'd levitated to an upright position without really meaning to. His mind began to swim. He looked down at his own prostate body, twisted and half submerged down a wide crack where the cushions met the back of the sofa bed. Clearly he was dead, and his departing consciousness was looking down on his spent corpse, just like in some fucked-up ghost movie.

As his head began to throb mercilessly, he recognised that it was actually his mate, Genghis lying on the couch, not his own expired self. He grabbed an exposed calf and shook it, just to see if his friend was still kicking. Genghis twitched and groaned wretchedly, sinking further into the inner reaches of the couch.

Jack let his instincts guide him to water. At a kitchen sink filled with the unwashed debris of countless meals, he laid his head sideways on the dirty plates and drank from the faucet, cooling his burning throat, and feeling his stomach swell. He imagined himself a camel, at a desert oasis.

Back at the sofa, he took stock, patting his pockets for his wallet and eventually locating it, to his considerable relief, under the nearby coffee table.

He checked it for cash. Empty.

He assessed Genghis to be a lost cause and made for what he assumed was the front door.

Down three flights of dark timber stairs – which reminded him of school days – he exited into a narrow laneway, where he ping-ponged along, bouncing off the brick walls, avoiding the rain puddles between the cobbles. A metal gate which took some opening, spat him out onto the pavement and he stumbled as it sprang shut behind him.

Chapel Street. He half-knew this, already. He had hazy recollections of at least one pub and a night club.

The ornate Neo-gothic gables of the residences above the shops opposite made him feel disoriented for a moment. The weak winter dawn cast everything in a febrile light. A dark vortex of morning cloud enveloped the low sun, with just one bright greenish-orange shaft, like some alien beam escaping from a ragged hole at its base, and detonating beyond the roofline.

To the south, he took his bearings from the corroded green dome of the old Read's department store, on the corner of Commercial Road. In the sickly light, and in his state of disheartened disrepair, it reminded him of a picture he'd seen of Hiroshima's skeletal Exhibition Building – with a similar dome – the only structure that had survived the world's first nuclear attack.

Such musings calibrated the depths of his mood. A brutal

hangover was setting in. He turned north and started walking, with no real plan. He had no money, no car; he would head for the city, maybe get a tram from there, and hope not to get done for having no ticket.

He got a few blocks before he had to stop and vomit up the water he'd gulped down, leaning against a pole, retching into the gutter. When he looked up, he was opposite an apartment block which looked familiar; Hermitage Apartments, 666 Chapel Street. He remembered a girl, whose parents had lived there. He remembered laughing about the street number, but in the end the joke had been on him, because the girl may well have been possessed – such a sick puppy – and the devil's number for an address. He shivered and pushed off the pole. The creepiness of the recollection, for some reason made him remember, for the first time since waking, just how much trouble he was in.

Chapel Street was shaking off its slumber. It seemed derelict in the yet dim light of an overcast dawn; peopled only by shift workers, cleaners, and somnambulant merchants, dead-eyeing the start of another fourteen hour day.

Some of the early morning workers looked up at the shambling young man, looking the worse for wear, but most ignored him. Jack plodded resolutely northward, towards the city, thinking now about Picasso, and the grief he'd depicted in Guernica and the Weeping Woman. Maybe grief was catching. He thought he'd heard something about the painting being cursed.

He cursed himself. Two nights of drinking, trying to blot out the worry of his predicament. But now the anxiety was back, only worse, exacerbated by a monstrous hangover. He remembered Genghis counselling him that he was over-reacting, jumping at shadows. There was no reason to think that Tate was really going to make him copy the Picasso. It was an outlandish idea, if you thought about it.

But Genghis didn't know his dealer like Jack did. He hadn't heard him talking about his plan, with that trademark smarmy coercion of his. Jack's gut – as fragile as it was this morning – told him he was still in trouble.

He reached the end of Chapel Street and crossed over Alexandra Avenue, so he could take the footpath along the south bank of the Yarra, heading towards the city, with stands of eucalypt and bush foliage, giving glimpses of the river below. He trudged along with nature on one side, and the elevated mansions of the South Yarra's elite on the other. By the time he crossed Punt Road the morning traffic was building, and he was starting to flag.

At a sweeping bend, he found a wrought iron gate, guarded by a garden-gnome Jesus, who granted him entry to the botanic gardens. As he passed through, into the gloriously treed and manicured commons, he thought darkly of Gethsemane, and betrayal. He navigated the web of paths with one eye on the city buildings and eventually came to a strange, small circular structure, like a Greek temple, overlooking the river. A patch of early morning sun illuminated an area of thick, sculptured ground cover of exotic origins, and a line of native shrubs bordering the temple. He sat down in the sun, just to rest for a moment.

He woke with a start, curled up and squashed into a silver mound of ground cover. He was shivering. The sun had moved on and he had no idea if he had slept for minutes or hours. His momentary panic subsided when he saw there was no one around. He brushed himself off and hurried down a path which he calculated would spit him out close to the city, on St Kilda Road.

He came out opposite a building he knew well – its imposing façade looking, for Jack's money, like Gestapo headquarters in Nazi-occupied Paris – the Victorian College of the Arts. Further along, at the jutting corner of the National Gallery he imagined he felt the gallery's fountains exerting some kind of curious gravitational pull, on his own depleted waters. By the time he reached the front entrance, and stood before the cascading water wall, he could see the gallery was just opening for Sunday business. There was nothing for it; fate had brought him to the NGV... He was going in.

He crossed the *theme park* foyer and rode one of the rinky-dink escalators to the first floor. He knew exactly where he was going, because he'd come to see the Picasso earlier that year, just after it had been acquired; the international collection, European gallery. Jack reckoned this part of the NGV had all the architectural charm of an underground carpark.

He exited the escalator and came around past a black sculpture on a pedestal; Picasso's Woman Combing her Hair. There, he was confronted by the ghastly magenta partition wall; and the wall was empty, but for four tell-tale screw holes marking the corners of the missing painting, and a small white card stuck to the wall, roughly at the centre of the vanished artwork.

Remembering to breathe, Jack exhaled hard and then sucked in a big breath. He looked around; panic gripping his chest, and there... There was a guard, hovering near the sculpture, his blue jacket and insignia, evoking more airline pilot than police. He eyed Jack suspiciously. Jack's gaze in turn must have seemed intense, beseeching perhaps, even fearful. He turned deliberately towards the missing Picasso, as if trying to draw the guard's attention to the alarming sight of the empty space. The security man gave Jack a stern and puzzled frown and nodded slightly towards the wall. Jack assumed he was drawing his attention to the hand-written card on the wall.

Jack leaned in and squinted*: Painting removed to the A.C.T.* the card read, hand-written in capital letters.

'What does it mean?' He posed the question with a breathless intensity, more like he was asking for the meaning of life, and barely even aware that he had spoken out loud. The guard looked at him depreciatively.

'On loan. Gone up to the National Gallery in Canberra.' The guard shrugged casually to back up his nonchalance.

'Are you sure?'

Clearly taken aback by Jack's questioning of his authority on the matter, the guard's back stiffened. 'I think you better move on, son.' Now he sounded more like a cop.

Jack floated back down to the ground floor, without even really knowing how he got there. *Removed to the A.C.T...* The words kept playing over and again in his head as he wandered the lower reaches of the gallery.

What did it mean? Could it be true? The Picasso was gone! This after Tate had told him they had something big planned. He had literally told him to practice his cubism. He bet Tate had connections at the NGV.

Removed to the A.C.T.? Could it be just a coincidence? Jack didn't believe it, not for a minute. He could feel it in his bones, even when he'd found himself standing outside the NGV that morning, even before he went inside. But he had really known, the moment he saw that blank magenta wall. His worst fear realised: They – whoever *they* were – had taken the Picasso, and Tate was going to make him copy it.

Removed to the A.C.T? Absolute bullshit!

He found himself in the Great Hall, where children were lying on the carpet looking up at the stained glass ceiling, so he found himself a quiet spot and did the same. In any case he needed to lie down. More importantly he needed to gather his thoughts. He fell into a kind of meditative spell almost right away, looking up at the kaleidoscopic ceiling; or perhaps he had become catatonic from a combination of shock, stress and a crippling hangover.

He lay there for a long time, letting the colours of the stained glass flow through his consciousness, and – in occasionally lucid moments – trying to understand why his life was spinning so out of control.

All the while the notion of '*removed to the ACT*' kept echoing faintly in his consciousness. *Such an innocuous-sounding lie. Doubtless it was a cover-up*. He would never be sure whether or not it happened right there, as he lay on the hard floor, staring up at the vast ceiling; or whether it happened sometime later... But certainly, by the time he made his way back to Brunswick, the acronym *A.C.T* had morphed into something else in his mind, and no longer stood for Australian Capital Territory – home of Canberra's National Gallery.

In future years, he would claim, quite fairly, that he couldn't pin point the precise moment, or exactly how A.C.T. had taken on an entirely new meaning, and through that re-invention, a life of its own. But Jack's intuitively divined iteration of A.C.T. – inspired or not by the artistry of the NGV's stained glass ceiling – would provide him with the escape hatch he needed, and a way to turn the tables on his arch-nemesis, his irretrievably bent art dealer.

*

Jack yanked the sheet out of his uncle's old typewriter and started reading it, from the top. He didn't even get half way, before screwing it into a ball and heaving it towards the waste-paper basket in the corner, to join many other crumpled missiles that had missed the bin.

'Fuck it', he muttered. *He had to get the voice right... That was the thing. It was sounding too much like something* he *would write. He needed to disguise it.*

In a moment of inspiration, he thought of his uncle. *Yes...Yes! He would love this shit. And he would know just how to stick it up them!*

Jack wound another sheet into the typewriter, and in a moment he was typing again, this time channeling his departed uncle: *Scratch the preamble – too much bullshit just get straight to the point.*

Okay: 'We have stolen the Picasso from the National Gallery...'

Jack paused and chewed his thumb. *A protest at the miserable funding... No, wait...* He remembered a word he might only have ever heard his uncle use. The story was, his uncle had heard a politician use this word once, and he'd exploded in rage – indignant at the use of such a racist word in public office – until he'd looked it up and found that it wasn't actually racist at all, but in fact was derived from Old Norse, via Middle English in the 14th century... A word meaning stingy or miserly.

Yes, that would do it.

Jack started typing again: '...as a protest against the *niggardly* funding of the fine arts in this hick state...'

Ha... that would confuse the shit out of them, I mean, who ever talked like that? ... Only Uncle Bill. He remembered fondly that his uncle would occasionally throw a *niggardly* into a conversation at the most inopportune time, always with a glint in his eye at the mischievous perversity of it, and only ever as a way of wrong-footing, or embarrassing someone pompous and entitled... and white.

He continued typing in the same vein: '...and against the clumsy, unimaginative stupidity of the administration and distribution of that funding.'

He kept the bullshit demands the same – red herrings they were, in any case – the increased annual funding, the art prizes. He added that the prize should be called the Picasso Ransom... *Ha ha.*

He'd decided early on that the ransom note would be addressed to Ross Maynard, his erstwhile, gas-lighting, asshole of a year twelve art teacher. After all, he was now a minister of the crown, and bizarrely, he had the dual portfolio of Police and the Arts... It was almost too perfect. The karmic irony and justice of it all had blossomed in his breast like a spiritual epiphany when he realised he could pull the rug out from under Tate and his cronies, and at the same time drag Maynard into it, and pillory him in public. It was beautiful. It was all meant to be. And righteous revenge was going to taste so sweet.

'... Because the Minister of the Arts is also the Minister of Plod, we are allowing him a sporting seven days in which to try to have us arrested while he deliberates. There will be no negotiation. At the end of seven days if our demands have not been met, the painting will be destroyed and our campaign continue.'

Perfect. And who exactly are 'we'?

It had come to him like a bolt from the cold, blue winter sky as he walked the last stretch from the tram stop to home. And when it had hit him, his hangover was instantly dispelled and he was energised with a rare clarity and purpose. It was the 'A.C.T.' written on the little white registrar's card at the gallery that had given it to him... It had lodged in his mind like a brain worm, as if it was a secret code, with a hidden message to convey. And he supposed in a way it was.

But how exactly would his uncle sign them off?... Yes, sarcastically, of course. Perfect.

'Your very humble servants,

Australian Cultural Terrorists.'

Jack hit the return bar a couple of times and read it through while the sheet remained in the typewriter. The irony and the beautiful symmetry of what was coming together was exquisite.

Whoever had taken the Weeping Woman off the wall at the NGV – presumably so that Tate could make Jack copy it – had done so with the utmost indifference, confident that the simple little card, indicating – a little prosaically – that it had gone for a visit to the National Gallery in Canberra, would cover their tracks indefinitely. He was going to fuck up their little plan, and someone was going to rue the day they'd written *removed to the A.C.T.* A.C.T. was about to take on a whole new meaning, when The Age newspaper received his ransom note, and then the shit would well-and-truly hit the fan.

Satisfied, he wound the sheet back to the top and engaged the Caps Lock: ATTENTION: ROT MAYNARD (MLA), he typed. No sooner had he typed it, than he thought putting *Rot* instead of Ross was a dumb joke, but at that very moment, he heard a key rattle in the front door lock... *Penny!*

*

Hearing Penny coming in the front door, Jack's mind began to race. She had only been gone for two days, but it might as well have been months, because so much had changed. Only two days since he met Tate down at Port Melbourne and learned about his rotten plan. Two nights carousing with Genghis, trying to forget his dilemma, now seemed lost in a fog of endless partying from one end of the city to the other. It had culminated in a long seedy Sunday, his dawn foot-slog home to Brunswick; detouring into the NGV to confirm his worst fear; and now here he was, typing a ransom note to the government and masquerading as the Australian Cultural Terrorists – his own bizarrely contrived criminal gang. All whilst Penny had been having a nice quiet weekend catching up with her mum and her old school friends.

Abruptly, Jack realised he'd lost his mind – or at least that was exactly what Penny would think. How could he explain any of this to her? She would have an absolute shit fit.

He took the letter out of the typewriter and folded it twice, and slipped it into the envelope he had waiting on his desk. If she read it, she was not going to understand.

Penny dumped her car keys on the kitchen bench and came two steps into the living area and then stopped dead. No *hello sweetie*, *hey babe*, or anything like that.... She just stared at Jack and said: 'What the fuck?'

He must've looked a fright. No sleep, still half drunk, unwashed and deeply fucked-up by the stress he'd been under; even more so because of his recent frantic project, involving a typewriter and Machiavellian madness. Screwed-up evidence of his insanity was strewn all over the place, together with coffee cups and plates and other shit he hadn't cleaned up since Friday.

'How's your mum?' Jack enquired dubiously as he slid the envelope onto the kitchen bench and gathered up a couple of cups and plates and pushed them tentatively across the bench towards the sink.

'What's going on? Are you alright?' Penny's brow scrunched itself up as she surveyed the room, taking in the mess, the typewriter on the table, and then refocused on Jack, who was clearly in the biggest mess of all.

Jack insisted on making Penny a cup of tea, and having her sit down before he would brief her. This made her think it was something serious, and her whole demeanor changed, from surprised annoyance, to ominous concern. She'd started to wonder if someone had died, until Jack got her settled with her tea and began his explanation.

He started by telling her his suspicions about Tate had all been well founded; the bastard *had* been selling his paintings as Fred

Williams originals. 'I'm an art forger!' Jack told her incredulously. Tate had tricked him into painting Fred Williams facsimiles, and the fucker was clearly willing to hang him out to dry for it. He'd threatened as much.

Jack told her everything that happened at his frenetic meeting with Tate at Port Melbourne on Friday, including him physically attacking his dealer, and finishing with Tate's not-very-veiled hint that they were planning to get him to copy the Picasso. Penny's expression waxed and waned from amazement and disbelief, to horror as she sipped her tea and listened.

A little shame-faced, he gave an abbreviated account of his and Mile's escapades during his week-end bender and finished with his impromptu visit to the NGV that morning, and his discovery that the Weeping Woman was indeed missing. He pulled up short of mentioning his imagined gang of cultural terrorists. He didn't want to completely freak her out.

'So what are you going to do?' Penny gave him a strangely intense and stern look.

'I'm gonna fuck their shit up.' Jack returned an equally intense and determined expression.

'But who are *they*?'

'I don't know.... Tate must be in cahoots with someone at the NGV.'

'Cahoots?' Penny suppressed a smile at Jack's country vernacular, then turned it into a frown and carefully placed her empty cup on its saucer.

Jack handed her the letter, already sealed in the envelope, and addressed to The Age newspaper.

'What's this?' Penny's frown deepened. 'News Tip?' She read aloud the annotation Jack had added – a little jauntily – at a forty-five-degree angle across the top left corner of the envelope.

Jack dead-panned his girlfriend and matched her serious frown. 'That's the cat amongst their pigeons... Big time. In fact a fucking *wild cat* amongst their bloody pigeons.'

'Jesus... The media? What does it say?'

'Well, these mother-fuckers think they can get away with this shit. Take the Picasso off the wall – Tate's got to have an insider at the NGV, I reckon – they've probably done stuff like this before. Leave a card on the wall – all official like – saying it's gone for cleaning, or up to the sister gallery in Canberra, or whatever... While they get a copy made.'

Jack thought again of his inspirational reimagining of ACT. The painting sure as shit hadn't gone to Canberra.

'This blows the whistle on them. It's telling The Age that the Picasso has been stolen. Tate's not gonna know what's hit him.' Jack nodded smugly, and put out his hand for the envelope. 'I'm going down the corner to post it right now.'

'Fucking hell!' Penny didn't give up the envelope, but continued to look at it with a worried frown, her expression becoming perplexed. 'What if you're wrong? You can't be sure Tate's involved. What if it really has been stolen... and why does it say A.C.T. at the bottom here?'

'That's the best bit, but it's a bit of a long story...I'll explain later. But it's them, I know it's them, one hundred percent.' Jack wiggled the fingers of his out-stretched hand.

Penny ignored him, still looking at the envelope. Thinking. She looked up at Jack, with a measured expression, and then back at the envelope. 'You can't post it down there.'

Jack tilted his head and gave an interrogatory grunt. 'Huh?'

'No fucking way! Because it'll end up post-marked with Brunswick PO, which is ten doors from our house.' Penny flapped the letter in the direction of the main street, not fifty meters from their front door.

Jack nodded and raised his eyebrows, conceding she had a very good point.

'I've got an assignment due at midnight. I've got to take it out to the Burwood campus this afternoon. I'll post it out there, at the mail centre.'

'Perfect.' Jack grinned and leaned over and kissed her on the cheek. 'Lucky I've got a criminal mastermind for a girlfriend, I hadn't even thought of that.'

While Penny went and put away her stuff from the weekend and searched out her assignment, Jack started tidying up some of his mess and hunted up a stamp for the envelope. Eventually Penny emerged, assignment in hand, and picked up the envelope from the kitchen bench. She looked at Jack with a troubled expression, she was clearly still not at ease with the situation – not at all.

Jack tilted his head sideways; a *what's up* gesture.

'So they think they've got the painting for as long as they want, just like that, so they can make a copy... Get *you* to paint a copy?'

'Right.'

'But *this* tells the media that the painting has been stolen?' She flapped the letter in the air. 'And then the absolute shit hits the fan... Someone has friggin' stolen the most expensive painting ever purchased by an Australian gallery, right out of the NGV, right?'

Jack nodded excitedly. 'Yeah, full on fucking art heist shit, awesome isn't it?' He grinned and popped his brows.

'Yeah, but the whole bloody police force, insurance companies, and god knows who else, are all going to be looking for that painting... It's going to be chaos – an absolute shit-storm.'

'Yes... So...' Jack gave his girlfriend a puzzled expression. 'Those fucking bastards are going to shit their pants. Especially Tate, that fucking asshole...'

'Yeah, but what if he turns up *here* with the painting? I mean before *this* gets delivered...' She held up the envelope. '...and *before* the shit hits the fan? What if Tate brings it around here? I mean after all, you're the one they were going to get to copy it, right? What happens if the fucking thing ends up *here*... In our house!?'

'Fuck me,' Jack exhaled the expletive and his mouth stayed open. He hadn't really thought this through. That was a horrifying scenario, and it could probably quite easily happen. He was looking at Penny with dismay etched on his brow.

Penny, meanwhile was reaching for something on the kitchen bench. 'I've got an idea, though.' She held up the video camera from the dance school. 'We use this.'

'Use it for what?'

'For insurance.' Penny nodded deliberately at Jack and smiled self-contentedly.

*

Time passed ever-so-slowly for the remainder of that Sunday afternoon and evening; slowest of all while Penny was out dropping off her assignment and posting the letter.

Jack paced.

He tried to read the paper, but couldn't concentrate. He made himself a coffee, but that only made him even jitterier, especially with the lingering after-effects of all the alcohol. In the end he resorted to cleaning the house, not just to pass the time, but to appease Penny. It seemed the least he could do.

They had set up the video camera before Penny left... Well Penny had, anyway. She concealed it on the sideboard in the front hall, pointing right at the front door. It was hidden behind a carefully constructed edifice comprised of magazines and books, a house plant and two stuffed toys from the bedroom. It had taken some time, but eventually she'd got it looking natural and there was no sign of the camera, its lens secreted with a direct line of sight to the entry, through the underarm of a nonchalantly reclining koala.

Once Penny came home, time dragged still. Jack cooked a simple meal for them – some pasta with pesto and cheese. They turned on the television. The news was on, and Jack couldn't help imagining the following night's news: *Shock horror – NGV Art Heist.* He turned the volume right down low, so they would hear the door.

Penny had posted the letter at the Blackburn Mail Center. She reckoned it would be cleared first thing, and probably delivered early the next day.

Jack paced some more and fidgeted. He couldn't settle. He could tell he was getting right on Penny nerves. She was just as uneasy. *What if he had it all wrong? What if he'd imagined the whole thing? Maybe he'd developed some kind of paranoia?*

They could wait all night and no one might come, nor tomorrow... Maybe never.

When the knock came, neither of them jumped, they just looked wide-eyed at each other for a moment, then Penny put a hand on his arm, indicating *I'll go.* Jack watched like a spy, half concealed by the post of the kitchen bench, as she strode purposefully down the hall, pausing deftly at the sideboard to push *record* behind the pot plant.

She opened the door and then he heard it – Tate's voice. A wave of emotion flooded over him. He had no idea whether it was relief or alarm. He took a deep breath and made a conscious effort to calm himself.

'Wait there, I'll get Jack,' he heard Penny say.

Yes, wait there, while we get you on film. He walked casually down the hallway. Suddenly adrenalin was coursing through him, making him feel sharp and clear-headed. Calm. Time even seemed to slow.

He saw Tate and grinned. 'Evening Logan. What brings you around on a Sunday?' His tone surprised even himself and clearly made an impression on Tate, who smiled warmly, seemingly disarmed by Jack's uncharacteristically friendly tone.

Jack could see he was holding a plywood box by a silver handle attached to the top edge. It was the kind of thing you would use to transport a painting, to protect it. *Fuck!* It could have been anything in the box. No smoking gun there for the camera. He felt a wave of panic, almost dread, but in his heightened state he hid it well. *What had they been thinking? ... That Logan would simply wander up the street with the Weeping Woman bare-faced under his arm?*

Jack sensed himself thinking fast, thinking clear. He stopped in the middle of the hallway right beside the sideboard, effectively blocking Logan's path. *Evidence is what we need.* Penny squeezed past him and called out something about putting the kettle on. Tate stepped inside and then stopped, with Jack effectively barring his way. He smiled awkwardly and patted the side of the box. 'Well... I've got a little surprise for you.' He carefully closed the front door behind him.

'Really? What is it? What's in the box?' Jack feigned his most enthusiastic smile but inwardly worried that he may have looked and sounded a little manic. Tate gave him a puzzled but pleasantly amused look and then nodded to himself. 'Well...' He placed the box on the floor, leaned it back slightly to protect the contents from falling out, then worked a small silver latch on the top, and carefully opened it.

'Jesus Christ!' The garish, vibrant greens and purples of the vaunted Picasso, seemed to fill the entry hall with colour. Jack whistled, because he thought – in his over-adrenalised state – that would be a cool and accommodating thing to do. Tate looked at him with a quizzical and intensely analytical gaze, trying to gauge his reaction.

Jack imagined for a moment he could hear the video camera whirring. Whilst Tate tried to read him, all Jack was thinking was: *Shit, I hope we're getting this.*

'What the fuck...' Jack whispered, trying to think of something appropriate to say – something suitably reactive, so as not to seem too out of character. 'How did you *get* that?'

Tate just beamed, with all-consuming self-satisfaction. Jack felt nauseated. He thought he was about to start trembling. At the same time he felt elated, imagining it all captured on video. 'You can't be fucking serious.' He tried to look surprised, and also a bit hostile, for the sake of the camera.

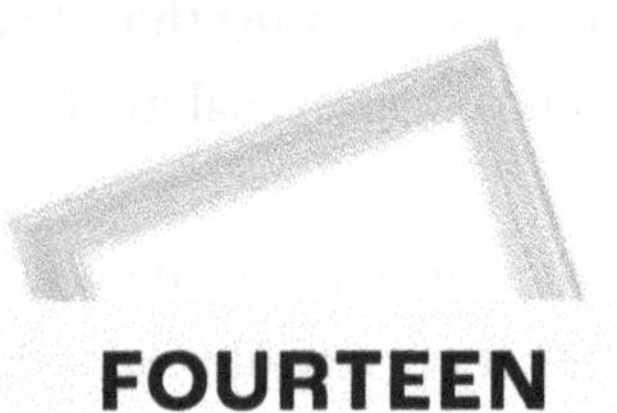

FOURTEEN

Monday, August 4th, 1986

Entities, sentient non-corporal beings, are everywhere. It's very crowded – hey, get out of my car!
Angry Buddha, 2001

Ellery hadn't slept well, and he wasn't sure why. Something had thrown him off balance, and when he thought about it now, it had been destabilising his mood for some time. His godson, Travis. Having him at the gallery as an intern was stressing him out, and he wasn't even sure why. There was just something off about that kid.

With Rosalyn away on interstate business he'd prepared his habitual bachelor's breakfast – a single poached egg on rye toast, with some wilted spinach from her vegetable garden – and a glass of freshly squeezed orange juice. Prepared it thoughtfully, almost ritualistically, a meditation of sorts, to centre himself.

Later he walked to the corner and took the tram up St Kilda Road to the gallery; which, even to himself, seemed a strange choice on a Monday morning, but he needed to stretch his legs and the crisp, blue-sky winter air cleared his head. He regretted it almost immediately. Rattling up the wide boulevard on an old tram that seemed far too crowded for mid-morning. Public transport made him self-conscious and he discerned, or imagined, surreptitious glances from the other passengers, identifying him as *that art gallery guy*. He tried to imagine being an ordinary commuter and was struck by the irony; all these people riding a tram with a genuine celebrity in the arts world, briefly brushing up against their mundane lives and them, barely even aware. He looked out the window at the passing landscape and traffic, trying to distance himself.

He thought again about Travis, and what sprang to mind was the project he'd given him – well, it was in fact Travis himself who'd come up with the idea – to send the Picasso on loan to the National Gallery in Canberra. He suddenly realised it was this week that the arrangements were to be made to send her off to Canberra, and for some reason he was suddenly quite anxious. His eye fell back inside the tram and onto a runlet of dried egg yolk on the lapel of a man sitting opposite him, reading the Sun. For some strange reason, the errant egg stain made him feel even more anxious.

The tram ride was mercifully short.

Walking into the gallery past the water wall, the security guard at the front entrance gave him a very strange look. Perhaps he just wasn't used to seeing him come in the front, especially with the gallery closed to the public for cleaning on a Monday.

It was almost midday, and he made his way briskly upstairs to his office. There he was confronted by the gallery's security controller, Glynn Llewellyn – ex-navy and urbane, with a second generation hint of a Welsh lilt – accompanied by his own private secretary, Grace. They were clearly waiting for him, and right away he detected an air of anticipatory angst.

He sidled past them with a smile and a greeting nod, but was unable to ignore the nervous flutter in his gut. The two of them followed him into his office and their demeanor darkened, almost like they were all entering a funeral chapel together. He put his briefcase on the floor next to his desk and turned on them with a questioning frown. 'Yes... good morning. And how is everything in the wonderful world of the arts, this fine day?'

They glanced first at each other, unsure of who was going to speak, and then back at Quinn, grim consternation written large on both their faces.

'We think the Picasso has been stolen,' Llewellyn said simply, dour and flat in his tone. His secretary concurred with a slight widening of her worried eyes.

'What? The Weeping Woman?' Quinn's mind raced. He had a sinking, irksome feeling in his gut – that the anxiety he'd felt in the tram on the way in, thinking about Travis – had been prescient in some way. He was already on the move, past the two of them and back out of his office and along the corridor. 'Nonsense! Come on, let's see.'

He made for the European Galleries at fast clip, the other two struggling to keep up, and as he rounded the corner, there it was, the magenta wall...Empty.

The Picasso...Gone!

Just four tell-tale screw holes and a white registrar's card, pinned at the centre of the blank space where the Weeping Woman should have been.

'Jesus!' He looked from Llewellyn to Grace and then back at the blank wall. 'What the hell...?' He could feel his face contorting and his mind was doing the same. 'But what's this?' He took a step forward and reached for the card on the wall.

'Don't touch it!' Llewellyn almost yelled.

Quinn recoiled and then recovered himself and frowned at his security chief. He leaned in to see the card without touching it. 'Removed to the ACT,' he read aloud. 'So, this says...' he gestured towards the card, '...seems to be saying...' He looked with puzzlement at Grace. 'This would seem to indicate it's gone to Canberra...' He screwed up his face even more and looked at Grace, with a sudden surge of irritation erupting inside him.

'Wasn't that meant to be happening this week...?' His eyes blazed and Grace looked worried. 'Where the hell is Travis!?'

Grace shrugged. Llewellyn looked confused.

'How... Why would it have gone earlier? ... I don't understand. Wait, was it there yesterday?... I mean all day Sunday, and presumably...' Quinn trailed off, with an uncomfortable feeling that he was babbling.

His two charges exchanged a glance that seemed to reference some sort of knowledge unavailable to Quinn.

He frowned.

They frowned back.

His security chief looked him in the eye, in a way that transmitted empathy and alarm in equal measure. 'We've had several calls from The Age newspaper this morning. They say they've received a *ransom note* from a group calling themselves the *Australian Cultural Terrorists*. They say they've stolen the Weeping Woman.'

Quinn shat himself... Figuratively, not literally of course, except perhaps on some sort of cellular level. Later, after the shock subsided, that would be how he'd describe it to himself... As if every individual cell in his body had simultaneously evacuated toxic effluent into his bloodstream and turned it to an ice-cold river of shit.

'Ridiculous!' he croaked. A febrile chill racked his body. 'That's impossible!'

And where the hell was Travis? Surely he was the *only* one could provide some kind of clue to this debacle.

'How? .... How on earth?' He started to imagine scenarios,

filmic images of masked bandits skulking in the dark, paintings under their arms. 'It can't have been stolen, surely...' He looked beseechingly at his secretary and then his security head. 'Surely it can't be true, I mean if this says it's in Canberra...' He looked to his hand-written card as if it was some kind of talisman, drawing their attention to it again. Only then did he realise that the handwriting on the card appeared to be his own. He shuddered inside again, and had a disconcerting sensation of being in a dream – or indeed, a nightmare.

When he looked back, the chief's face wore a puzzlingly ironic half smile and he was nodding his head.

'Clever buggers aren't they?'

'What?'

'My men saw it was missing of course, all day yesterday, but were sure it had gone up to Canberra... *Removed to the A.C.T.*' He let the acronym hang.

'Yes...' Quinn nodded his head impatiently, perplexed, and distracted by a horridly vivid memory of Travis suggesting the Canberra loan, and him agreeing, thinking it would be a good and challenging project for him.

Llewellyn was looking at him strangely again. Consternation with a hint of panic, like his boss was missing something obvious. Annoyingly the security chief repeated himself: 'A.C.T.' And then, when all Quinn gave him was a blank stare, he said it again. 'A.C.T.... Australian... Cultural... Terrorists.' He said it slowly, like he was teaching a child.

Quinn closed his eyes and his mouth gaped. He let out a small gasp. His gradual understanding that all logic really had departed his world, set off a new storm of torrid neurochemicals in his brain and he was dumbstruck for a moment... *What the actual fuck was going on here?*

Where the hell is Travis! ... The silent scream reverberated in his dazed mind.

Llewellyn went on: 'Bloody clever dicks.... Calling themselves the Australian Cultural Terrorists, and leaving behind a card with their initials, knowing we'd think it meant the National Gallery in Canberra.' His chief held his boss in a piercing glare. 'It's almost as if they knew something about gallery procedures.' This in thoughtful tone. 'The damnedest part is, it's given them a head start. We think the theft must've occurred on Saturday night and so they've been away with it all day Sunday, with nobody any the wiser.' He took a step towards the barren wall and indicated one of four screw holes. 'What I can't figure out is how they unscrewed the snake eyes. You need a special tool to do those.'

'J...Jesus...' Quinn ran a hand up through his hair, trying to grasp all the implications. 'Stolen?... Cultural terrorists? This can't be.' His mind's eye flashed him an image of the security screw-driver in the top draw of his desk. As far as he knew it was only one of two in the whole gallery.

And so it was, with a confidence he didn't feel, he consigned himself to the path of the unexpected and startling new reality which had been foisted upon him. The way he saw it he had no choice. *Yes. The Picasso had been stolen by the Australian Cultural Terrorists... whoever the flying fuck they were.*

'Let's get back to my office, I'll need to make some calls.' Quinn regained some of his composure as he spoke. 'Has anyone told Wendy? We need to schedule a special board meeting. The police have been informed I take it?'

'Yes,' affirmed his chief of security, 'and we'll need to do a thorough search of the gallery. We can't discount the possibility that it's a hoax and the painting's been hidden somewhere in the gallery.'

He hurried after the other two, calling out to his secretary: 'I think we'll use your office as the war room for now Grace, if you don't mind. Let's reconvene there in about fifteen minutes.'

This would give him time to get hold of Travis and, if necessary wring some sort of explanation out of him.

*

Back in his office, Quinn snatched up his phone and speed dialed Travis. It just kept ringing until he was ready to wrench the thing out of the wall and hurl it. He slammed the phone down hard, and looked up to see Travis himself, standing in the open doorway of his office.

'What's all the fuss?' Travis' tone was casual, a little jocular even – as though arriving for work at noon on a Monday was nothing to be remarked on – and him apparently oblivious to what the fuss *was* all about.

'Have you seen? Have you been up to the European Gallery?' Quinn glared at his charge.

Travis frowned and screwed up his lips. The expression angered Quinn more than it should.

'The Picasso... It's fucking gone!'

Travis wasn't sure he'd heard his godfather swear like that before. 'Which Picasso?'

'The bloody Weeping Woman! Gone! Vanished.... Over the weekend sometime... She's... she...'

'Do you mean she's gone up to Canberra?... Already?' Travis' tone and manner was calm and almost condescending in contrast to Quinn's agitation. For a moment it robbed Quinn of words – then angered him and confused him in equal measure.

'No.... No!' ... Has she?' Quinn blinked and twitched involuntarily. 'No!'

Travis gave him a worried expression. Ellery seemed to be losing his grip. Travis had wondered how he would react. He hadn't really given much thought to how he would explain bringing forward the *dispatching* of the Picasso. He'd figured he'd just wing it – as he usually did – blame it on the specialist freight forwarders, striking transport workers, storm and tempest ... Something.

But Quinn's extreme state of agitation, right now, was more than a little concerning.

'Well, you know we were intending to send the painting up to Canberra this week...' Travis trailed off, because of the expression on his godfather's face. He was quite sure he hadn't seen Ellery look like that before... Aggrieved and sad, with fear and anger battling for supremacy on his clouded visage.

'No!' Quinn's tone was hard and emphatic. As he continued, it became disconcertingly matter-of-fact. 'Llewellyn has just told me, the newspapers have received a ransom note from a group calling themselves *The Australian Cultural Terrorists...* Saying they've stolen the Picasso, and if their demands are not met, they will destroy it.'

The two stared at each other and no one blinked for some time until they both did. 'That's impossible,' Travis breathed.

'What?' Quinn's eyes became even more penetrating. 'Do you know something about this?'

'No, no...' The grievous look on the director's face told Travis *it being impossible,* was not a good line for him to take. 'It just – surely that can't be...'

Travis had a horridly clear image of himself handing the de-framed Picasso stretcher to Tate the previous afternoon, and an equally disturbing mental picture of the big chunky and oh-so-recognizable frame, which he'd carefully removed from the masterpiece, and hidden on top of a high cabinet in the gallery where, he'd assumed no one would ever look, until he was ready to retrieve it.

'Trust me... The media have been calling all morning, the police are on the way, and I've just convened an emergency board meeting. She really has been stolen...' He gave Travis a plainly suspicious look, '...Apparently.'

'Christ...' Travis inserted a croaky bit of emotion into his voice, trying to sound as surprised as possible, which wasn't hard, because his head was spinning trying to understand what the fuck had just happened. *How and why could anyone be claiming to have stolen the painting, when in fact it was still in his own safe-keeping?...Well in Tate's keeping for the moment. The Weeping Woman wasn't stolen, it was safe, albeit away from the gallery briefly... for undisclosed purposes.*

As he stood there in Quinn's ominous glare, a ghastly reality was dawning on him. His world had now split into two alternate realities, and somehow, he was going to have to navigate between the two, until the fabric of his personal universe could be repaired. With that, Travis' mind suddenly filled with every platitude he'd ever heard about the problems posed by weaving a web of lies and the inevitability of that web ultimately strangling its creator.

*

While Quinn went to his meeting, Travis made a bee-line for the European Gallery, ostensibly to *see for himself.* Once there – and mercifully with no one else in sight – he deftly plucked the registrar's card off the wall and put it in his pocket.

On the way back he stopped at the tall cabinet where he stashed the frame, and did a little jump and craned his neck to see if it was visible, which it was...Just. He checked the area left and right and then, standing on his tip-toes, reached up and pushed it further back with the tip of his finger. Thank God he'd had the presence of mind to give the thing a really good wipe before he stashed it.

Evidence – what else was there? He'd already put the snake eyes tool back in Quinn's desk on the night. *So that was about it.* Now, back to his broom-cupboard office, *and call bloody Tate...* Tell him what had happened – not that he even knew exactly what the hell had happened – and tell him to bring the painting back.

'We need to meet.' The clenched urgency in Travis' voice couldn't help but transmit down the phone line.

'Okay...' There was an uneasy and exaggerated uncertainty in Logan's voice.

'Urgently!'

'What the hell's going on?'

'We're in deep, deep fucking shit.'

'Jesus... Okay, where?'

'Get down here to the café around the corner. I'll see you there in an hour. If I'm late, wait.

'Are you going to tell me what this is all about?' Tate asked this a little tetchily, somewhat taken aback by Travis's urgent and inflexible tone.

'Not on the phone. One hour.' Travis hung up, leaving Logan to stew.

*

The hastily called meeting in Quinn's secretary's office with no particular agenda and an overriding sense of doom, was not going well. Wendy was on the warpath, furious to be dragged in without notice, only to find herself part of a train wreck in progress. There was no way to spin this to the board. It was an unmitigated shit show.

Derek Tillery, the gallery's chief conservator, kept interjecting with questions that made everyone uncomfortable; questions about insurance (the complete lack of it), security measures (also lacking) and all the embarrassment *that* was going to cause when the media, and probably the police too, inevitably asked the inescapable questions.

Meanwhile Llewellyn told them his security people had already found the empty frame, thrown up on top of a display cabinet near the missing painting.

Grace was racing back and forth between the meeting and her outer office – fielding calls and relaying. The other papers and at least one television station were onto it, and were calling incessantly looking for quotes, wanting an interview with the director.

'We'll need to schedule a press conference,' she said.

'Christ,' intoned Wendy.

'What are we going to tell them? We don't even know what's happened ourselves yet,' Derek complained.

Glynn Llewellyn pointed out that without some sort of appraisal by the police – some sort of investigation – it would be premature to announce anything to the press.

'And where the hell are the police?' Wendy demanded with rhetorical candor.

'We don't even know that it's gone,' continued Llewellyn. 'I mean it could still be a prank, we need to search the gallery. It might still be here somewhere.'

'I don't think so.' Derek shook his head morosely. 'Finding the frame like that – that's a bad sign. Without the frame you could just carry it out under a coat, I mean the stretcher itself is only a foot and half.' The conservator held his hands out in front of his face, estimating the dimensions of the missing canvas, and eyed them gloomily. 'And it means whoever took it knew what they were doing – had some expertise in handling a valuable artwork.'

'What, you mean someone just walked out the front door with

it?' Wendy was aghast. 'Surely security would stop them?'

'Well, we're a public art gallery – hundreds of people coming and going every hour – especially on a Sunday.' Derek shrugged and smiled faintly. 'You know, they could've come in late on Saturday, and hidden 'till the gallery closed, then removed the painting in the middle of the night, and when the doors opened on Sunday morning, out they go, with the stretcher under their coat.

'Fuck me, really!?' Wendy was incredulous. She switched her attention to Quinn and gave him an incendiary scowl. 'Could they do that? Is there anywhere to hide in the gallery?'

Quinn bowed his head and sighed. A humorless chuckle came from Llewellyn and Derek simultaneously, drawing Wendy's ire back on them. 'So many places,' said Llewellyn glumly. 'The place is a labyrinth – false walls, partitions, storerooms – they could have just hidden in the toilets. In fact one of my men found a couple of empty beer cans in one of the toilets; could have been left there on Saturday night.'

'What? What about security? Surely the security patrols would have discovered them if they were there all night?' She looked at Quinn again, increasingly puzzled and annoyed by his apparent detachment.

He sighed again and said: 'After closing there are only two guards on duty. They do hourly patrols, just through the main galleries. They don't even turn the lights on... Just with torches.'

'You have to be shitting me.'

'I shit you not Wendy. It's a budgetary thing – your budget. Something about weekend penalty rates.'

Wendy sat back with a loud groan and proceeded to smolder. Quinn checked his watch. 'I'm going to need to put something together for this press release...What are we going to say?'

'All we've really got for now are these so-called Australian

Cultural Terrorists.' Llewellyn ran a hand through his grey stubbled hair and Quinn swore under his breath.

'I suppose we have to assume they're serious, that they really have stolen it, to draw attention to arts funding. Doesn't seem very plausible though...'

Derek cut Llewellyn off. 'Or it's a ruse to distract everyone while they get the painting out of the country. Seems more likely it's an old-fashioned art heist and their intention is to sell it.'

'Surely it's too hot, they'd never get away with it.'

'Hm, well, you might be surprised, there's a very healthy and extensive black market out there for stolen art; you know, some far flung millionaire with a private collection in his basement, just wants to show off to his mates – look here, I have a Picasso – and the mainstream art world, none the wiser.'

'Or maybe the whole thing's a prank,' interjected Quinn, 'and with a bit of luck she'll be returned unharmed, sooner rather than later, I hope.' The rest of them looked at him with a more or less similar quizzical expression, perplexed by his optimism and surprised he wasn't taking the theft a lot harder.

He adjusted to a more somber tone and said; 'In the meantime, I really should get something down on paper for the press, so perhaps we should wrap this up.'

As if on cue, Grace hung up the phone in the outer office and poked her head around the corner. 'The police are here.'

Quinn got to his feet and the others roused themselves. 'Right, Glynn, why don't you take Wendy and Derek, go and sort out the police... We'll start working up a press release.'

*

Travis strode into the café and looked around impatiently until he saw Tate in a corner booth, at the back... Pretty good privacy, no one much about, the café getting ready to close.

As he sat down Tate gave him a look of impatient annoyance at being kept waiting, opened his hands and shrugged his shoulders. *Well?*

'We are royally fucked!' An emphatic whisper, fixing Tate with a penetrating stare which turned Tate's annoyance instantly to fear.

'Why?' A frown and a belligerent tone.

Travis didn't answer right away. He took a deep breath and exhaled slowly, keeping his partner in crime fixed in a hard and ambiguous glare. 'The Weeping Woman has been *stolen*.' He used his index fingers to put quote marks around the word.

'What the... What!?'

Travis lifted a brow, tipped his head and gave the slightest of nods, unnerving Tate with the fire in his eyes.

'Are you fucking crazy?' Tate switched to a condescending tone that seemed to imply he was talking to someone in a delusional state. 'No... No, it hasn't...'

'Listen, in about half an hour, Quinn's giving a press conference right outside the front entrance of the gallery, to the assembled Melbourne media in all their rabid glory, telling them that the Picasso was stolen from the gallery on Saturday night by a group calling themselves the Australian Cultural Terrorists, and that said group are holding the painting for ransom.'

'You, my friend, have surely been chewing on the insane root ...' There was a tremulous tone to Tate's voice – half humour, half fear.

'Listen! The Age newspaper... This morning, received a ransom note from these so-called fucking terrorists with a list of demands, saying they have the painting and if their demands aren't met in seven days – seven days for Christ's sake – the painting will be destroyed.'

'No...'

'Yes.'

'How... How is that even possible? *We* have the painting... I mean, it's just us. *We* have it. No one knows...' Tate looked uncertain, like a child trying to spin a story to a parent.

'No one?...'

'Well...'

'Who else knows?'

'Well, only my painter, Jack, I mean, he's the one doing the work...'

'Where is the painting right now?' Travis demanded belligerently. His tone shocked Tate – always the senior member of their little partnership. But it was almost as if there had been a role reversal of sorts, with Logan struggling to absorb the facts, and Travis seemingly calling the shots.

'I took it around to his place last night...He was going to start work on it today... Jesus!' Tate exclaimed and exhaled, as the implications cascaded in his head.

Travis glared at him. 'Jesus won't bloody help us. Get around there – get around there right now – and get it back!'

*

Tate peered in through the stained glass side window and strained to hear any noise coming from inside. He couldn't see much at all, just a dim distortion of Jack's front hall; no movement, not a sound.

He knocked again, louder this time, and put his mouth close to the key hole and tried to project his voice into the house, feeling awkward and embarrassed at the plaintive sound of his own voice: 'Hey, Jack!... You home?'

Nothing.

'Fuck!' He spat the whispered expletive at the lichen-crusted porch and looked around self-consciously at his own parked car, and then up and down the street.

What the hell was he going to do? Where could he be at five o'clock on a Monday... on this particular Monday of all Mondays. 'Jesus Christ!' He tried to look through the window again and then the futility and tension of the situation overtook him and he lost his shit altogether. 'Fuck it... Fuck!' He literally stamped his foot on the ground and threw a senseless air punch at the front door, following it with pinched groan and then a weary sigh.

'Alright....alright, shit!' *Calm down.* He went down off the porch and followed a cracked and overgrown concrete path to the side gate. The gate yielded to his touch, and he looked over his shoulder furtively, like a burglar, as he pushed it open and went down the side path. Only then did he realise he was actually going to break in... He didn't know how, but he had to get in. No fucking way was he waiting for Jack to get home from where ever in the galloping blue blazes he was... He had to get that painting back.

He'd heard Quinn on the car radio on the way over, announcing to the gathered press that the Picasso had been stolen. Any doubts he had – any lingering sense that Travis had lost his mind, or was involved in some elaborate scheme – had vanished and a cold tremble had gone through him from nape to toe. They *were* in trouble... But exactly what sort of trouble, no one seemed to know. In some ways that made it all the more disturbing.

He tried to look in the windows down the side of the house, but they were all about chin-high and seemed to be shut tight, so he continued down to the small back yard. In the gathering dusk, it seemed quite secluded and shielded from the neighboring houses by shrubbery, so he went up onto the small timber deck and tried the sliding door. To his surprise, it slid open.

Maybe this was going to be easier than I thought.

He paused just inside and called out: 'Jack!... Penny! Anyone home?'

Silence.

He started by doing a thorough search of the open-plan living area, Jack and Penny's workspace. No sign of the painting or the carrying case anywhere. He checked behind a stack of paintings leaning against the kitchen bench, the big bookshelf against wall, where Jack kept most of his painting materials, Penny's study area, her make-shift bookshelf, under the desk... behind the couch.

Nothing.

He worked his way into the kitchen, opened a couple of cupboards, and even the fridge for no particular reason. He made his way up the hallway, already thinking the bedrooms were likely to be more fertile ground. He hesitated in Penny and Jack's bedroom, suddenly feeling a bit weird about invading their privacy. But he checked the wardrobe and under the bed, had a look on their dresser and behind it. Nothing.

He realised he was doing only a cursory search – hoping it would be easily located. He started to wonder what he would do if he couldn't find it – would he really have to turn the place upside-down?

Only one room left.

In the spare room he checked in the cupboards of the old TV cabinet and under the coffee table, behind the couch. Still nothing.

He went into the hallway muttering expletives and wondering what to do next; go and come back later, do another more thorough search, call Travis? The late afternoon winter sun was hitting the stained glass beside the front door, giving the front hall a stage-lit glow. Something caught his attention on the sideboard by the front door; an envelope, a bulky one, propped up against the shelf, right in the middle. He approached it with an odd, prescient tingling at the nape of his neck and when he got closer, he saw why – the envelope had his name written on it.

He ripped open the envelope with a mix of urgency and trepidation. A hand-written note fell out of it onto the floor. Inside the torn envelope was a VHS video cassette. It also was labelled with his name. It said: *Tate Delivers.*

With a growing sense of morbid unease he reached down and picked up the hand-written note:

Dear Logan,

Penny and I are taking a little break. We hope you enjoy the video, your performance is really quite convincing.

Regards

Jack

PS: If anything happens to me or to Penny, copies of this will AUTOMATICALLY be delivered to the police AND the media.

Tate rushed back into the front room, turned on the television and shoved the cassette into the VCR on the shelf below. He hit play.

The television immediately came to life with snowy static which gradually resolved itself into Penny, shot from behind, opening the front door. Then Tate entering – with the plywood carry case. Tate fell to his knees on the shaggy carpet in front of the television and groaned. He could tell from the angle, that the camera must have been on the dresser, right where he'd just found the tape. He sat transfixed, horrified as the small drama unfolded in a sickening predictable tableau.

He groaned again weakly, like something was dying inside him as the camera caught the case opening to reveal Picasso's lurid greens and purples in all their splendor. And at the top of the frame, his own highly recognizable face, wearing what he knew Jack would describe – had described – as his shit-eating grin.

*

Jack booted his old Corona up the Midland Highway into the deepening dusk with a smile on his face and the radio up loud, to get over the road noise and vibrations of his aging bucket of bolts. Half an hour earlier he'd been delighted to hear the NGV director's press conference broadcast live on the ABC. It was just as he'd thought – big fucking news – Melbourne's media were in a frenzy. The story would probably even go international.

He'd hooted out loud hearing Quinn solemnly mention the Australian Cultural Terrorists, and their ransom demands. Fifty kilometers north of Ballarat and he was smiling still, thinking about Tate watching himself on video. It was a safe bet – almost a certainty – that Tate would go to their place, and Jack reckoned he wouldn't be able to resist going in once he found no one home. To that end, he'd left the back door unlocked. It filled him with a warm and happy glow every time he thought about the little surprise he'd left on the sideboard for his conniving dealer.

He glanced at the shopping bag full of art materials beside him, and the rolled up blank canvas on the floor, beside the plywood carry case – the case containing the nation's most valuable artwork.

He hadn't expected to feel this way. *Why didn't he feel guilty or afraid?* Instead he felt elated – a pure high better than any drug – and excited, like anything was possible. Maybe this was how boosting priceless artworks made a person feel. *Maybe he should take it up as a career.*

He also felt vindicated... A deep sense of satisfaction, like he was in the employ of the god of Karma, helping to nudge the wheel of cause and effect. After all, it wasn't him – he hadn't stolen anything, not really – he was just minding it, while the real perpetrators were dished up some well-deserved consequences.

He laughed again, and glanced again at his plunder, on the passenger seat. Whilst Maynard's minions were chasing their tails around Melbourne's art scene, who would guess the two million dollar Picasso was in the front seat of a rust-bucket Toyota in country Victoria halfway to Woop Woop.

Stranger still that he'd acquired the technical paraphernalia Tate had mentioned. It had come to him through the auspices of a tall lanky stranger – with the appearance of a drug dealer and the manner of an undertaker – who had appeared at his house just moments before he departed.

'Are you Mr. Jack Curran?' He'd enquired delicately.

'Who wants to know?' Jack had replied, momentarily freaking out, with the Picasso sitting in the front of the car, as he loaded up the rest of his stuff.

'I have a delivery for you,' he'd intoned morosely, slightly lifting the shopping bag he held in one hand. Only then did Jack notice a rolled up canvas under his arm and he remembered Tate telling him about his technical expert – the aged canvas and the historical paint mixes.

Fuck me, you've got to be joking. 'Did Logan Tate send you?'

'I'm afraid I'm not at liberty to say.' He bent at the knees and placed the shopping bag on the nature strip and held the rolled canvas out to him like it was a precious religious scroll or something.

The recollection brought yet another smile to his face. He had no idea Jack was loading up his car with the Picasso, no less – and the moment this guy turned his back, with all of his bespoke forgery materials too – ready to blast the hell out of Melbourne to parts undisclosed.

The gods were surely smiling on him.

He wondered about Penny. She was going to spend a couple of nights with a friend in Northcote. They'd agreed it might be better to vacate their place in Brunswick for the moment. She would go around and lock up on Tuesday... Check to see if Tate had found his little present. Then after her Tuesday class, Penny would join him up at the farm.

He hoped she wasn't freaking out. Once she'd understood the whole story, she'd been determined, just like him, that they had little choice. He had no qualms about putting himself at risk – if it seemed the only way to extricate himself from the coercive grip of Tate– but the thought that he might be dragging Penny into danger, troubled him.

As he took the St Arnaud Road out of Maryborough, the sky to the west had only the faintest ribbon of orange below a band of dark cloud, the purple sky above graduating to darkness with glimmering Venus emerged like the Bethlehem star, and marking his destination to the Northwest.

He switched off the radio and punched in his new Talking Heads cassette and turned the volume right up.

...We're on the road to nowhere... The rhythmic nihilistic quatrain of his favorite funk punkers filled the car and the aptness of the lyrics gave him a prescient shiver.

FIFTEEN

Tuesday, August 5th, 1986

They would have let Donald Duck walk point that day.
Angry Buddha, 2001

Detective Sergeant Ted Doherty threw back the covers in disgust. He'd had enough; tossing and turning endlessly, or lying staring into the blackness, pondering his fate. It seemed like he'd been tormented by it all night, but when he checked the clock radio, it was only just past midnight. Clearly he hadn't slept at all, and in his current state, probably wasn't going to.

He sat on the edge of the bed and put his head in his hands and massaged his scalp. *What the hell is a frigging cultural terrorist when it's at home, anyway? And why his department? Why the major crime squad? Don't we have an Art and Antiques unit, like the Met do in the UK? And if not, why not?*

The unease had been creeping up on him all evening, ever since getting the late afternoon call from the assistant commissioner himself, telling him the Major Crime Squad had been assigned the Picasso case.

'Your wife's an artist isn't she Ted?' He'd asked him solicitously. 'This one should be right up your alley.'

Like hell it was. Was he serious? Just because my wife paints?

He'd seen the gallery director's press conference on the news, and it already sounded dodgy as hell; something about it just didn't add up.... The painting missing for well over twenty-four hours and nobody notices until the newspapers get a ransom note from these weirdos, making their demands...And the note itself, the language in it just not sounding right; something *off* about it. And the gallery director, with his bow tie and haughty bloody manner...

I mean, who are these people?

They certainly weren't Doherty's people. His world was populated by professional criminals, snitches and all the other fringe dwellers and bottom feeders that circulated in Melbourne's underworld; including bent cops, bent cops in denial pretending to be good cops, and the ones like himself – straight-shooters trying to navigate a path through the bullshit and depravity and violence without being infected by it.

But gallery directors, artists, and bloody cultural extremists? These he knew nothing about. It was like asking a pest exterminator to suddenly take on the work of grooming poodles. He wouldn't even know where to start.

His job normally involved working long established networks of contacts and relationships throughout the underworld. When something big was on, something always sent a shudder out through the web. Crims just loved to talk – contrary to the stereotype of honour among thieves and tight-lipped solidarity – gossip and innuendo was rife throughout Melbourne's underworld. You just had to know where to look and who to talk to – sometimes applying just the right amount of duress or inducement – and eventually the network started leaking information, and that was when his team – just like a bloody big spider – pounced and wrapped up the perpetrators.

But the art world? No contacts. No web. No idea.

Ted made two cups of chamomile tea and took one down to the back room, where he knew Nancy would be working late – as was her wont – in the sunroom she'd re-purposed as her studio.

'Can't sleep, honey?' Nancy didn't look up, but continued delicately working her tiny brush around the petals of a native orchid she'd created in exquisite detail as part of her latest native botanical still-life.

'Hmm...' Ted groaned as he lowered himself onto the daybed by the window, and took a moment to examine his wife's latest work. 'That's looking very nice, isn't it?'

She let the obligatory compliment pass. 'Is it this new case, the stolen painting?... I knew it was going to upset you, the moment you told me about it. It's just not your cup of tea is it?'

'Exactly. I mean what do they expect *us* to do with it? Right outside our remit, isn't it? Bloody artists, students, galleries and all that palaver. My lot wouldn't even know where to start and the whole thing sounds like a bloody prank to me anyway.'

'It's worth millions isn't it?'

'So they say. Can't see why, I have to say. Looks like it was done by a drunk if you ask me... bloody colour-blind drunk at that.'

'Darling, Picasso is one of the most important artists of the twentieth Century. That Quinn's no idiot. Thing'll be worth ten times that one day. 'Nancy dunked her small brush into a glass of liquid and selected another even smaller brush and delicately loaded it with a speck of blue paint.

'Well, I dunno... I already think something stinks about the whole thing, and I don't like the look of that gallery director...'

'Quinn, isn't it?'

'Yeah... I haven't met him yet, but that press conference ... Something just seemed to be a bit off...First impressions anyway.'

'Oh... well I'm sure he was just in shock. It can't be much fun for a gallery director to lose a million dollar painting.'

'Two million,' Ted corrected. 'I think what's really bothering me is that I just haven't got the faintest idea what an investigation like this even looks like.'

'Maybe just follow your instincts, like you always do.'

'Maybe... Only problem is my instincts are telling me this one smells all wrong... My instincts tell me this one is all going to end in tears.' Ted drained the last of his tea and sat contentedly for a few moments watching his wife applying tiny grains of paint with the utmost concentration and a steadiness of hand that defied belief.

*

Audrey turned off the gas under the stove-top macchinetta and carried her glass of orange juice out through the sliding door to the patio. It was bracing after a cold clear night and the low sun barely peeping through the denuded vine twisting over the pergola. She didn't care. After months cooped up in the squash court above Mietta's, it was exquisite to have a garden again – a real house, with a patio no less – with a grapevine canopy and trees along the back, all leafless now, but in the summer it would be a beautiful shady refuge.

It was surprising what you missed. The artist's garret in the city centre had sounded all romantic and bohemian, and it had been fun at first, but the cramped kitchen, the distant bathroom down the long haunted hallway, and the makeshift living space – which had to be cleared every few weeks for exhibitions – had worn them both down. She had begun to long for the simple pleasures of a real house. And they were lucky to get this one, a beautiful renovated terrace in Fitzroy, not far from the main drag. And they could afford it now – with her working for Max and four sell-out Private View exhibitions under their belt – their financial situation had improved dramatically from six months earlier, when they'd first been offered the squash court.

This was their first morning in the new abode, and Audrey was relishing the fresh air and sunshine of their north-facing kitchen and patio.

Beautiful.

At the sound of the sliding door she turned to see Daniel grinning in the doorway, clutching a bag of treasures from the Brunswick Street café and a newspaper under his arm.

'What have you got?' He'd gone down for bread, but Audrey knew he wouldn't resist the temptation of pastries and other morning treats.

He opened up the paper bag and showed her the croissants and a Danish he'd acquired. 'Someone's stolen the Picasso from the NGV... Front page of all the newspapers.'

'What?' Audrey gave him a dubious frown that clearly conveyed she thought he was joking.

Retreating inside Audrey poured the coffee whilst he arranged the pastries on top of the bag and laid the newspaper beside them. Audrey sat next to him and they read the front page story together, drinking their coffee in silence, but for the occasional grunt or breathless expletive at one part of the story or another.

'If their demands are not met in seven days, they're going to destroy it,' Daniel said at last.

'What demands?'

Daniel's finger went to the break-out of the ransom note printed beside the story. 'A ten percent increase in Arts funding...'

'What? Ten percent of bugger all?' Audrey huffed.

'And five $5,000 arts prizes.'

'Doesn't sound like much for a Picasso! What are they calling themselves?' Audrey found the relevant paragraph and answered her own question. '...Australian Cultural Terrorists.'

'Name like that, sounds like they mean business.'

'Sounds like a bloody joke, to me.' Audrey broke off a piece of croissant and popped it in her mouth. 'It has to be some kind of prank, don't you think?'

'Maybe.' Daniel got stuck into the Danish and then took a small sip of coffee to wash it down. 'Look at this, Quinn says *he does not believe gallery security was lax in any way*... No, not very; just lax enough to let a two million dollar painting waltz out the door. Fuck me, embarrassing...' He offered Audrey the Danish he'd half demolished. She declined. 'And bloody hell, it sounds like it wasn't even insured. Although... *Mr. Quinn would neither confirm nor deny this*. What a bloody wanker.'

'Yeah, well, pants down and red faces all around I'd say.' Audrey got up and took her cup over to the sink. 'Going to be interesting to see what happens. I've got to get to work though. Are you going to start setting up your studio?'

'Yeah, gotta hit the hardware store first.' He said, licking his fingers and still reading some of the further background about how the Weeping Woman had been purchased only about six months earlier. He looked up at Audrey and grinned. 'All pretty damned amusing, if you ask me. Nice work those cultural terrorists.'

Audrey shrugged and headed for the bathroom. 'It's gonna be a shit storm if they really do destroy it.'

*

Quinn left his office and ducked his head into his secretary's office.

She gave him a crookedly sympathetic smile and asked him how he was holding up.

As well as could be expected he supposed, he told her. 'What are they all *doing* up there?'

She knew he meant the public. A Tuesday morning in the middle of winter, no major exhibitions and attendance was through the roof. 'They're all going up to look at the empty wall,' she said, somewhat redundantly; he already knew that's what they were here for.

'Christ ... Really? And have you seen the newspapers? Implying the security is lax, as if we didn't know...'

'And they seem to know it's not insured...' Grace's eyes darted to the folded newspaper beside her. 'Maybe you need to do something... maybe announce some initiative to improve security.'

'Well, maybe now we'll get some budget to do just that.' Quinn brightened slightly at the thought, briefly wondering if there might be some kind of silver lining to the shit storm that had descended on his domain.

'What do we do next, do you think?' Grace looked a bit forlorn.

'Well, right now, I'm going down to see Derek. He must be beside himself.' He knew his head conservator had been completely blindsided by the events of the previous day, and he detected in him, above anyone else, an air of skepticism about what had transpired. He knew him well enough to know Derek had suspicions, and so Quinn wanted some one-on-one time with him, to compare notes.

*

Derek Tillery flipped through the first few pages of the report and then stopped, reading carefully from the subheading, Microscopy. He flipped a few pages and scanned again, moving his index finger slowly down the familiar paragraphs. Closing the folder, he stared into space, looking absently in the general direction of the conservation laboratory door. He sighed heavily and stood up, scooped the file off his desk and crossed his office to the filing cabinet. There he opened the drawer marked departmental budgets and misfiled the inspection report for the Weeping Woman between budget folios from about six years ago.

No one would ever find it there.

Whatever had happened to the Picasso, he was going to make certain of one thing; until it was recovered, no one but him was going to access the inspection report in which he himself had detailed every defect and imperfection of the Picasso; the conservatorial fingerprint which would be the only way to authenticate the painting if it ever returned.

It was his responsibility to maintain the integrity of the collection, and this, it's most valuable single artwork had just disappeared under highly questionable circumstances. As an art conservator he had heard too many stories casting doubt on the authenticity of great masterpieces in the world's most revered galleries; too many stories about forgeries being passed off for the real thing; too many stories of dodgy deals in the highest echelons of the art world.

He had not the foggiest idea what was really going on in real time, here at Melbourne's premier gallery, but when and if the Picasso was returned, he and only he, would authenticate it beyond doubt, according to the meticulous report he had prepared six months prior.

'What the hell do you make of it, Derek?'

Derek flinched slightly and slid the filing cabinet draw shut, as he turned to see Quinn standing in the doorway, one hand on his hip looking a little disheveled in comparison to his usually dapper self.

'It's hard to believe, isn't it? Barely seems real, does it Ellery?'

'Place is crawling with police cadets... Searching the place top and bottom. There's still a chance they might find it and that'll be the end of it. Whole thing a harmless hoax.'

'Let's hope so,'

'More people are coming to view the bloody empty wall than wanted to see her in the first place. And the papers are already baying for blood.' He looked at his conservator, hoping for signs of sympathy, but detected instead only a dour and cool detachment.

'Travis told me you and he were planning to send her on loan up to Canberra,' Derek said casually.

'We were. It was going to be Travis' big project for his internship. Would've been a feather in his cap.'

'Bit bloody bizarre then isn't it?

'What?'

'Saturday night, just before she's going up to the National Gallery, and some crackpots hide in the gallery and steal our most precious painting, and leave what looks for all the world like a real conservator's card on the wall, so all day long on Sunday, everyone, including security, think it *is* on loan to Canberra...'

Quinn conceded it was strange with a shrug and a murmur, keeping his own profound discomfort about that very thing to himself.

'What did the card say... On loan to the A.C.T.?'

'Removed to the A.C.T.' Quinn corrected him.

'And then it's not until two days later, these ratbags pop up with a ransom note, calling themselves the Australian Cultural Terrorist – same initials, A.C.T. – Absolutely bizarre.'

'It certainly is.

'And you know it's gone missing now...?'

'What?'

'The card,' said Derek. 'Gone missing, before the police even arrived, no one can find it. You're probably one of the only ones who even saw it.'

'Well, except for everyone who came through on Sunday,' said Quinn, with a slightly scoffing tone, which he regretted immediately. It evoked the disquieting memory of seeing that the hand-writing on the card looked just like his own – a detail that stuck in his mind like a thorn and gave him a sinking feeling. And as usual, that sinking feeling made him think of Travis, and he wondered for the umpteenth time whether he knew more than he was letting on.

Putting that thought aside, he asked Derek, 'Do you think we'll get her back in one piece?'

'God I hope so. By the look of the frame, whoever removed it knew what they were doing. Hopefully they'll protect the canvas...'

'Unless they put a match to it,' Quinn ruminated.

'Bite your bloody tongue Ellery.'

*

Tate was in his showroom when Travis entered. The gallery was closed and Tate looked small and cowed in the morning light, spilling in from the street. He stood in the midst of a dozen towering works of a Western Australian abstractionist whose show had opened that previous Friday. Travis had met the artist, when he'd helped bump in the show the week before; during which he'd developed a strong dislike for the artist and his work.

As he approached, Tate gave him a bemused stare and mechanically lifted a tumbler of brown fluid to his lips and took a big swig. He looked like the sole survivor of some kind of bloody and apocalyptic battle, surrounded as he was on all sides by the garishly grotesque and affronting canvases. The crisp morning light reflecting from the paintings made Tate's eyes appear glassy, and his Scotch seem to glow with a rare golden hue.

'Logan...' Travis just let his name hang as he drew up a few meters short of the clearly drunken dealer.

Tate eyed his young lover vacantly then glanced around the room, shaking his head slightly and said sadly: 'Fuck me, what a shit storm,' careless of the obvious ambiguity; because as far as Travis was concerned, he could just as easily have been referring to the paintings on the walls, as the unalloyed disaster of the missing Picasso.

Travis glanced again disdainfully, at the abstracts depicting all kinds of mayhem; images erupted unfettered from the diseased imagination of the painter from the West, who Travis reckoned had descended irretrievably into a rabbit hole of depravity and rude technique.

'So, have you got it?'

Tate's eyes filled with a fierce sorrow and he purposefully drained the last of his drink. It was very obvious by now, that it was by no means his first for the morning. Instead of answering him, he turned and shambled over to the bar in the back corner of the showroom and helped himself to another generous measure of Scotch. 'You want one?'

'No, I don't bloody want one. Jesus Logan, get a grip. 'Where is the painting? Have you got it?'

He took a gulp and swallowed hard. 'Gone!' He almost gagged on the word and coughed weakly for a moment or two. His face was forlorn and angry, looking up at Travis from where he was now slumped against the bar. 'It's fucking gone....!' He showed him an unaccountably empty hand. 'And he's gone too... Jack is. Absent without leave. Decamped to parts unknown, the fucker!' He did a little flourish with his free hand, making something imaginary vanish – just like Jack had – into thin air.

'Tell me you're shitting me Logan, for Christ's sake. What do you mean he's gone? Gone with the painting?.... How can he be gone?' Travis demanded. '...With the friggin' Weeping Woman under his wing? Please tell me this is a joke. Fuck!'

'Yes... Fuck!' Tate agreed. 'You've hit the nail right on the head, my friend. Fuck is absolutely right. We are all fucked!'

'Just tell me *exactly* what happened... You gave him the painting on Sunday night, right?'

'Yep that's a fact... Fuckin' matter of record.' Tate looked like he was about to cry. 'Not only that, my technical guy went round there on Monday and gave him all the materials; aged canvass, period oils, all the good stuff,' he concluded with fake cheer.

'And...'

'And... I went round there last night, right after we met at the café. Went round there and fuckin' broke in – bit of breaking and entering, you know – *Big city art dealer burgles art thief's premises; Picasso still missing.*' He gave this a newscaster's voice and made a banner in the air above his head.

Travis pinned Tate with a long hard stare that didn't let up. Tate squirmed and took a sly sip of his Scotch. Travis was quickly cooling on Tate as a desirable or even remotely dependable partner in romance or crime. He worried whether he was going to be any use at all in managing the debacle foisted upon them. In fact, if he was honest, it scared him to see the normally urbane and confident dealer losing his shit. Drunk at eleven in the morning.

As the two men glared at each other in the empty gallery, Travis fancied that he saw Tate's sagging features firm up minutely, and his glazed eye clarify a little. Did he intuit that Travis was already thinking about throwing him under the bus? ... That he was calculating Tate's low place in the pecking order; resolutely and instinctively drawing up the gangplank to protect his own connections to the high echelons of the art world through the auspices of his mother and godfather?

In truth he *was* re-thinking their relationship at that very moment, and calculating the connections that could be drawn between himself and Tate, should push come to shove, as he suspected it would. And so they eyed each other for a moment or two, like predator and prey; with each trying to access which was which, except in Travis' mind there was no doubt at all on that question, even though he had always let Tate think he had the upper hand.

But perhaps it wouldn't come to that. If they really had lost control of the painting, there was only one course of action, and it would be Tate's problem whether or not his young forger could be connected back to him.

'If that little rabbit of yours has run off with our painting, then there's really only one thing to do...'

Tate slid his tumbler away from himself, as if he'd lost his taste for a brunch of Scotch. He squared his chin at Travis, a thoughtful expression now crossing his face.

'We drop him through the hatch,' Travis affirmed. 'You know we have no choice. He's got his greasy little mitts on it. He's got form as a forger. Jesus, we could probably even mount a pretty good argument that he's the ransomer. Case closed.'

Tate pursed his lips and sighed a big sigh with his whole body. 'We can't do that.'

'What the hell do you mean, we can't? We have to. If you're worried about him fingering you, it'll be his word against yours. They'll have their culprit, the painting will be back. Everybody happy. No one's going to listen to his bullshit.'

Tate had started moving toward the back corner of the gallery, towards his office. He didn't answer, but just looked intently at Travis and swiped his head sideways, beckoning him to follow.

He followed, and found Tate fiddling with a video recorder slotted in under the television occupying a corner cabinet in his office. 'For one thing, I don't know where the hell he is. I don't *know* where he'd go – I think his family lives somewhere up in the country, but no idea where.'

Travis gave him a puzzled and contemptuous look which seemed to censure him for his lack of diligence with his young protégé. 'You don't know?'

Tate shrugged as he slotted a tape into the player. 'I never asked him. Why would I?'

'It doesn't matter, you don't need to know where he is. The cops'll find him.... Statewide man-hunt, it'll be.'

'Yeah, well that's not the real problem anyway. *This* is the real problem.' He hit play on the recorder and nodded at the TV screen.

Travis watched quietly as static on the screen resolved itself into a woman, videoed from behind, opening a door, and then all the rest of it, which Travis watched in silence – an increasing stunned silence – as the brief but graphic amateur movie, depicting Tate's fall from grace, unfolded.

At the end Travis bowed his head as though in prayer and swore softly. 'That cunning little fucking worm!'

'He says he has copies ready to go to the police and the media if anything happens to him.'

'Christ almighty! What the fuck were you thinking?'

He didn't specify which part of Tate's mishandling of the situation he was referring to. Tate was miffed at being judged. *How could he have anticipated this?* 'None of us could've seen this coming,' he protested.

'Jesus Christ! What the bloody-actual-hell is going on here? Your so-called tame painter has gone completely off the rails, taken the painting God knows where to do God knows what with it. Quinn's got the Major Crime Squad crawling all over the gallery, and meanwhile the media is making heroes of these Cultural-bloody-Terrorists, whoever the flying fuck they are...' Travis paused for a hurried breathe and glared at Tate with undisguised reproach. 'But this...' he waved at the TV screen, now consumed again by static. 'It doesn't get any more fucked up than this...' He harpooned Tate with a jagged and plainly hostile glare. 'This means, *you*, my friend are completely fucked!'

Tate dead-panned him with a stare just as antagonistic. 'You mean *we're* fucked.'

A dropped pin could have been heard making a resounding thud out in Tate's empty art gallery as the dealer and his soon-to-be-ex-lover quietly eyed each other with newly edged hostility.

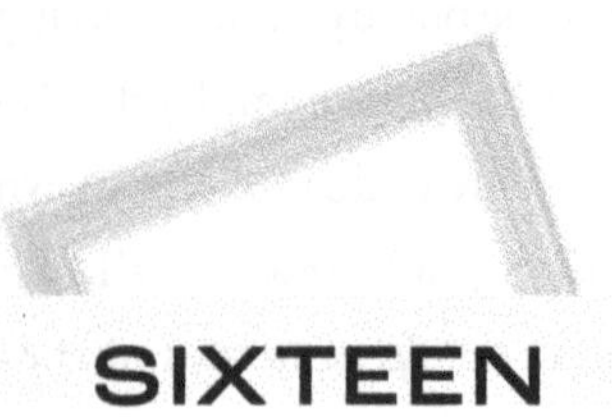

SIXTEEN

Wednesday, August 6th, 1986

He was a shaman who taught me fox magic when I was a very young child. I could dematerialise by being very still, I could shape shift... and I could fly.
Angry Buddha, 2001

Jack lifted the silk coverlet from the painting on the second easel and stared at the Picasso for a long moment, before folding the fabric and putting it under the bench. He'd been doing a lot of exactly this for the last two days – staring at the Picasso – looking at it from every angle, in every light, dissecting it with his eyes. Trying to figure out the layering and the structure, attempting to analyse and understand the painter's technique. Meditating on it. Mentally rehearsing. He knew he was getting close, when he started to imagine he could understand what the painter was thinking all those years ago – what he was *feeling* – when he slavered on the layers of colour in a wild and passionate storm of creativity.

Was *she* there in the room with him, his muse Dora, when he painted her? Or was it all done from memory? Memory of a time when he'd hurt her?... An offence, committed by the notorious abuser, channeled into a depiction of agonising grief – The Weeping Woman – a woman of Guernica, grieving the loss of her child.

Dora Maar said it was all a lie, the way he painted her, always torn by grief. But hadn't their relationship been a tempestuous one? Certainly from what Jack had read about it. Dora, his muse, and political mentor, his photographic chronicler and his lover. But he was cruel, and she, they said, something of a masochist. Perhaps Picasso painted the grief he saw buried deep inside her as an act of atonement, or an attempt at exorcism; perhaps he alone saw her hidden grief because he was the one who had instilled it in her.

Jack told himself he was ready to begin. This was probably a lie, and he was most likely a fool. But he told himself nonetheless, he was as ready as he would ever be.

His course of action had been unclear when he left Melbourne and headed home with the painting. It had felt for a while now that he was being swept along by destiny or fate. He'd relinquished control. It was the only way for him to remain calm. Some kind of higher power – a universal intelligence of some sort – was clearly directing proceedings. That's what he knew Penny would say, in fact, she *had* said so, more or less.

But once he'd set the Picasso up on the easel in his old studio, he'd been overcome by a strong intuition, one which couldn't be denied, even though he tried to for a day or so. But something inside him knew he couldn't ultimately deny it. He would never have done Tate's bidding and tried to copy the painting – not for Tate – that was definitely a line in the sand.

But who was he to stand in the way of fate? Maybe he would do it for Penny and for himself, or maybe for shits and giggles – or maybe indeed, because destiny had demanded it.

In any case, the next day he'd set up a second easel right beside the Picasso, with the aged canvass, gifted to him. Erecting it there had seemed like a lark or even a provocation... To himself, or maybe to the fates. He'd also set about carefully cataloguing and assessing the so-called historical paints he'd been delivered, and he felt that he now knew how to proceed.

All the while in the background was the radio. He couldn't resist keeping tabs on the news coming out of Melbourne. The latest thing, earlier in the morning, was the security staff at the NGV had called a strike and the gallery had to close. This had made him laugh out loud. Apparently the director, or someone in management, had removed the security guards' chairs; necessitating that they spend their time patrolling the gallery – doing what to Jack's mind was actually their job – but instead they'd called a strike. *Fucking hilarious.*

Against the background banter and music on the radio, he mixed some dark grey; a suitable substrate for background and outlines, and began to make some lines on the canvas. It felt right as he painted lines and shading, confident they were just like the layers he intuited were below the surface of the masterpiece before him. Presently there was a flutter in his chest and he felt an old familiar clarity of eye, and the quiet fusion of mind and hand, as a soft surge of dopamine propelled him into the flow state the artist in him habitually craved.

*

When Penny appeared in the studio unannounced it gave him a start as he looked up from loading a brush. Not least because the project going on in the studio had, of course, been declared top secret. He'd banned his mother unconditionally – telling her he was working on a surprise – he didn't specify for whom. Neither his father nor any of the farm staff ever ventured into his studio, but for good measure, he'd positioned the Picasso facing back into the studio – away from the door, which in any case gave it the best light, from the side windows.

'Look at you – getting stuck into it,' said Penny with one hand on her hip and the other waving back and forth between the two easels. 'Looks like you've been forging masterpieces your whole life.'

'Oh, don't... Fuck... Please, don't.' Jack gave her a contrived frown and put his brush into a jar of turps. 'I'm just mucking around, seeing what some of these colours look like.'

Penny came around and kissed him on the cheek, then turned and examined the partially painted canvas, and nodded appreciatively, and said 'Hmm... Have you heard the news?'

'About the strike? Yeah, so fucked... Because they took away their chairs. You couldn't make this stuff up, could you? So funny.'

'And the cops searching the place – did you see it on the telly? Like Keystone cops. What a joke.'

'Did you go around home? Was the tape gone?'

Penny's eyes widened, remembering that that was her real news. 'Yes... Yes! Tate must've gone down the back – and in through the back door, just like you said he would. It was gone! Nothing else touched though. I locked up before I came up here.'

'Fuck me! Wouldn't you like to be a fly on the wall when he sees it?' Jack raised both brows and blew a little raspberry though his lips.

'He will lose his shit, won't he?' Penny's expression took on an intensity and her smile changed into a frown. 'Are we going to be alright? I mean this is serious shit. It's all over the news, overseas too apparently, and the government's up in arms.'

'You mean that bastard Ross Maynard? Did you see him on the news? Pompous bloody dickhead.'

'You've really got it in for him, haven't you?'

'For good reason, and this'll be so bloody perfect... The funniest part is, he won't have a bloody clue. He wouldn't even remember me... But I'm going to fuck *him* right up.' Jack's tone was vehement, with an intense passion that worried Penny a bit.

'And I've got another letter for you to deliver when you go back down. This one's even better.'

'Seems a bit like poking the bear – are you sure we should be doing that?'

'Calling the Arts Minister *a tiresome bag of swamp gas*, is the least of our crimes, given that we're currently baby-sitting a borrowed Picasso.'

Penny looked over her glasses at him, a dubious and inquisitive expression on her pretty face. 'That's what you're calling him this time, is it?'

They both laughed.

'Yeah and a whole lot more besides. Uncle Bill would fucking love it. It's like I'm channeling him, and it'll confuse the shit out of them, because it doesn't sound anything like a bunch of young artists. They'll be chasing their tails 'til the cows come home.'

'They already are – the ransom note's being touted all over the media. They love it, because it's kind of... Funny.' Penny sighed and looked a bit sad, and bit her lip. 'I'm a bit scared Jack... We've got ourselves in the middle of something really big here. We could get in a lot of trouble.'

'Well, too late to worry about that now.' Jack unfolded the coverlet and draped it over the original painting. 'It's like you said, fate has got us caught up in something bigger than both of us, and the only thing to do is just forge ahead.'

Penny shrugged and nodded, with a smile that seemed a bit forced.

Jack said, 'let's go up and see if Mum's got anything on for tea, and I'll give you the next letter.'

As they left the studio together, Jack swung the door shut and locked it then turned to Penny. 'You know, the funny thing is – I reckon I can do it. I reckon I can make a copy even old Pablo himself'd be hard pressed to pick.'

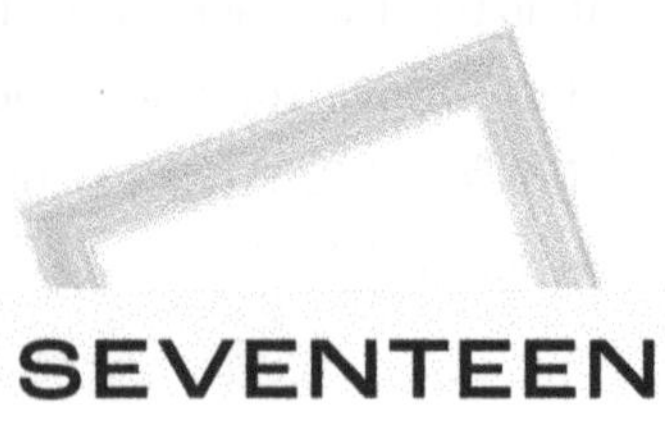

SEVENTEEN

Saturday, August 9th, 1986

Hollywood (Babylon) and the media wish to limit your perceptions to those of a six-year-old dog.
Angry Buddha, 2001

The ABC television journalists were really starting to give him the shits, making an absolute picnic of the whole thing. Watching the television in his office, Quinn felt like he was under siege. There they all were; milling around out in front of the water wall, talking up the weekend deadline by which time, the so-called Cultural Terrorists' demands needed to be met, or the Picasso would be destroyed.

Destroy the Picasso? Who the hell were these people, these cultural terrorists? Were they even real? His peace of mind and his usually sound sleeping habits had been brought undone with questions like this rabbiting around in his mind every night.

And meanwhile the city's press and television were having a field day; as if a bunch of daring, anonymous, hard-done-by young artists – calling themselves terrorists of all things, and holding the state for ransom for their meager and strangely reasonable demands – was the most fun they'd had in years.

He flicked off the television in disgust and sagged into the big high-backed swivel chair, and stared forlornly at the phone on his desk.

The discourse between the press, the gallery and the police had somehow backed him into a corner, in which he was now obliged to see out a vigil in his office throughout the weekend, waiting for a call from the so-called Australian Cultural Terrorists.

'No one's going to call, are they?' He looked forlornly at Travis, slouched grumpily in an armchair on the other side of his office, drinking coffee.

'You know there's no such bloody thing as the Australian Cultural-fucking-Terrorists, don't you, Ellery? Bloody phantoms, I reckon.' Travis saw the look of sudden consternation on Quinn's face and knew right away he'd said too much. But Travis was seriously pissed off. He should've been down the coast surfing. And the surf was banging.

But Quinn had twisted his arm and eventually pulled rank – saying, if he was to be stuck in his office on a Saturday, then the least Travis could do was keep him company, while they waited in vain for the ransomers to make contact. Grace and some of the others had hung around all morning, but now it was just Quinn and Travis.

'What do you mean, phantoms?'

'Well the cops can't find any sign of them, can they?' Travis thought with a resurgence of fury, how Tate's young forger – whom even Travis had wrongly assessed as being quite meek and mild – had taken off with the Picasso. He wondered darkly whether it could be Jack sending the ransom notes.

'Well who's sending the ransom notes then, if *they're* phantoms?'

The second ransom note had sent the media into a whole new frenzy, with its renewed invective against the Police Minister. The press couldn't wait to print it in full, with its wild lampooning of Ross Maynard for calling in Interpol; addressing him as '*you tiresome old bag of swamp gas*', comparing him to *Clouseau* and asking him if he called on *Red Adair* to read his gas meter.

Maynard was livid and had called Quinn more than once, seemingly just to share the burden and project the blame onto him. Getting pilloried in the press all over again, was so galling to him, he was baying for blood... Looking for a scalp.

Why were the perpetrators going all out to embarrass *him*? Why Maynard and not Quinn? The gallery director would have seemed the obvious target. After all, the Picasso was his baby from the start. *His* reputation on the line. It was almost as if they were affording *him* the respect of the recently bereaved, whilst focusing all their ire and condemnation on the minister; saying Maynard would soon be carrying about him '*the smell of kerosene and burning canvas*', and signing off with '*good luck with your huffing and puffing, you pompous fathead.*'

Quinn stared again at the phone on his desk, with a rare mixture of angst and resentment. Why would Travis say they were phantoms? He was hit yet again by the sense that Travis knew more than he was saying. Ever since childhood, Travis had had a disconcerting air of deviousness about him. Quinn had always thought so. And now, it was crystal clear; there was no way he'd have had him anywhere near the NGV if he wasn't Betty's first born son – and Quinn's godson. And it really *had* been Travis who'd come up with the idea of sending the painting up to Canberra as his internship project. And then there was the infuriatingly ambiguous conservator's card, which had now disappeared.... What the hell had happened to that?

Travis sat back with his coffee cup on his belly, taking Quinn's last comment as rhetorical, and effusing surly indifference.

This angered Quinn: 'Well if they're not Cultural Terrorists, then who the hell are they? Listen, Travis, if you think you know who these people are... If you're holding back on something, now would be a very good time to unburden yourself.'

Travis looked up at Quinn with contrived affront. The last time he'd spoken to Tate he'd asked him the same thing. *Who the hell was sending these ransom notes? Could it be Jack?* Travis would have liked nothing better than to let Jack take the fall for the whole thing. They all would. But that was impossible, because young Jack had turned out to be a devious little bastard; if Jack went down, they all when down.

'Ellery, if I knew anything, I would tell you. Of course I would.' Travis tried to sound a little hurt. 'I do have an ear to the ground, I mean if anything bubbles to the surface, you'd be the first to know.'

During his last conversation with Tate, it had been obvious he'd been drinking a great deal, and really starting to lose his composure. On the subject of finding Jack, he'd told Travis that Blackthorn's bright idea was to have Jack *wacked*.

Travis' response had been sharp and acerbic: *What planet are you on? We don't even know where he is, do we?*

And old mate Blackthorn's a psycho, by the way.

We just need to find him, get the painting back, that's all.

Well good luck with that, Tate had said. *Because the little bastard's fully gone to ground. There's no sign of him....*And something about how Tate would like to kill him himself, if he could get his hands on him.

*

Detective Ted Doherty paid for a round of beers for his team and expertly transported them back to the booth in the corner, where Grant Mallory, his head investigator, was holding court; giving the other detectives the benefit of his wisdom in respect of the investigation so far.

'It's a weird world out there isn't it? I mean fuck...Some of these fuckin' knuckleheads in the so-called *art world; they* make our usual smooth-brains look like bloody rocket scientists.' He slid one of Doherty's beers towards himself, lowered his lips and sucked the foamy head off the top of it. 'If you ask me, none of 'em's got the nous to nick a porno from the newsagents, let alone a Picasso from the bloody NGV.

'But they sure as shit think it's all a big joke, don't they? And they don't seem to give a fuck about us traipsing through their shitty little studios, either... Don't even bother hiding their dope... Good job we're not the fuckin' drug squad.'

There was a general murmuring and mumbling of concurrence as the other three all claimed their beers and drank.

'And no one's heard of these Australia Cultural Terrorists, either,' said Doherty. 'Just gets more smirks and giggles, because they all bloody-well know we're getting played. All a big fuckin' joke.'

'Maybe. Or it could be cover for an actual art heist,' countered Mallory. 'I've had plenty of bullshit about fakes and forgeries, and a lot of talk about art being sold on the so-called black market. But ask for any details and they just clam up. All crap and gossip, most likely... Or some fucker tryin' to big note 'emselves.'

'It's gotta be an inside job, I reckon,' piped up one of the other detectives, plucking a Winfield out of its box and igniting with his Bic. 'I interviewed the head conservator today, down at the gallery, and ...'

'Did you get a collar on him?' Mallory interjected with a muffled guffaw, prompting a weary groan from some of the others.

'He's as straight as a die, but he reckons whoever removed the painting from the frame knew what they were doing. Says they must've had experience handling fragile artworks.'

'And then there's the matter of the snake eye screwdriver,' said Doherty.

'The what?' Mallory reached across the table and slid the other guy's Winfield's and lighter across to himself and helped himself to a cigarette, lit up and hungrily filled his lungs.

'The Picasso was attached to the wall with snake eye security screws – unique to the gallery – you need a special screwdriver to remove them.'

'Shit.' Mallory let go a cloud of smoke which drifted over the assembled squad. 'Has anyone talked to the director –the guy with the bow tie?'

'Yeah, he says any employee could've got hold of one of those screwdrivers, but the conservator had quite a different take on it; said there were only a couple of the special screwdrivers in the whole place.'

'What do you make of the director?' One of the other detectives asked Doherty.

'I think he's in shock. Someone's just pinched his two million dollar painting, and it's not bloody insured.'

'Isn't it?'

'Nope, they say there's no way the gallery can afford the premium. Same deal in big galleries all over the world, precious artworks on every bloody wall and none of 'em insured because the premiums would break the bank.'

'So what happens when someone pinches a priceless painting?'

'They have to try and get it back themselves – that's how it works. The big galleries in Europe; they have their own investigators, and pretty often they get the stolen art back – sometimes they even nail the perps. More often they offer a reward and the art gets returned.'

'That's like paying a bloody ransom, isn't it?' Mallory objected.

'Yeah pretty much, I suppose.'

'What do you think Ted? What's your gut say? These cultural terrorists are bullshit aren't they? Maybe someone's really taken it to try and get it out of the country and flog it.' This from the quietest member of the team, Thorpe, sipping his beer thoughtfully in the corner.

'Well, they just don't ring true, do they?' Doherty responded. 'Something very bogus about those ransom notes.'

Mallory chimed in: 'I had one bloke, reckoned they'd try and move it out of the country, sell it on the black market. He said there were plenty of potential buyers – you know, Middle East, Russia maybe – dirty money, oil money. Fuckin' super rich cunts. Love to get their hands on a Picasso, and you know, have it in their private collection, just to show off to their mates. No one would even know or care that it was flogged from some gallery in Melbourne.'

'Fucking hell,' said Fink, the detective who belonged to the Winnies. 'Maybe... But I still think it's an inside job... Some of those gallery people, y'know, some of 'em just seem a bit sus to me... Especially that young intern, what was his name...' The detective flipped over a couple of pages in his notebook. 'There it is... Travis McRae.'

'The young bloke interning under the director?' asked Mallory.

'Yeah, under Quinn, the director,' said Doherty instructively.

'You know who Quinn's father is, don't you?' This from the quiet detective in the corner.

'No.' said a couple of the detectives in unison.

'He's the Governor.'

'The what?'

'The Governor ... Of Victoria.'

Everyone went a bit quiet then, until Mallory blew out a sideways puff of smoke and looked his boss square in the eye and said: 'Fuck... You better hope it wasn't *him* then.'

And this got a nervous laugh from everyone.

*

Blackthorn craned his head and held a finger aloft to attract the waiter's attention. 'Fucking useless little cunt,' he muttered – loud enough that the other two could hear him over the hubbub in the cocktail bar – and then, when that didn't work, he tapped his tumbler four times hard on the table and held the empty glass up over his head. 'Jesus, who do you have to blow to get a fucking drink around here?' He gave his two ex-students an angry sideways glance, and a half sneer, half smile, until he saw the young waiter reluctantly approaching.

'Who wants another one?' He pointed a crooked finger at Travis. 'It's your shout. Three more?'

Travis gave him an almost deadpan look, which nonetheless conveyed a combination of disgust, resignation and a kind of loath admiration. 'Fuck you, Dougy,' he said in tacit agreement.

Blackthorn looked to Max, the more timid of his acolytes – clearly drunk and yet still not particularly at ease in the company of his old teacher. Max held up a hand in protest with the usual thinly veiled look of morbid fear he had whenever he was around Blackthorn. He opened his mouth to speak but Blackthorn shut him down.

'No. You shut up. Three more. Single malt,' he instructed the boy standing grimly at his elbow. 'Let's go right up to the top shelf this time, shall we, because he's paying,' he scoffed, with a sideways tilt of his head towards Travis.

The young waiter gave the slightest of nods and turned to go, but Blackthorn grabbed his arm and wrenched him back. 'Let's hear a yes Sir, right away Sir, shall we?... And don't keep us waiting all fucking night this time.'

The boy twisted his arm away in fear; offence blazing in his eyes as he retreated towards the bar.

'Sulky little prick, isn't he?' Blackthorn cast an eye around his favorite haunt, a kind of art nouveaux cocktail bar, with a bohemian twenties feel and décor. It was popular with students and young party-goers alike, and his favorite place to start a Saturday night's drinking.

'Did you bring the stuff?' he asked Travis, when the waiter was out of earshot.

Max averted his eyes and Travis gave his old teacher a dubious glare across the table. 'Of course I did, but I wasn't going to give it to you right here.' He turned a palm upwards. 'We're in public.'

'No one gives a fuck, it's dark. Everyone's drunk. Don't be a pussy.' Blackthorn reached a hand out under the table and he felt Travis put a small plastic pouch into it. A small burst of anticipatory pleasure surged in his body. It had been a while.

'Thanks.'

'You're very bloody welcome.'

Blackthorn slid the small package surreptitiously into the inside pocket of his sports jacket and gave his two companions a humorless smirk. These two were classics – talentless wannabes, who, even several years after completing their training, were still trying to bathe in the reflected glory of their master and teacher... Pathetic.

Max poured some water for himself and took a sip. 'What do you make of all this Picasso bullshit at the NGV? Pretty fucked up, eh?'

Blackthorn eyed him critically, trying to figure out whether he thought he knew something about it, or whether he was just making casual conversation. Then he threw a sideways glance at Travis. Had he said something to his little mate Max?

Surely not. But you never knew with Travis; he was a complex and interesting person. Some would say toxic and psychologically unwell, but who was Blackthorn to say? He quite liked Travis, as much as he liked any human. Or perhaps he just tolerated him because he sensed, at some deeper level that they were similar in some ways – peas in a pod. Maybe even fucked-up soul mates.

The theft had been all over the media for a week – one of the biggest local news stories Melbourne had ever seen, so it was an obvious topic for conversation – nothing more than that. Blackthorn himself had been keeping a low profile since the shit had hit the fan, calculating that he was a good long step or two removed from Tate and his boyfriend, Travis. Plausible deniability he had, and the less he heard about it the better; although he had had Tate on the phone to him twice; both times in quite a state and the second time, apparently quite drunk. He'd told him to fuck off and sort it out himself; other than to suggest that if his young forger had run off with their painting, they could and should pay someone to off him, the little bastard.

'Humph, bit careless of them wasn't it – letting a two million dollar Picasso walk out the door.' Blackthorn made himself sound nonchalant and looked around for the waiter, thinking now, he should've ordered doubles.

'But who do you reckon these cultural terrorists are?' Max persisted.

'Fucked if I know. Scumbags. Wanna-be attention-seekers.' *Who indeed*, thought Blackthorn. They were fucking ghosts, as far as he and Travis were concerned. They could not, by any rational consideration, be real and yet, somehow these phantom villains had become the centre of attention. They both reckoned Jack must be behind the ransom notes in some way, so it was a good thing overall, focusing police attention away from them... Except for the odd occasion he'd heard a detective or someone on the radio posit the idea of an inside job... No one wanted to hear that.

'Well, I reckon I know who they are,' said Travis, eyeing Blackthorn over the top of his water glass.

Blackthorn stabbed a fierce scowl across the table and seeing it, Max flinched, but Travis just gave a satisfied grin. He liked riling the grisly old coot.

'How would you fucken' know?' Blackthorn wondered what game Travis was playing.

Travis shrugged, as if to say, *alright if you're not interested...*

'Well, go on then... Who?' Blackthorn calling his bluff, now.

Travis gave him a long hard stare before he replied. 'Fucken Hardman and Burke,' he said finally. 'I mean, they're up there lording it up in the big city – trying to make out they're God's gift to bohemian-friggin'-eighties art. And you know he's a loose cannon. You know that. Who else would try and pull off something like that? Trying to make a name for himself ...Just like Picasso did himself, when he was fingered for stealing the Mona Lisa.'

Doug Blackthorn glared at his defective protégé – a fiercely intense look, but tinged with admiration. Travis turned away, as he caught sight of the waiter coming with their drinks. He was relieved to have Blackthorn's attention off him, because he'd been looking at Travis like he was going to garrote him. When he looked back, Dougy was smiling, because what Doug was actually thinking was; *you're a clever-dick, Travis - planting a nice little rumour like that with your gullible mate,* Max.

The three of them watched the waiter deliver the drinks without a word. The young waiter appeared both disappointed and relieved to be ignored this time. When he'd gone Blackthorn caught Travis's eye again and picked up his drink and held it aloft as if to make a toast: 'I like the way you're thinking there, Travis,' he said simply, and they all took a sip.

Fuck me, thought Blackthorn... *Why didn't I think of that?* Of course he hadn't thought of it, because he knew there *were* no cultural terrorists. He hadn't thought of it because he knew damned well it *was* an inside job – their inside job – and he knew that Tate had the painting, ostensibly, right up until that little fuckwit of a forger had run off with it.

So naturally he wouldn't have thought that his arch-nemeses, Hardman and Burke had been involved in an art heist that he knew had never actually happened...

But he had to admit... It was a very appealing idea.

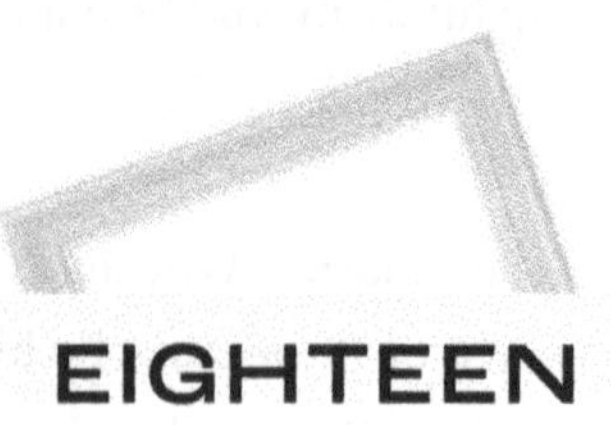

EIGHTEEN

Wednesday, August 13th, 1986

In the face of ...(it)...we allow ourselves to be hypnotised by notions that it's all being managed, or coped with by experts, governments and specialists.
Angry Buddha, 2001

Ross Maynard stood in the window for a few long moments with his back to Detective Sergeant Doherty, and surveyed the green canopy of the Treasury Gardens stretched out below his parliamentary office.

'You realise don't you, these people are a threat to the very fabric of our society. What they're doing is challenging the very rule of law in this state, with their threats and their disrespect... And calling themselves terrorists, for goodness sake; that's the biggest affront of all.

'I mean, terrorists... Christ! Terrorists blow up airliners, murder innocents... Terrorists have no respect for civilised society or the laws that keep us all safe.' Maynard turned to face the policeman in his office, still standing over his desk, looking at the note Maynard had just shown him – the third ransom note from the so-called Australian Cultural Terrorists – this one addressed to Ross Maynard himself and delivered to his office that very morning, together with a half-burnt match.

Thank you for your support. Phase Two begins shortly....' It was much briefer and more cryptic than the first two notes, and lacking the cutting personal invective against the minister which had characterised the first two; content which had so excited Melbourne's media.

'Phase Two...What the hell could they possible mean by that?'

Doherty was struck again by the minister's resemblance to a miffed teddy bear – with his curly blond hair, round face and mild demeanor – all this seemed at odds with his smoldering anger over the events of the last week, which everyone knew, would end up defining his tenure as a minister in the state government.

'This is why we have to hunt them down – route them from their filthy little garrets and bring the full force of the law down on their damned heads. Criminal charges of the highest order. If I have my way, we'll be locking them up and throwing away the key.

'But first... first we need to find them!' Maynard peered over his glasses at Doherty and let the pause sink in. 'That's why I've asked you to come in. It's been over a week, detective. Surely you must be getting close. Please tell me you have some *leads*, some salient information... Because up to date they seem to have managed to make themselves invisible, undetectable, somehow; even whilst managing to get their agendas, their demands – and their bloody insults – aired all over the dammed Melbourne media, as if they're some kind of celebrities. Surely we can track them down? Surely there's a trail?'

Ted Doherty was thrown by being summoned to the minister's office. It was unheard of – in his experience, a complete circumvention of the chain of command – and it only added to his misgivings about being lumbered with this miserable case.

'My best men are working on the investigation, minister.' He kept his tone neutral, considered. 'We're looking very carefully into every lead. But it's not uncommon in this kind of investigation for there to be blind alleys.

'You would have seen the identikits published in Monday's paper? They were based on information received from people who visited the gallery on the weekend in question – people who thought they saw someone behaving suspiciously. It's kind of a long shot to begin with, because it's all a bit subjective, and once they were published we had many many calls, all of which have to be sorted and assessed. We investigate each one, if at all plausible, but frankly...'

'Frankly what? Surely ... it will lead you to the perpetrators. Someone must've seen something.'

'Well yes, but people call in for so many reasons... They get carried away with their imaginations, or they just want to feel important, or maybe they genuinely think they know something... Sometimes they might have a grudge against someone. It takes a lot of work to sort the wheat from the chaff. Most are dead ends.'

'Jesus, have you got any suspects? Anyone at all?'

'Not yet, nothing concrete, anyway.'

Maynard glared at Doherty for a moment and the detective perceived a milieu of emotions in the politician's sad eyes; foremost frustration, and also a bit of fear.

'We must do better detective. This is the sort of case that can make or break a career, you know.'

Doherty wasn't surprised Maynard pulled that card out, sooner rather than later. He was under enormous pressure because the cultural terrorists had targeted him personally. He'd want a quick arrest, or he'd be looking for a scapegoat. This was precisely why Doherty's heart had sank when he was given the case; *a bloody poison chalice, it was.*

'We're throwing every resource we have into it. But it's an

unusual case, and it keeps kind of folding back on itself.'

Maynard gave him a dubious and weary look, then asked what he meant, but in a tone that suggested he really didn't want to know.

'Well, for one thing, the feedback we're getting out on the street – in the art scene, that is – is that no one's heard of the cultural terrorists. Many of them think it's a hoax. And their demands; they're kind of generic... Pretty much any struggling artist would ask for those same things. Pretty modest really... I mean it's not exactly a million bucks in unmarked bills and a jumbo to Fiji.'

Maynard stiffened and frowned disapprovingly, but bade him continue with a nod of his head.

'On the other hand, some aspects of the case point to an inside job... But of course that doesn't gel with the ransom notes and the cultural terrorists. There's a strong feeling around that it's a hoax; which is why we've done an even more thorough search of the gallery and arts school, just to be sure.

And there's quite a bit of talk about forgeries – paintings being copied and sold. A black market right here in Melbourne – and offshore as well, of course – for the buying and selling of forgeries and stolen art. So...'

'So what you're telling me is we don't have a clue – we're still no closer to solving this thing?'

'No Minister, that's not what I'm saying. Every lead we chase down, every suspect we eliminate gets us one step closer. What I am saying is; this one's going to take some time; time to untangle all the strands, because it really is a knotty bloody mess.'

'What if we don't have time? What if these people are trying to get it out of the country and sell it on the black market? What if they *destroy* the bloody thing, like they're threatening to... If we lose this Picasso...'

Maynard trailed off, giving his attention again to the tree-tops beyond his office. He sighed heavily: 'Okay, so tell me detective; what do you *really* think? What does your *gut* tell you has happened to it?'

'Someone took the Picasso off the wall at the NGV, probably on the Saturday night, before it was reported missing. Somebody has it still, somewhere, hopefully. What they're doing with it, God only knows. Holding it for ransom? Maybe, seems unlikely though. Trying to sell it? Maybe, could be difficult though, so perhaps trying to get it out of the country.

'Or maybe someone's trying to make some other sort of point... Or it was just a random act, or a dare; or maybe someone wants to get the contract to sell the NGV a new-fangled security system... The possibilities are almost endless.'

The Minister looked deflated. His eyes seemingly beseeching the detective for some glimmer of hope.

'What I can tell you is this: As long as we keep shaking the branches, eventually something will drop. Someone will talk, because somebody knows something and eventually, someone always talks. We just have to keep an ear to the ground and eventually the ground will start rumbling.'

While Doherty was talking, Maynard moved across his office towards the door, moving a little like a despondent ghost, with his head slightly bowed and an air of disappointment. He slowly opened the door – without another word – a clear gesture that it was time for the detective to depart. He'd heard enough, and none of it was what he'd hoped for.

'Thanks for coming in,' he said simply as Doherty gathered himself and moved uncertainly to the doorway. As he went through he turned to say goodbye, but something in the minister's expression stopped him, something haunted and deathly. His cheeks seemed hollow and his eyes full of ire.

'Do your job, detective,' he said in a low voice. 'Find my painting.'

*

There were seven of them seated around the big old dining room table which always reminded Daniel of Christmases spent here, at his grand-parent's old house in Anglesea. The long table set in front of the windows in the big lounge room was adjacent to a wide opening where food could be passed through from the big country kitchen. At the other end, the lounge room narrowed into an alcove lined with books, where, as a boy he would sit for hours reading from his grandmother's strange and eclectic collection of books and looking out the picture window at the bush garden beyond. The unique set up and the smells of the old place evoked all kinds of memories, which he knew he shared with Will, who also must've felt the nostalgia, reaching back to school holidays when they used to invade Daniel's grand-parent's house.

But this night was different – with Will's new wife from Germany, Lidia, and their two young children at the table – it felt like a quite different place, like the old house had been shifted forward into a modern era. And Audrey's friend, Bianca – who'd been at art school in Geelong with Audrey, but more recently had returned from a year-long exchange program in Paris – added a further measure of sophistication.

Roast chicken, gravy, heaps of roast potatoes and a big pan of beans and other greens in a tomato and garlic sauce – Daniel's signature menu, would feed them all – nice and simple. Plenty of wine, some good cheeses for later and a night of cheer and amiable conversation was guaranteed. Daniel was bemused by the two little girls – unused as he was to small children – and impressed by their behavior and language which seemed way beyond their years. But he *had* begun to wonder what time was bed-time...

Mid-August and the old pot-belly fire was stoked up to the maximum, making the living room and kitchen area toasty and warm. The bedrooms would be icy and stacks of extra blankets obligatory. He and Will had braved the surf earlier, on a darkly overcast mid-winter day, with the sort of fierce north-westerly that dragged cold air from way down in the Southern Ocean, up over the divide, to dump bucket-loads of snow on the Alps before swinging back over the south-west coast to freeze their bollocks off in the surf. They'd lasted about forty minutes, and that was all, before packing it in and jittering up the track to the empty carpark. There, they'd wrestled off their wetsuits with frozen fingers barely operational for the job, and even more unworkable for unlocking the car, to access dry towels and clothes. Then straight back home, for long, hot showers – making feet and hands sting with bursting capillaries – and hot strong tea in front of the fire.

After dinner the talk turned to politics and world events. While Will was busy tucking the two girls into bed, Lidia told stories of working with anti-nuclear groups in the UK before their return to Australia. She'd been arrested, more than once, and as she talked, it evoked a world of hard-core activism and radicalism that seemed far removed from Daniel's life of artistic endeavor. His constituency was peopled mainly by elite and privileged yuppies; most of whom were oblivious to the wider world and the dangers there-in. He was impressed, maybe even a little envious of Lidia and Will's commitment and involvement.

When Will returned, the talk had turned to the changes in the Soviet Union, since the ascension of Gorbachev to the presidency – Perestroika and Glasnost, the so-called restructuring and openness – which on the surface seemed a good thing. But Will said the Soviet

Union was falling apart and that Gorbachev's policies could lead to the disintegration of the Soviet empire, which, he said could lead to chaos. More worryingly, it would mean loss of central control of the Soviet nuclear arsenal, with weapons falling into the hands of disparate groups or opportunistic governments seizing control in newly independent states. 'It might look like progress, but it would actually make the Soviet nukes even more dangerous. I mean Christ knows who'd end up in control of them. Friggin' nightmare, really.'

As they all got stuck into a dessert of apple crumble, Audrey changed the subject and got Bianca talking about her time in Paris, which was a welcome shift to something a bit lighter – and who didn't want to hear about what, to most of them, would be a dream come true – studying art at the Sorborne. After she'd regaled them with a couple of classic Parisian anecdotes and rather a bit too much detail about an affair with a young French professor, Audrey asked her about being back in Geelong, whether it was hard to adjust to home after having so much fun in Europe. 'I mean it's a bit of a come down from Paris, I would think...'

'Yeah, horrible, at first. I was actually really depressed for the first month or so, but I've adjusted now. Just gotta finish one more semester in that fucked up art school, and then I'm out!'

'Jesus, yes, it must've been a shock to go from European sophistication to having to deal with Blackthorn again,' observed Daniel, drily.

'Thank God, I don't have him anymore,' replied Bianca, 'but if I did, I'd bloody-well kick him right in the balls if he came near me, the prick.'

Everyone laughed, but in a way largely devoid of humour – knowing what Bianca was referring to – and Bianca smiled too and then looked around the room and then said brightly, 'So where have you got it stashed? Is it here in the house?'

A chunky silence descended on the diners and after a moment or two Audrey ventured: 'Got what stashed?'

'The Picasso of course, the Weeping Woman... It's all over the art school, if I heard it once I must have heard it three or four times. Hardman and Burke, they say... *They're* the cultural terrorists.'

A minor whirlwind of protest erupted around the table and Will almost gagged on a sip of wine, while Daniel and Audrey looked at each other, mortified.

'You are fucking joking, aren't you?' Daniel gave her a hard quizzical stare.

'Well *I am*, course I am, but I swear to God... I heard it straight from one of Blackthorn's latest bevy of baby acolytes. Practically wetting themselves, they were. Rumors all over the art school.'

'And I'm sure we can all guess who started them,' said Audrey.

'That piece of fucking shit.' Daniel spat. 'How is he still even there?'

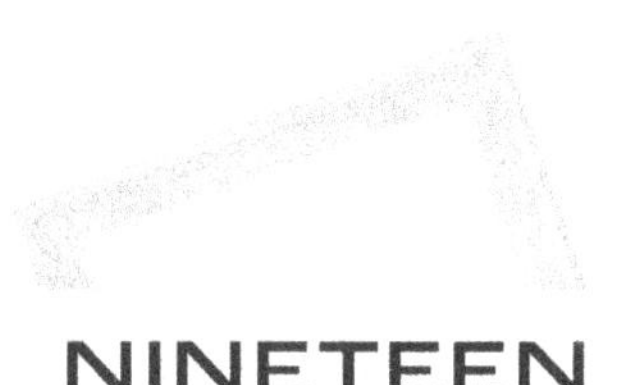

NINETEEN

Friday, August 15th, 1986

Art had its beginning as pure ritual and magic...
Angry Buddha, 2001

Jack bent down and angled his head to get the light from the high windows reflecting nicely from the finished canvas, and then he moved his head back and forth to see how the changing angles affected the finishing varnishes, now they were dry.

It looked good.

He took a couple of steps back and stood right next to Penny and she reached down and took his hand and squeezed it. 'It's incredible,' she breathed. 'It looks realer than the original.'

She was genuinely awe-struck and it gave Jack a pleasant, full feeling in his chest hearing her praise his work. He himself was pleased with the result. He'd been uncertain throughout most of the job. It was all so new. He'd had to figure out what he was doing step by step – from first principles.

First, he'd had to get the foundation coats right, and that had involved a lot of guess work and some trial and error. If anyone ever x-rayed the thing, the jig would be up – well, that is, if they had an x-ray of the original to compare it with.

Next had been mixing the colours – a nightmare, until he hit on a method, which, when he found it, had activated an oddly powerful intuition, that it was just how Picasso may have done it himself. As the work progressed he had that same feeling on a number of occasions – a sense that he was psychically connecting with the old bugger across time – almost as if something of the mental processes that created the Weeping Woman in the first place, had been lodged somewhere in the transcendental ether and had downloaded into him in fits and bursts as he progressed.

Inspiration across the ages.

The brush strokes had also been a big challenge at first, and so he'd practiced over and over on a spare canvas until eventually – just like the colour mixing – he'd felt like he had the connection, and was inside the old fellow's head. And yet still he was uncertain and his progress had been halting at first. But as he got closer to the finished product, his confidence grew until finally, at the end of it, *she* had emerged on the canvas; a sublime twin, wretched in all her glorious misery and identical to her sibling.

Penny moved forward and looked more closely at the original, and then deliberately at the copy, and then back at the real Picasso again.

'How have you done that? It doesn't look like it's been freshly painted. It looks old, just like the original.' She peered at it again. 'If anything, this one looks like it might be even older. That's amazing.'

Jack stepped forward and touched a finger to the edge of his work. 'The canvas has been aged. But it's really more about the glazes. The old masters used them to protect the paint from oxidising. We use similar sorts of varnishes today – modern ones. But I've used what they used in the 30's – with something added to them to make them seem to have yellowed a bit with age. Pretty cool, eh?'

'Remarkable. You're a fucking whiz at this.' Penny laughed and lifted herself on her toes and kissed him on the cheek.

'And check this out,' said Jack as he lifted the new canvas off the easel and carefully rotated it, to show her the backing board he'd attached to the back.

'What is it?'

'It's the original Masonite backing board from the Picasso... And see these? Jack indicated the faded labels glued to board.

'What are they?'

'Providence labels they call them. One of the ways they authenticate old paintings. They've got information about who owned the painting, when it was sold or exhibited... Sometimes there's receipts or even notes attached by the artist. This lot was on the back of the Picasso.' He gave Penny a cheeky grin.

'You've swapped them over?'

Jack nodded, still grinning. 'Swapped the whole backing board.'

Penny crinkled her brow. 'So what does that mean, exactly?'

'Well, they'll end up with the original back – they would know if it wasn't the real one, because someone will have examined all the tiny imperfections in the original, probably photographed them too – but they won't have the old backing board with the providence labels, and they won't have this either...' Jack went to the bench and picked up a small plastic sleeve and handed it to her.

Penny turned it over in her hands, examining the faded receipt protected inside the plastic and then looked at Jack questioningly.

'It was taped to the back – looks like an original receipt for a sale, or maybe for an exhibition.'

'So, yours will have all this stuff attached. Won't that make it more *authentic* than the original?'

Jack nodded with a cheerful smirk. 'Well it certainly clouds the issue. Things start to get pretty grey. Shit like this has happened all through art history, you know. They reckon anything up to ten per cent of the so-called masterpieces in the big galleries might be fakes. In this case they'll have the real one back in the NGV, but *this* will look more like the genuine article than the original itself.'

Penny gave a little whoop and then laughed quietly. Lowering her voice to a whisper she said: 'So are you saying that we could potentially sell this one as a real Picasso?'

'Well, we'd have to wait a few years until all the fuss had died down, and we'd have to pick a buyer very carefully – you know, someone far from here, someone very rich and someone who didn't want to ask too many questions – a private collector of some sort. But yeah, you know with all these stuck to the back of it...' Jack waved a hand over the back of the painting. 'Pretty good argument they'd be the proud owner of the real one.

'Fuck me,' Penny breathed and then laughed quietly. Then she looked at Jack in a way that Jack thought curious, like he was a new acquaintance. 'You really are a great big sexy bloody art forger, aren't you?'

*

Detective Sergeant Doherty could feel himself imploding, somewhere deep inside. Somewhere beyond the gruff exterior he showed to his team, beyond his perceived persona of punctilious purveyor of the foundation principles – *Patience, Enthusiasm, Persistence*. Something vital and structural, he felt sure, was crumbling to dust, deep down in his detective's secret heart and his dogged grip on propriety and exactness very suddenly felt alarmingly precarious.

It had only been two weeks since this, the most vexing investigation he'd ever been handed, had been foisted onto him, and it already felt like it was threatening to de-rail his professional life. Two weeks was nothing in the normal scheme of things. But this investigation was different; this was well outside his usual purview, and in addition, there were way too many players with fingers in the pie; a pie he couldn't help thinking he was going to end up wearing all over his face.

The media was in a frenzy, and no detective, going about the business of investigating, wants *that* level of media scrutiny. And it was political as well, with the shadowy *cultural terrorists* persistently ridiculing the police minister, embarrassing the government and bringing even more pressure for the culprits to be found. In the space of a fortnight he'd had more calls from the assistant commissioner's office than could reasonably be expected to happen in the course of an entire career... And being summoned himself to the minister's office for a personal de-brief... What was that all about? It was unprecedented.

At times he conceived himself in some kind of waking nightmare; wandering the unfamiliar streets of Melbourne's peculiar art world, a world filled with strange and enigmatic characters and suspects – completely unlike the criminals he was used to dealing with – people whose motivations and agendas were unfathomable to him and whose cooperation was uncertain and at times downright suspect.

The result was he and his team had seemed to have been going around in circles for two weeks: two weeks during which the pressure for unrealistically quick progress, had been unrelenting.

As Doherty stared vacantly through his office window to the squad's muster room, he felt a bleak emptiness in the pit of his stomach. Mallory and Fink were already in there, preparing for the Friday morning end-of-week briefing. Mallory was standing up by the big white board, pointing at one of the names surrounded by connecting arrows making some kind of point, or more likely, some sort of joke.

From a distance, the flow chart of names and arrows and events scrawled on the board had a disturbing circularity which seemed to symbolise the continuing dynamic of the investigation. Watching his men, Doherty thought they looked more like they were skylarking than seriously preparing for a meeting, and it lent some heat to the emptiness inside him, transforming it briefly to a caldera, volcanic frustration threatened to erupt. But he held it back.

Nonetheless it irked him that even some of his crew might be starting to see the investigation as some kind of joke... Not a serious crime, but a lark by students, or possibly some nefarious scheme gone wrong, perpetrated by gallery staff – no blood in the gutter, no corpses in the morgue – and with everyone they interviewed trailing boat-loads of red herrings, why take it seriously? It burned him and it hurt him that some of his squad, Mallory in particular, seemed disinterested and glib.

Their careers weren't at stake. As the detective in charge of the major crime squad, his was. It might be time to knock some heads together and demand a bit more commitment.

It was five minutes to nine as he gathered the file he'd been reviewing into its tatty manila folder and put on his coat. He had little appetite for the Friday review, but he had to remain positive, had to maintain motivation and morale. Somehow he had to break the impasse, and soon.

As he reached for his office door, the phone on his desk rang. His first thought was to let it go through to messages. But intuition told him to pick it up.

As Doherty listened to the low, uneasy voice on the other end of the line – himself speaking only occasionally to ask the odd question – he watched his men gather in the ante room, and they watched him, wondering no doubt, what was so important? Minutes ticked by and Doherty held the receiver to his ear, writing feverishly on his big yellow note pad.

Eventually, every eye was on him – his four team members gathered around the meeting room table – each of them gradually coming to the same conclusion, as the delay dragged on to fifteen minutes and Doherty continued to scribble furiously, the phone pressed to his ear...*The boss must be on to something.*

When he finally hung up the phone and gathered up his files and came into the meeting, there was an expectant hush. Doherty wore a faint but discernable smile on his customarily dour face. He placed his papers neatly on the end of the table and took up the white board marker. He looked around advisedly at each of his squad members and said, 'Right then – I think we might be on to something.'

They watched silently, and even a little wide-eyed, as Doherty took to the whiteboard with the eraser and carefully cleared a patch, right in the middle of the mind map of names and arrows, and neatly printed a name smack in the middle of it all.

The name was *Logan Tate* and underneath it he wrote: *Helicon Galleries.*

'This is our new target – we need to focus major resources on this guy. New information puts *this* guy at the centre of all *this* palaver...' He drew a new arrow linking Tate to the top left corner of the board where the words *art forgeries* had been underlined heavily in blue. 'And there's also a connection here...' He drew another, linking to the area on the board that referred to the NGV. 'And possibly to here as well...' A third arrow came down to a circle at the bottom of the board which contained the word *Forger*, with a large question mark.

*

Quinn untangled his bow tie and then ripped it away from his throat in annoyance and started again, chin up, folding and looping and watching in the mirror as Rosalyn passed behind him into her own dressing nook, and sat down at her make-up table.

'You saw the thing on the ABC, didn't you? Making a goddamned parody of the whole thing now; journos tearing around like the sodding Sweeney, on their way to that bloody thing in Adelaide.'

His wife leant back slightly and peeped around the corner of the walk-in wardrobe. 'What thing in Adelaide, darling?'

'Oh, some silly outfit calling themselves the Experimental Arts Foundation. Students, I suppose. Someone had them paint a whole swag of Picassos – you know Weeping Women – nineteen of them apparently. How very droll. Trying to jump on the bloody bandwagon.' He gave a derisive grunt as he finished his tie. 'And the ABC – supposedly still the national broadcaster, aren't they? Supposed to have some sort of journalistic integrity or at least some decorum, I would've thought – they send a film crew over there, hamming it up like they've solved the crime of the century, pretending the missing painting might be there. Embarrassing really, someone should be bloody sacked.'

'Well, I thought it was quite amusing.' A pause, and then: 'One has to keep a sense of humour don't you think?'

Ellery Quinn harrumphed as he shrugged on his jacket. 'Worst part was the real police showed up there while they were filming; checking all the ridiculous looking fakes as if they thought the Picasso might actually be there. Made them look like a bunch of witless bloody keystone cops and the ABC made a meal of it. Just what the police back here in Melbourne need – that sort of rubbish on the nightly news – especially when they've made no progress what-so-ever recovering my masterpiece.'

'Oh, it's *your* masterpiece now, is it?'

'Well it's my neck on the chopping block if we don't find it.'

He hadn't mentioned to Rosalyn his sneaking suspicion that Travis was in some way involved. After all, it was just an uncomfortable intuitive niggle, and because Rosalyn's life-long best friend was Travis' mother, and wife of the Chief Justice, best not to mention their son – Quinn's godson and current bothersome intern – might just be mixed up in the country's biggest ever art heist. She didn't need to know, and hopefully never would. Nonetheless he felt a slight shiver at his nape, as he slackened his collar with a finger, thinking about chopping blocks and necks.

'Still nothing from the police then... No progress? Do you think you'll ever get her back?'

'Of course!' Ellery asserted. 'I mean one way or the other we have to get her back, it's inconceivable that she could vanish, and honestly I'm not sure the gallery would recover if she's gone for good.'

'But she really *is* gone, isn't she? I mean it's been two weeks hasn't it?'

He grimaced as he reached for his good shoes, his back to his wife. Typical of Rosalyn, he thought, playing the devil's advocate, denying him any respite or comfort. His reply was only a simple grunt as he seated himself and pulled on a shoe. As the second shoe went on he added. 'Well, God only knows what a scandal like this could mean for my career if she is lost.'

'Surely you'll be okay Ellery, I mean you've already got your position in London. That's locked in, and we'll be in the UK by the spring, so ultimately, not your problem – and not your fault either, by the way – if someone's walked out the door with Picasso. It's not like you're head of security or anything, and you've got it firmly on the record with Wendy that you've been asking for better security for ages.'

When Quinn didn't reply and after a short pause she said, 'Tell me again who's coming tomorrow night, royalty of some sort aren't they?'

'The king of Norway, Carl the second or fourth, or something; wife Sonka and daughter Princess Astrid, I think it is. Had them through the gallery today and we seem to have gotten away with it. No mention of the theft anyway.'

'Perhaps they were just being polite... What do we call the wife, the queen I suppose she is...Is it Your Royal Highness?'

'Only the first time, but most likely she'll ask you to just call her Sonka... or Sonja, or whatever it is, I'll have to check... Let's just get through this recital thing tonight and we'll brush up on the rest of it tomorrow, before we go out there. I think my secretary gave me some kind of protocol sheet with all the right guff on it.

'What is it with these Scandinavian countries? They all seem to have royal families, still with their heads on their shoulders. Didn't you have to host the Swedish lot a few years ago? I thought they were all terribly modern democracies over in those Nordic regions?'

'They are. It's all just ceremonial. Constitutional monarchies, they are, just like Australia.'

'And is it some kind of protocol thing that your father has to host them for a dinner out at Government House?'

'Sort of, not really though, not obligatory. Father knew Carl in Cambridge; so I think he just wanted to make a fuss, and extend a bit of hospitality...Cooked it up with foreign affairs. Quite the artistic family apparently – the mother paints and daughter is into ceramics or photography or something – so mother thought we better come along too; make it a nice family get-together sort of thing.'

'Alright then, but what are we going to talk about? How's their English, by the way? Presumably quite good...'

'Very good. Just be yourself dear, you know you're always

brilliant once you get going. The wife, Sonka, she's right into sailing, so you'll have that in common. I think she represented Norway in the Olympics years ago, so you could ask her about that.'

'Splendid. And then there's always art. I might just let you talk the paint off the walls about art... That should keep them entertained.'

'I'll just have to remind myself not to stray into early century expressionism.'

'Hmm...Don't mention the war!' Rosalyn said in a strangely stilted voice that may have been an attempt to imitate Cleese's Faulty Towers character.

'Amen to that. No politics. No religion. No Picasso.'

*

Blackthorn snatched up the phone angrily, irritated with himself for not just letting it ring out – it was late and he normally would've been well gone from his campus office – but given the current state of his world, he thought he'd better at least see who it was. And sure enough, his instinct to take the call was right... It was Tate. And it was obvious from the get-go, he was in quite a state.

'How *are* things down there in Sleepy Hollow?' Tate enquired with solicitous sarcasm. 'Staying well-insulated from the shit storm are we? Nicely upwind of all the fall-out down there in the provinces, I trust?'

Being obtuse and talking in circles, was a sure sign Tate was upset or drunk, and probably both. Blackthorn found himself increasingly disenchanted with their acquaintance, but for the moment, he knew, he was stuck with him. And besides, regardless of his emotional instability and drunkenness, he was well-connected and could still be potentially useful, once the current catastrophe passed. He just had to hope Tate wouldn't lose his shit altogether over the Picasso thing.

'What's wrong?' He asked carefully, trying to gauge the extent of his woe.

'Oh nothing much, nothing at all really.... Just had three friggin' goons from the major crime squad down here tap dancing up and down my gallery, that's all.'

'Jesus! What did you say to them?'

'Just that they should fuck off and get a warrant, that's what I said to the mother-fuckers!' Tate sounded distraught and very drunk.

Blackthorn groaned.

Tate retaliated. 'Alright for you – you haven't had the friggin' Gestapo busting down your door...' an uncertain pause '...Have you?'

'No.'

'Well count yourself lucky. Some fucker's been talking, some mother...' Tate's voice became muffled and after a moment Blackthorn heard the tinkling of ice cubes and the sound of Tate swallowing and gasping to the sting of the liquor.

'Who was it? What did they ask you?'

'I dunno, Detective Sergeant something-or-other... Doherty, I think. Two other cops. Fucking macho bloody bone-heads, trying to intimidate me they were, but I sent 'em packing...'

'Okay, just tell me what they said. Did they know anything?'

'Just heard some bloody rumors that's all, rumors about fake landscapes... Could've heard that anywhere. Just fishing, the bastards. Asked me if I had any Picasso's out the back, the cheeky pricks. Just trying to scare me... They know nothing...' Tate sounded like he was trying to convince himself. It sounded like they *had* done a pretty good job of scaring him.

'Are there any more of those landscapes in your storeroom? You better get rid of them, in case they come back with a warrant.'

'Already done.' Tate slurred. Blackthorn felt his skin crimp. *Thank Christ for that at least.* Nonetheless a shiver of uncertainty and worry went through him... Drunk Tate was a liability.

But then, the dealer seemed to gather himself and his voice suddenly took on a child-like quality, and he sounded quite sober: 'Do you think they *do* know something? I mean, why would they question me, if they didn't *know* something? They asked me about my relationship to Quinn, and whether I knew his assistant Travis McCrae... I mean fuck me...'

'Jesus, what did you say?'

'Nothing... Told 'em to fuck off.'

Blackthorn assumed he hadn't literally told them to fuck off. All this was bravado, and the drink talking. He wondered vaguely whether Tate had been drunk when the cops interviewed him, or whether he'd gotten that way subsequently.

'Did they ask about me? Blackthorn asked delicately.

'You? No. Why would they? *Mister anonymous* down there in Geelong? There's nothing to connect you and I, not really.

'Let's keep it that way.' Blackthorn's tone carried a none-too-veiled threat.

There was a long pause, and he could hear Tate's ragged breath and he sniffled, which made Blackthorn wonder if he'd actually been crying, or if it was just the drink.

'We could be in a lot of trouble. What if they really do have some sort of information?'

'They don't. Don't worry. They would have arrested you if they had anything. Like you say – a fishing expedition. You didn't say anything about your young painter, what's his name... Jack?'

'Fuck no. Fucker's got me on video... A video he'll be wearing up his arse, if I ever see him again.

Thinking about the damning evidence this young punk had on Tate made Blackthorn shudder, and a sudden dark fear rose up in him, and immediately turned to anger; murderous anger, and he thought again about what he'd said to Tate previously – if only it were possible – to just get rid of the little bastard.

'We just have to find that little rat-fuck forger of yours, that's all,' Blackthorn intoned with menace.

'Well good luck with that, because he's gone. Fucking vanished.'

'Okay, so get someone to track him down, for Christ's sake. Can't you hire someone? I can't believe you don't have anything on him, I mean didn't you get his next of kin or something?'

'Are you serious? Why would I?'

He heard Tate swallow over the phone and in the background the tinkle of ice cubes.

He realised Jack wasn't the only one he wanted to get rid of. Drunk, sober or otherwise, Tate was a nerve-wracking liability and now the police were sniffing around his carcass, it was clearly time to cut him adrift... If only it were that simple, push the drunken sod overboard and let the sharks have him.

But in reality he knew neither option was feasible. If Tate went down, so would he. Even the most inept investigators would eventually make the connection. And as for disposing of the boy – in spite of the fact he knew someone who knew someone, who would do it for a good price – the risk that Jack's video really would go to the police if something happened to him, could not be ignored.

What they needed was a diversion. He'd come to this conclusion some days ago. There'd been too much talk about the possibility it was an inside job; and that theory seemed to be gaining ground as time dragged on, with the police getting no closer to identifying the cultural terrorists.

The cops needed a breakthrough, they needed some good solid information to point them in the right direction, and away from Tate. And it was just such a diversion he'd been working on. It was the very thing that had kept Blackthorn working late in his office that Friday afternoon.

'Well, let's not worry about your little forger,' Blackthorn said quietly. 'What we need is a distraction. Get the heat off you. But the last thing we want to do is point them in the direction of your boy...' He paused. Tate was quiet on the other end of the phone line. Listening. 'Because if he goes down, we go down... Right?'

A muffled grunt of agreement from Tate, as he took another sip.

'We need to give the cops what they want... A couple of fully-fledged cultural terrorists. Plausible ones, that everyone will believe are the real culprits.' As he spoke Blackthorn's free hand straightened the half-completed pencil drawing on the desk in front of him and he allowed himself a small smile of satisfaction. It was coming along quite well.

'What do you mean?' Tate's voice sounded plaintiff and small. Again, child-like.

Jesus. Thank God someone's got some balls. Blackthorn looked from his drawing to the photograph he'd liberated from student records. The drawing of his ex-student was only half done, but already it was a very good likeness. Unmistakable.

'Don't you worry about that, I've got a plan... A very bloody good plan. But we'll have to get the timing right.'

'What do you mean timing?' Tate sounded worn out. Miserable.

'Well, the way I see it, my little plan will work a whole lot better, once the painting's back where it's supposed to be. We have to find that little fucker of yours and find out what he's done with the painting. And we better hope he still has it, and it's still in one piece. The tricky part will be getting it returned to the gallery without implicating us, or him.'

'Yeah well good luck with that, because he's fucken gone.' Now he was sounding, positively morbid and depressed.

'Listen man, just get a grip on yourself... Or do you want to end up in bloody jail. I mean, have you even been keeping an eye on his house? We should have the place under twenty-four-hour friggin' surveillance.'

'I have, I've been around there every second day or so. I tell you, he's fucken gone! I think his girlfriend might have been there once or twice, but I missed her...'

'What? So they're not *gone*. You need to be watching that place, *every day*. We need to know when he comes back. Someone needs to talk to that little bastard. I mean not scare him, just talk to him. Get him to cooperate.'

'I've got a friggin' gallery to run, you know. I'm not a bloody private eye.' Tate's tone had switched to argumentative. 'I feel weird creeping around his place all the time. The neighbours have been giving me suspicious looks.'

Bored and annoyed with Tate's whining tone, Blackthorn switched off for a moment, as he pursued another train of thought: 'Travis – he's the one should talk to him. No police. No argy-bargy with you. Travis... Or maybe even Quinn, could talk some sense into him, reason with him...'

'Maybe so, but you're forgetting we don't know where he is... Could be in Timbuctoo for all we know...'

'Will you stop pissing and moaning and just bloody find him!?' Blackthorn hung up the phone, cutting off the tinny, whining voice of Tate still complaining in the ear-piece.

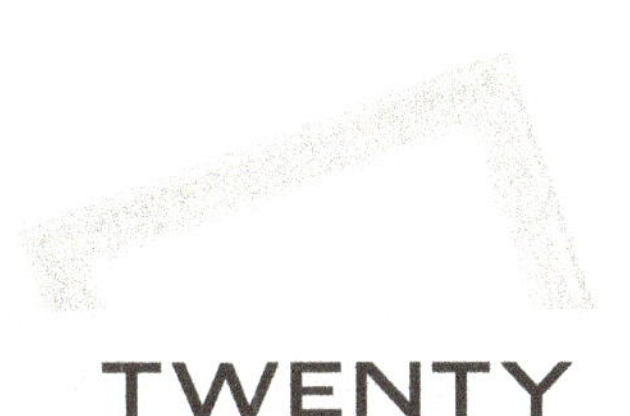

TWENTY

Sunday, August 17th, 1986

My God, it's full of stars.
Angry Buddha, 2001

Overhead a plump gibbous moon, rising over the old mansion, threw a dark shadow across the wide driveway, as the limousine bearing the Norwegian sovereigns pulled away and crunched down Government House Drive and into the King's Domain.

The governor, his wife, his son and *his* wife Rosalyn stood steadfast in the frigid night, formed up in a semicircle and dutifully waving them off until the tail lights vanished from view.

'Well, weren't they lovely,' said Ellery's mother with a satisfied sigh.

There was general agreement and indeed it was obvious the King and his father had enjoyed their catch-up immensely, waxing nostalgic for much of the evening about their glory days in Cambridge. His mother, who genuinely reveled in her role as vice regal hostess – always exuding a surfeit of gracious hospitality – had hit it off nicely with Sonka the Queen and her daughter, and the meal as usual had been exceptional and had drawn genuine and unsolicited compliments from all and sundry.

They had hosted them in the informal family dining room, just to give it all a relaxed and intimate atmosphere, which seemed to have done the trick.

Rosalyn, despite her misgivings, had done her usual thing and charmed them all with her delicate probing, getting the royal trio to loosen up and divulge, with engaging candor, various intimacies of their lives at home in Norway, to the mutual gratification of all. And by the end of the night, the bond between the King and his father, had expanded to envelope them all in a convivial bubble of warmth.

Ellery however had experienced more than his usual sense of disconnection from it all – more observer than participant – other than the obligatory interactions which he carried off, with his usual aplomb. He was more than a little distracted. With another week drawing to a close, and no sign of any resolution of the Picasso debacle, it had been difficult for him to enter into the spirit of the evening.

Throughout the dinner, he'd had a faintly prescient awareness of something approaching, of something about to shake loose in respect of the grotesquely distorted aberration of normal life he'd been suffering through for a fortnight.

It was perhaps for this reason, when he received the first of two strange and unsettling phone calls – the first of which, stranger still, reached him at Government House – that he was not entirely surprised, and perhaps even a little relieved. Something, at least was shifting.

He took the call in his father's office, in the library wing, overlooking the piazza, with first his father and then the footman who received the call, each giving him a similarly quizzical frown as he retreated inside to take the unexpected late-night call.

The strangeness of the evening stepped up a notch when he picked up the receiver and found Travis on the line. *Why would*

Travis be calling him so late and night...And out here? What could be so important that it couldn't wait until morning, at the gallery?

He was about to make that exact point, but Travis' first words stopped him in his tracks.

'The major crime squad now thinks it's an inside job.'

'What did you say?' Quinn heard him well enough, but incredulity prevented it from sinking in. 'How do you know that?... What do they mean an inside job? How?... Who? What the hell are you talking about?'

'Well, I told you I'd put my ear to the ground and let you know if I heard something... Well I heard something.' Travis paused deliberately for a moment. 'There's this dealer, a friend of mine. The cops have got him in their sights. I'm not sure why.'

'Which dealer?'

'Never mind, you don't know him... Or you might, but that's not important. The cops think he's got something to do with it – but it's not him. But he thinks he knows where the painting might be. He thinks it's still in Melbourne, and he thinks the people involved want to give the Picasso back, if it can be done without involving the police.'

'Jesus,' Quinn whispered.

'He reckons whoever did it – they've had their fun, or they're getting scared, and they just want it to be over. They don't want there to be repercussions.'

'Repercussions...Christ!' Quinn exploded slightly and then recovered, lowering his voice to a low hiss. 'They've stolen the country's most valuable painting – calling themselves terrorists, for God's sake – and antagonised the absolute be-Jesus out of the Police Minister. How can they expect there to be no repercussions?'

'Listen, like I said, the police think it's an inside job. They've come to the belief that the Cultural Terrorists are nothing but a hoax. They raided this guy's commercial gallery – with a friggin' warrant, for Christ's sake – interrogated him for hours. He said they asked him all kinds of questions about the NGV and all kinds of questions about you, too.'

'What? That's preposterous!' *It's you they should be asking questions about, boyo.* He almost said it out loud, but held back.

'The point is, everyone's going to be better off once the painting's back in place, no? Takes the heat off my dealer friend. Takes the heat off the NGV. Everything's more relaxed. Balance restored, you know.'

'Why are you telling *me* this?'

'Look, my guy has a name and an address. A young artist. If he hasn't actually got the painting, my friend is pretty sure he knows who does.'

'For Christ's sake Travis, what has all this got to do with me? You shouldn't be telling me this. I can't be involved.'

'You want to get her back, don't you?'

'Of course, but...'

'The cops think *you* might be involved.' Travis said quietly and precisely, and just let it hang.

Quinn seized up for a moment. Mute. Rage boiled up precipitously, but he held it down, not without some effort. He couldn't believe his bloody dodgy and disreputable godson-come-intern, was blatantly trying to manipulate him. But somehow, in the moment it was working. He promised himself he would take it out of the kid's hide in due course.

'But what am I supposed to do?'

'It's obvious isn't it? To get her back without any fuss, no questions asked, no police; it has to be someone official, but not too official, someone they can trust... Someone who can make a deal.

'But how? How the hell do we actually do it? I just wander into the gallery with the Weeping Woman under my arm and say; *Look what I found! Don't ask me where...'*

'You'll think of something, I'm sure. I'll give you the details tomorrow at work.' With that the phone went dead. Travis was gone. Quinn stared in disbelief at the receiver and muttered vehemently: 'Bloody obnoxious, precocious little bastard...'

*

The further south he went, the more apprehensive Jack became. He was driving into a fog of doubt. A gathering storm of consequence.

It was completely unlike his northward flight with the Picasso in hand, two weeks earlier. That had felt like an escape. He'd been filled with an almost unbelievable lightness of being, as if some small oppressed part of himself had been freed from long incarceration. Recalling *that* feeling, now filled him with a heavy nostalgia and a sense of foreboding. His mood could not have been more different.

Even his tired old Corona – which had borne him away from the city like a nimble steed – seemed reluctant to make the return journey, and he felt the old engine miss and surge yet again, as if in protest. It troubled him. What if the old beast actually broke down with its infamous contraband onboard? He hadn't even considered this on the way up, but now, with the engine sounding decidedly sick, it gave him cause to fret, and the knocking noise – which most likely had been a problem for some time – now played on his mind with every mile.

Returning to Melbourne was a necessary part of the plan. Penny had caught the train back a couple of days earlier, almost as if she was the advance party; testing the ground. He tried to tell himself it was no big deal, that he himself was nowhere on the radar. But after the last few weeks of media furor it felt dangerous, coming back to the city...Like some kind of ambush might be waiting for him.

Even though the police and media were still running around trying to find the cultural terrorists, Tate knew Jack had the painting. And it was a pretty safe bet he was pissed off. He'd certainly had plenty of time to nurture his anger, and also time to hatch some sort of scheme to counteract Jack and Penny's so-called *insurance*.

Before his departure Penny had reported nothing out of the ordinary at home; no contact from Tate, although a neighbor told her they'd seen someone hanging around the street a few times, *acting suspiciously*. Probably Tate, they surmised. But what if it had been someone else watching their house? Police... Or some other unknown agents or gangsters of some sort? Jack tried not to dwell on the possibilities.

By ten o'clock in the morning, he was nearly home, zooming along the Western Highway with Ballarat already behind him and the western suburbs of Melbourne ahead. It was either a failure of nerve or his rumbling stomach that had him spontaneously turn off the highway for Ballan. One last stop to gather his nerve and get himself a coffee and a sausage roll.

Leaning against the car and sipping his coffee, gathering his resolve, his eye settled on the typewriter sitting on the back seat. He crinkled up his nose as if the coffee was not to his liking – which in truth it wasn't, but that wasn't the problem – it was the typewriter, which suddenly constellated the creeping sense of dread with which he'd been wrestling.

The friggin' typewriter – the very one used to type all three ransom notes. The notorious ransom notes of the cultural terrorists – published all over Melbourne these last two weeks.

All kinds of notions started racing through Jack's head – a lot of it, to be fair, based on Hollywood tropes or books he'd read – but he was pretty sure still with a basis in real forensic practice.

Typewriters! ... Each machine with its unique idiosyncrasies – a crooked striking arm here; a tiny casting defect on a letter there, or some other distinctive maladjustment. In this way, a typewritten letter could be linked back to a specific machine. How many times had he seen it on film? The damning evidence, the smoking gun; the typewriter used by the culprit.

Jack crunched his empty cup and binned it, and as he got back to the car, he cast an accusing look at his old typewriter, sitting innocently on the back seat. Jesus, what had he been thinking? This was exactly the sort of sloppy thinking that could sink them.

A mile or so out of town, before the byway re-merged with the Western Highway, he pulled over on the narrow verge of a small bridge – checked both ways to make sure nothing was coming – and jumped quickly out of the car. He raced around and pulled open the opposite back door and checked once more, ahead and behind. A quiet country road, ten o'clock Sunday morning, not a soul in sight. He hefted the old typewriter out and in one fluid movement hoisted it over the guard rail and watched its brief descent before disappearing with a modest plonk into the murky shallows of the Werribee River.

*

It was a wintery August night in Melbourne, with a gusty southerly wind driving squalls of intermittent rain across the city as they made their way through the back streets of Brunswick. Quinn had convinced Hans Mueller, who was on the NGV's board, to come with him to follow up on what he'd told him was a possible lead on the whereabouts of the Picasso. Hans was a retired Melbourne dealer and artist, and one of Quinn's oldest if not closest acquaintances, and he thought it would be a good idea to have a witness with him when he visited Travis' mysterious contact.

Travis had given him the address, but had offered no useful intelligence on the chances of finding him at home. Then in a more sober tone Travis had advised him to *tread very carefully* if he did manage to talk to him. *The kid's probably going to be a bit nervous, especially once you show up at his door unannounced.*

Hans had of course suggested that perhaps it was a task best left to the police, if it was a genuine lead... Quinn had convinced him otherwise.

The two of them must have seemed like a couple of clichéd gumshoe detectives, sulking around the backstreets of inner Melbourne with no regard for the finer points of procedure, or the brutal winter weather. The image was reinforced when they finally stood at the front door of the nominated house – buffeted by a freezing southwesterly, driving swirls of light drizzle around their ears – Hans in his thick woolen overcoat and beret and Quinn in his bone-coloured trench, with the collar up, like some sort of misplaced Poirot.

As Quinn prepared to knock, Hans had another go; suggesting that their actions might not be entirely appropriate.

'We can't involve the police, not at this early stage,' Quinn had whispered in reply. 'You know, if the police went barging in with their jack boots, it might just spook the lad – and if he does know something, or knows someone who really is involved – they might go to ground.'

'Hmm, I suppose so,' conceded Hans as Quinn rapped on the door.

Much to their surprise the door opened and before them, in

the warm glow of a classic terrace-house hallway, was an attractive young woman smiling at them uncertainly, and giving them both the *once over* with a frankly appraising eye.

'Hello,' Quinn said mildly, 'we're looking for Mr. Jack Curran, if he's at home.'

'And whom should I say is calling?' Penny asked this with mock formality, looking from Quinn, who she recognised perfectly well, to Hans, who could have been anybody. She flicked a quick glance past the two men, to see if there was a squad of police backing them up.

Satisfied there was not, her manner – which had been polite but taut – relaxed a little, and she surprised even herself, at being largely unperturbed by the director of the NGV turning up on their doorstep, looking for his Picasso, no doubt. She had to suppress a grin; but on the other hand she *was* a little nervous about what Jack would make of it, so she made them wait right there on the doorstep, while she went and sought his advice.

Once admitted they made their way down the hallway, past a bedroom and a spare room where they could see the glow of a television, and found Jack down the back in the living area-come-studio standing expectantly beside the easel with its half-finished still life, his hands on his hips. His posture plainly posed the question: *What do you think you're doing here, disturbing our Sunday night?*

Penny introduced everyone as best she could, but got Hans' name wrong. Quinn explained to Jack that they were visiting various artists around town, in the hope that they might gain some intelligence about the missing Picasso, because it *had* been two weeks, and so far the police had drawn a blank... *So, just asking around, on the off chance.* Even as he spoke, Quinn was aware of how banal and implausible he sounded, but it was what he and Hans had decided on; a non-threatening low-key approach. In reality, it was Quinn's code to Jack to let him know that he wasn't accusing *him*.

Jack looked at Quinn and then Penny, with a deeply ironical frown and then back at Quinn. Meanwhile Hans was looking around the living room and through into the kitchen, noticing the various newspaper cuttings about the stolen Picasso plastered around the place, on the fridge and on the big cork board over Penny's desk.

Jack watched Hans taking it all in and frowned a little more deeply at Penny. It was all Penny's work – the cuttings – and he'd taken her to task about it when he'd got home a few hours earlier, because it seemed ill-advised... *And this was why*, his frown told her.

She shrugged.

Hans took it all in, a bit wide-eyed, and then stared at Quinn and raised his eyebrows, nodding pointedly at the display of clippings on the corkboard.

Quinn ignored him and continued: 'You see no one at the gallery wants any recriminations of any kind... We just want the painting back.'

Jack gave him a fake smile and said: 'Of course.' Wondering if Quinn had lost his marbles. What was he doing here, really? Had Tate sent him? It was Tate he'd expected to see, and he'd planned how he would handle that. But having the gallery director himself show up was just weird. *Did he think Jack would just hand the painting over? In that case why on earth would he bring a witness? And who the fuck was this Hans, anyway?* Perhaps, he mused, the stress of losing his two-million-dollar painting had sent Quinn over the edge.

From the kitchen, Penny made some diversionary small talk, something about the latest media speculation, and then quickly switched track and asked if anyone wanted a cup of tea. After some momentary indecision from Hans and Quinn, about the tea, they decided no, and there followed an uncomfortable silence. Then there was some more polite chat, by Hans this time, which left Jack shaking his head derisively. He half expected the front door to burst off its hinges at any moment and Special Forces police to storm down the hallway. But there was something about Quinn's guileless manner and the awkwardness of the two men, which reassured him that wasn't going to happen.

'Look, if anyone has the painting and wants to return it, we don't expect it to be delivered to the front door of the gallery.' Quinn smiled a solicitous smile. 'I mean it could be just left somewhere, you know... In a locker at the airport, or at Spencer Street Station, or some such. No questions asked, all well and good just as long as the painting's returned... That's what we've been telling everyone.'

In the kitchen Penny let out an involuntary whoop of laughter and then quickly stifled it. Jack smiled at Quinn and tipped his head sideways as if perplexed by a strange specimen.

Things got awkward again and Hans cleared his throat and shuffled his feet. Suddenly Quinn seemed to notice the unfinished painting on the easel and then turned his attention to the others leaning against the wall and took a few steps closer to look at them more carefully, as if appraising them, and then made a few gratuitous complimentary observations about them, which no one took seriously.

Then almost as quickly as they'd arrived they made their way back up the hallway and took their leave; Quinn, pausing at the front door to make the same speech about the possibility of the stolen painting being returned via a railway station locker, or something.

As Jack closed the door on them, Penny burst out laughing and put a hand over her mouth to suppress it. Jack looked at her with a mien of puzzlement and wonder and said: 'Fuck me, what the hell was that?'

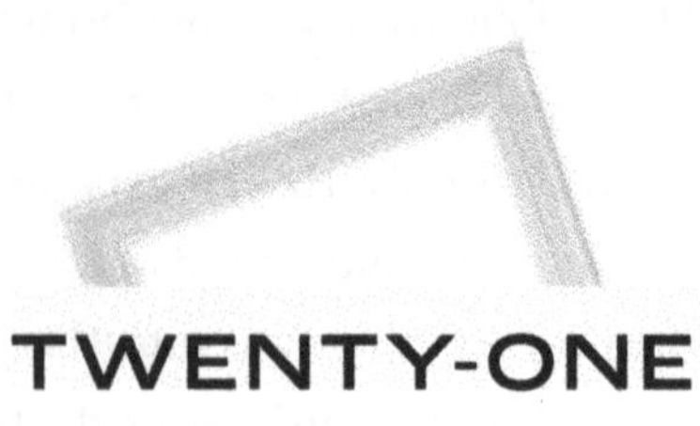

TWENTY-ONE

Monday, August 18th, 1986

'Your friends are terrorists.'
Angry Buddha, 2001

Penny folded another large piece of tissue paper in half and then in half again and smoothed her palm along the fold, before carefully placing it on the painted surface of the canvas.

'Are you sure it's properly dry?' She looked across at Jack on the other side of the work table. He gave her a dubious and quizzical frown, atop a half-submerged smile.

'You know this is the original. We're sending them back the real one... You know that, don't you?

'Oh...Well I can't even tell the difference. I thought this one looked like the one you did, so, there you go... Can't even tell them apart.' She flashed a cheeky grin. 'Are you sure you didn't mix them up?'

'Very funny.' Jacked returned her smile, but a little tentatively.

Penny shrugged and changed the subject. 'Did you see the look on that guy's face when he saw all the newspaper clippings?' Penny smiled approvingly at the protective layers she had around the painting, and then looked up at Jack smugly.

'Yeah, like he'd seen a ghost or something.' Jack gave his head a little shake. 'What were you thinking, really – all that stuff plastered all over the house? You could see his little brain ticking over, couldn't you? And Quinn too... Ah ha! We've uncovered the lair of the cultural terrorists...'

Penny chuckled and brandished her big dress-making scissors. 'If only they knew... It was right under their noses ... Well under the bed anyway.' She sliced along the roll of brown paper, cutting off a piece more than three feet long, and letting it slide to the floor.

'But what *was* that all about, I mean it was fucking bizarre wasn't it?' Jack held the painting up off the table while Penny retrieved the paper and laid it across the table underneath. 'Was it Tate, do you reckon? ... Did he send them around? Or was it just Quinn off his own bat? How the hell would he know?' Jack answered his own questions with a shrug.

Penny shrugged too, and then folded one side of the wrapping paper right over the painting and tucked it in on the other side, then did the same with the other side, so that both ends were tucked in beneath the stretcher.

'Can you pass me those stickers? ... Who knows babe. He's a strange one isn't he? What did he say? He'd been *doing the rounds... Talking to various artists around town.* So funny!'

She carefully turned the painting over, holding the wrapping in place. 'Can you hold down here?'

While Jack put a finger on the edge, she applied two big white stickers, and gave them a pat and let out a satisfied grunt, seeing they were holding the wrapping nice and snug.

'Done! All ready to go,' said Jack.

'No... We need string,' said Penny. 'If we're gift-wrapping their friggin' Picasso it's gotta be done right.'

While she searched for the string, Jack said: 'What about all that shit about putting it in a railway station locker? Was he serious?'

'What? You mean because it obviously sounds like a set up... Like some kind of trap?'

'Yeah... Does he think we're bloody stupid?'

Penny cut a long piece of string and Jack lifted the painting so she could lay it underneath and then she joined and looped it on top and went back under at right angles. They flipped the package and Penny tied it off with a nice bow.

'Hmm...' Penny looked thoughtfully at the finished parcel. 'But if you think about it, if they wanted to arrest us they would've just brought the police with them. Maybe they're still running scared, because they know we've got the video of Tate, and if Tate goes down, so does his insider at the NGV – whoever the hell that is – maybe it was Quinn himself... Ha!'

'I reckon he just wants the painting back. He must be bloody desperate after two weeks. Maybe he was genuine... Just letting us know to return it, no questions asked. Put it in a locker and all is forgiven.'

Jack looked at Penny and then down at the parcel, twisting his mouth into a fake grimace. 'Maybe, but I wouldn't put it past them to set up some sort of ambush... Police, media, the whole circus... And us right at the centre of it... Marched off in chains to appease the cheering masses.'

'Maybe. But you saw him on the telly again this morning... He was saying the same thing... Putting it out there for everyone to hear... *Just put it in a locker.* I reckon he really does just want the painting back.... I mean you know it's not insured? ... I've been reading about historical art thefts. Often they negotiate to get the paintings back. They're too valuable. Irreplaceable often... And galleries can't afford to insure them all. So it's a different set of rules.' Penny patted the wrapped painting thoughtfully.

'And at the end of the day, if we go down – they all probably go down, whoever they are… Your mate Tate for sure, but maybe Quinn too, and who knows who else. I reckon he wants to protect *us*, because that protects all of them too. Once the painting's back, the heat's off everyone.'

'You're probably right,' said Jack. 'But the one thing we're not taking into account is that prick Maynard; he's gonna pursue this until hell freezes over. He seriously wants heads to roll.'

'Yeah, mainly because you rubbed his nose right in it!'

They both laughed, and Jack thought with satisfaction about his final message from the Cultural Terrorists, typed at the farm, on the now submerged typewriter…*If we have also drawn attention to your own inadequacy… so much the better.* He'd tucked it inside the parcel with the painting. One last bit of salt in the wound, for old mate.

In the end, they decided to do exactly what Quinn suggested, because Penny was right, and the way Jack had rationalised it in the end, there was a kind of symmetry to returning the painting according to Quinn's wishes. He'd actually offered them an olive branch, because essentially, they *were* all in this together – adversaries in the same boat; co-conspirators, really – and they were all going to either sink or swim together.

So the plan was set… And the sooner the better.

First thing in the morning they would go down to the station – early, before any nine-to-five detectives or gallery directors were out and about – but plenty of commuters rushing about for cover. Jack would go in and get a locker – go down and measure it up for size, just to be sure it would accommodate the parcel – and then come out and give Penny the key. Penny, looking all pure and innocent, would walk down nonchalantly and deposit the package. Job done.

The only thing left was for Jack to find a public phone and telephone his old friends at The Age newspaper… *Hi! Remember us?*

TWENTY-TWO

Wednesday, August 20th, 1986

We're all immortal, clairvoyant light beings, I keep telling them – for a dollar a minute.
Angry Buddha, 2001

Quinn took a sip from his flute and smiled for the cameras. He was in his element, standing in front of the recovered Picasso; looking small and fragile, naked on a small easel, rigged up especially for the press conference.

A strong protective impulse had him fixed in a tight orbit around the painting. He was disinclined to let her out of his sight, but he was more than happy to exude unadulterated joy and relief for the cameras, at the recovery of the gallery's signature masterpiece.

The press and television had been lapping it up, every bit of it, as Quinn hammed it up for them: *It's going to be bolted to the wall and placed behind glass. If you want to take the painting, next time you'll have to take the entire air conditioning duct... Ha ha.*

The only dampener on proceedings was Maynard, who seemed incapable of letting go of his persona of vengeful police minister, bent on biblical retribution for the affront to himself personally, and to his bumbling police force.

No doubt it irked him even more that the Picasso had finally been recovered, not by the police, but through another tip-off to The Age newspaper; saying the painting had been left in a locker at Spencer Street railway station, and giving the locker number. Right to the end, the cultural terrorists seemed bent on embarrassing the government and their instrument of oppression... Maynard's Keystone Cops.

The Age had immediately telephoned Quinn at the Gallery; whereupon himself, Derek, a journalist and a photographer from the newspaper, together with an ABC news crew, had descended on the locker at the railway station. What followed was another embarrassing debacle. It took more than an hour for police to arrive; by which time a crowd had gathered –people having recognised Quinn from his numerous media appearances and, with the cameras all around – guessing it had something to do with the Weeping Woman saga.

Finally when police and forensics did arrive, the farce continued, with the station master being unable to find a master key that would open the locker, and having to resort to jimmying it open with a crowbar.

Eventually, a Picasso-sized parcel wrapped in brown paper and string was extracted from the locker and whisked away, out of the station and into a waiting car, like some kind of Hollywood starlet, with the bourgeoning media contingent and interested onlookers pursuing her all the way. After being checked by police at the forensic science laboratory, in Spring Street – and more importantly by Derek, to confirm its authenticity – the Weeping Woman was declared safely restored, undamaged, and a hasty press conference was arranged, which quickly took on a festive atmosphere.

The fact that the Picasso's Masonite backing board was missing from the returned painting, was not the first thing Quinn noticed. But he saw, by the look on Derek's face – right there in the forensics lab – it was certainly the first thing that struck Derek. Quinn heard his conservator's sharp intake of breath and saw the fleeting hint of panic in his eyes. The look that passed between the two of them then, acknowledged the fact that it was missing, and all the implications.

They both new intimately the faded remnants of labels and stickers adhered to the backing board: Receipts and exhibition notices, some of which had been encased in polyester for protection, and attached to the backing board. They were all missing; backing board, sheathed providence labels; everything that attested to the painting's journey through the art world since its creation.

Something in the hooded, haunted expression on Derek's face had made Quinn shut up about it, and to his surprise Derek hadn't mentioned it either, as if it was a detail just too troubling to consider in light of the prevailing euphoria at the painting's return.

A kind of conspiracy of silence ensured, and Quinn was already wondering how long it would last, before the troubling detail of the missing providence labels became common knowledge.

Meantime, even Wendy seemed content if not ebullient, and even accepted a glass of bubbly which she sipped sparingly. Derek was two sheets to the wind on his second glass and even Glynn had treated himself to a light beer. But not Maynard. He publicly turned his nose up at a celebratory glass, and as good as rebuked Quinn in front of the assembled press.

'Not for me – I'll wait until an arrest has been made, if you don't mind.' And he told the assembled press that the fifty-thousand-dollar reward for the capture of the Australian Cultural Terrorists was still in effect.

'All of Victoria's art treasures are going to remain at risk, so long as these people are at liberty,' he said, also making the spurious point that funds which might have been spent on the arts, might now have to be spent on improved security.

Christ, thought Quinn, *Ross must be the only one left in Melbourne who thinks the Cultural Terrorists actually exist.* Their lack of any kind of corporal credibility – which had gradually dawned on most people involved in the debacle – had so far eluded Maynard, possibly because he was blinded by his need to avenge himself for the public shellacking they'd given him.

For Quinn's part, the relief was absolutely immense, and he wasn't going to let Maynard's churlishness spoil it. Two-and-a-half weeks of purgatory, in which he'd felt like he was tip-toeing through a minefield, was finally over.

Travis had proven himself to be erratic, shifty and almost invisible throughout the crisis until, in the end, passing on the advice from his questionable colleague that had turned the tide. And this fellow Jack – or whoever his shady friends were – had taken his advice to return the panting in good faith, obviously seeing it as their best last chance to avoid repercussions, and putting an end to the matter.

As he helped himself to another glass of bubbly – careless of the possible impact on his afternoon schedule – his relief almost bordered on elation. No one could really know the extent of the turmoil he'd endured in the last fortnight. But now, the Picasso was back in the NGV, his reputation was intact. Maynard and the police department would eventually lose interest in chasing red herrings, and in a few short months, he and Rosalyn would be safely ensconced in Oxford with the whole sorry business of the missing Picasso behind them.

But best of all, the short and inauspicious patronage of his dodgy godson – of whose complicity he was more certain than ever – would finally be at an end. *In fact that can start right now,* he thought as he drained his champagne and smiled at the young TV reporter advancing towards him in the hope of another witty sound bite.

*

Blackthorn looked up from his oysters and squinted down a long line of white-clothed tables toward the front entrance of the narrow, dimly lit restaurant. He could see the young aproned waiter who'd been serving him, talking to someone at the front door and gesticulating in somewhat clichéd Italian semaphore, but he couldn't make out much more without his bifocals, which he'd left in his car. *Was it Tate?* Surely it was – he was already half an hour late.

For reasons best known to Enzo – the owner and host of the vaunted Lygon Street Trattoria, Blackthorn's favorite – they'd put him all the way in the rear of the long dining room; his back to the wall and facing the entrance, like he was some kind of security-conscious mafia don, habitually taking up a defensive position in case of ambush by rival gangsters. Maybe that was the way the old maître d' saw him, in his colourfully jaded European imagination. Indeed, perhaps Enzo had some intuitive insight into Blackthorn's perfidious heart. But in the gangster movies *he'd* seen, the rival family's assassins would just come in through the kitchen to surprise the doomed godfather, as the bullets and spaghetti sauce started flying.

The figure at the door resolved into Tate, as he approached through the near-empty restaurant, which seemed to Blackthorn strangely quiet for the popular eatery. Normally it would be packed and noisy, any day of the week; filled with Melbourne's Italian community and everyone and anyone who enjoyed good hand-made pasta and Enzo's renowned wine list. There would be families, couples, after-work diners; young punks fueling up for a night out, together with the serious, well-dressed young stallions deliberately exuding gangster shtick for its imagined allure, and yes, even the odd reserved and aloof ensemble – who might actually be the real thing – quietly going about their business over plates of linguini and sauce.

'Did your horse throw a shoe, or something, did it?' Blackthorn jutted out his chin and flicked the bottom of it, deliberately mimicking the vernacular gesture which Blackthorn thought – incorrectly – was the universal *fuck you* in Italian, just to see if he could get a rise out of his tardy companion.

Tate ignored it or didn't understand it, and greeted Blackthorn with a scowl and a nod and slid quickly into the seat opposite him, almost like something was chasing him. He glanced nervously around the restaurant and said: 'Sorry. Traffic.' He dead-panned the old bugger and twitched a fake smile. 'Also I had a bit of trouble getting past the phalanxes of fucking cops surrounding my goddamned place of work.'

'Well, that sounds like a mild exaggeration,' observed Blackthorn. 'Surely they're not still interested in you; not now that old mate has his painting back. I mean, you've seen the news haven't you?'

'Hmm... Yeah. Quinn looking like he's swallowed a whole family of Cheshire cats. Loving himself silly with bloody champagne and press conferences, and everything all rosy and gorgeous in the garden. But that fucking detective has got a whiff of something and he won't leave it alone.' Tate glared accusingly at his dinner companion. 'They *did* come to the gallery again today, asking more bloody questions...'

'Tell 'em to fuck off. Painting's back... Case closed, surely to God.' Blackthorn sniffed dismissively and drained a last bit of red wine from his glass, then looked around for the waiter.

'Maybe *you* should tell them.' Tate said with peevish resentment.

Blackthorn's attention sprang back on Tate like a piston, with a dark, furious frown, as though searching for some invective to punish him, but then he relaxed. 'Well, anyway, I started without you, you fucking late, fuck.' He gestured to his plate of shells. 'The oysters are good, you should try some.'

Tate took up his menu and studied it, while Blackthorn snapped his fingers and waved the waiter over. 'Let's get a bottle of this Shiraz; it's bloody good... The Coonawarra,' he told the waiter pointing a finger at his empty glass, as if it held the specifications of the wine he wanted. '...And another glass for my friend here.'

'I never know what to order in these places – all the bloody pastas sound like origami or something to me, and the sauces all look the same. I don't even like tomato,' Tate complained.

'You should order the Faghottini,' Blackthorn suggested solicitously.

'You should shut the fuck up.' Tate glared at him desolately and gave a condescending shake of his head. 'You really are a cunt sometimes.'

The waiter, who had returned with the wine observed this exchange with mute passivity as he filled their glasses and then waited with pen poised for their order.

'I'll have the veal,' Blackthorn told him.

'What's the lasagna like?' Asked Tate.

The young waiter gave him the Italian gesture for delicious – lips pursed to the tips of his fingers and then opening his hand with an ironical flourish; his face remained impassive, eyes dead. Tate pushed the menu away from himself in exasperation. 'That'll do me, and a side salad, please.'

'So what did they want? What did they ask you?' Blackthorn slurped his last oyster and drank the juice from the shell. '... And what the fuck did you tell them?'

'Nothing, of course. No fucking comment. But it's starting to get a bit tiresome. You know what these pricks are like – just keep niggling away at you, trying to get you to slip up, and every time you refuse to answer, they reckon that makes you look guilty as hell.'

'Well you are fucking guilty.... The whole bloody thing was your idea, after all.' Blackthorn gave him a smarmy smile and slugged down a big gulp of Shiraz.

'Well that's a great fucking help, that is.' Tate projected his coldest death stare, and took a sip of wine and then twisted up his nose as if it were bad.

'But do they actually know anything or are they just dicking around?'

'How the fuck would I know? But why would they keep coming back if they didn't have something?' Tate frowned at his colleague over the top of the over-size wine glass. 'What if that little prick has been talking? I mean where has he been all this time? ... And then he suddenly turns up, and Quinn spouting off all over the place about how... *oh, someone could just put it in a locker at the railway station or something....*' Tate made a pretty good fist of imitating Quinn.

'That was my idea by the way. Soon as it looked like Jack and Penny were back, I got Travis to tell Quinn to go around there and talk to him. Not the whole story, just that maybe Jack might know something. But it would have put the wind right up him, having Quinn turn up on his doorstep like that. And it worked a treat... He did just as Quinn told him, the little fucking prick.

Blackthorn re-filled his glass without taking his eyes off Tate, appraising him. He was sounding pretty frazzled. 'Listen, you need to just settle down. There's no way that young punk is going to say anything to the police – no way he's gonna stick his head up, especially now after he's gotten rid of the painting.

'Think about it – there's nothing to connect him to the painting, except you, so the last thing he's going to do is put you in it – because that puts him in the shit too.

Tate gave him a long hard quizzical stare, and said: 'Except the cops still want to nail someone for the theft. All that bullshit with the Australian Cultural Terrorists... Was that Jack too, do you reckon? ...' Tate looked mildly confused for a moment then continued. 'Embarrassing the government, putting shit on the Police Minister... They want someone's head to roll, and right now it looks like it's my head they're after.' Tate was leaning forward over the table, his eyes looked alarmingly bulbous and, Blackthorn thought, full of fear. As the waiter approached with their meals, he sank back in his seat and they both remained silent until he left.

Blackthorn eyed him critically and gave a small grimace. 'No,' he said firmly. 'No... You're being melodramatic. They're just fishing. Some fucker – probably some poor fucken' painter you've screwed over in the past – has been shit-talking you to the cops, but they haven't got anything solid. If they did they'd already be arresting you.

'You just need to keep playing them with a straight bat, and keep your head down. Besides which, I've got a plan to take the heat off.' Blackthorn hacked at his veal and stuffed a forkful in his mouth. 'Take the heat off *us all...*' he added, chewing mechanically.

'What is it?'

Blackthorn pointed his steak knife at Tate, like he was lining it up between his eyes, and smiled humorlessly. 'Eat your lasagna and then I'll show you.'

When they finished eating and Blackthorn had ordered a second bottle of red – having consumed most of the first bottle by himself – he hoisted his brief case out from beside his chair and took out a folder.

'Have a look at this,' he said casting a leery glance up and down the restaurant to check for observers.

He made a space in front of him and carefully wiped the table with his napkin to get rid of any crumbs, or wine spillage, then slid a piece of paper out of the folder and spun it around so the drawing on it was right-side-up for Tate.

'What is this?' Tate squinted in the dim restaurant light. 'Wh... Who is this?' In front of him was a coloured drawing of a woman, standing full length, in profile. It was quite detailed, depicting her clothing and high heels, and her red hair. She was holding a large flat rectangular package under her arm – wrapped in brown paper and string – identical to the one he'd seen the police and Quinn recovering from the railway station locker on the TV news the night before.

He looked up at Blackthorn quizzically and the old academic smiled – to the extent that his craggy face was capable of arranging itself into something resembling a smile – and he raised one eyebrow and nodded. 'Yeah, don't worry it's a perfect bloody rendering of the package they got out of the locker. Did you see it on the news?'

Tate nodded vaguely, and went back to studying the picture. Something was gradually dawning on him. Blackthorn watched him, content to wait for it to sink in.

'Wait a minute, I recognise this woman.' He pointed at the picture and clicked his fingers, as if trying to jog his memory. 'It's that woman... The artist's girlfriend.' He looked up as if startled by his realisation. 'Mietta's.... The exhibition!'

'Bingo.' Blackthorn's face wore a satisfied smirk. 'Audrey Burke.' He nodded and kept on smiling.

Tate looked puzzled still.

'Her and that fucking Hardman prick. They're a perfect fit for it.

Christ, half the art scene back in Geelong already think they did it. Rumors all over the place.' He took a big satisfied slug of wine. 'No one's gonna doubt it – they've got cultural terrorists written all over them. It's *fucking* perfect,' he said with passionate emphasis. 'We get rid of these mother-fuckers and the heat's off us – off you – for good. It's brilliant... Look I even added in the lockers.' Blackthorn gave himself a self-satisfied chuckle.

'But how... What the...' Tate frowned unhappily.

'Don't you worry.' Blackthorn returned the picture to his file and winked. 'I've got a woman... Impeccable credentials. Respectable as fuck. She's going to identify Burke; say she saw her down at the station, hanging around the lockers with the package. Red-fucking-handed. She's going to the police with this, tomorrow.' Blackthorn's smile faded and he gave his colleague a stern look. 'They'll be fucked. And you'll be home free, so relax.'

He lifted his glass, as if proposing a toast. Tate did the same and their glasses clinked. But Tate's expression was far from celebratory. He still looked puzzled. Worried. This annoyed Blackthorn and his mood soured. 'Fuck man, just relax,' he said dismissively and drained his glass. 'I've got this sorted, but don't thank me *right* now.'

TWENTY-THREE

Friday, August 22nd, 1986

A naked man was painting and dancing in my studio and we all watched and wondered at his intentions, his meaning and the portentous nature of his presence in that sacred place. He was my teacher nevertheless. I had tried to free him, and yet I was forced to watch as he lost everything for foolish comfort.
Angry Buddha, 2001

'Fuck!' Daniel swore and speared a brush into a jar of turpentine. *Something wasn't right, but fuck it.* It would have to do. He crossed to the kitchen bench and flicked on the kettle, then grabbed his tobacco pouch and rolled a cigarette.

Later, sitting in the big raggedy old armchair sipping his tea and smoking, he realised, as usual, he was being too hard on himself. It was fine. What he'd perceived as a technical error, was so small and insignificant, no one would ever notice. He could barely notice it himself now, as he surveyed his latest landscape from a safe viewing distance. And as he rewarded his neuro-receptors with a cocktail of caffeine and nicotine, his creation softened before his eyes. It was another good one. Good, as in saleable. Agreeable for domestic consumption, hanging on the lounge room walls of middle Australia.

But he knew that eventually the *itch* would have to be scratched, and the itch was becoming more and more persistent; that niggling discomfort of spirit, telling him it wasn't good enough. The whole landscape thing wasn't good enough; because it had ceased to be a challenge and no longer satisfied his innate urge to push the artistic envelope.

That progressive impulse had informed his whole artistic career. Without progressive intent, he reckoned, the frontiers of art itself could not advance. Without it, there was just stagnation, and capitulation... And decoration. *Might as well get a dealer.*

But the landscapes were good, weren't they? Beautiful works of legitimate art. Some said they were like Fred Williams, but with better use of colour. And they sold. And right now, *that* was the name of the game.

But once the itch started, it was hard to shake the feeling that he was selling out. Hadn't he just last night, been joking with the cocktail barman, James, when he asked how he got inspiration for painting the landscapes: *A six-pack of beers,* he'd told him. *After drinking each one, I smash the empty can against my forehead.* (He'd done the joke with actions) *Then, I'm ready to pump out one more landscape.*

Daniel knew he should ease up on himself. They had a plan. Audrey had the business acumen and he knew she knew what she was doing. They were laying the foundation for a future career – in which there could be plenty of opportunity for experimentation and innovation – but right now it was about seeding the market, getting recognition and putting a body of work out into the world. And the landscapes were the right vehicle for the present moment.

People fucking loved them.

His thinking was interrupted by the sound of someone coming along the hallway; in fact, multiple footsteps. *Who could this be?* He wasn't expecting anyone, and his squash-court studio didn't exactly attract a passing trade. He got up and extinguished his rollie and turned down the volume on the radio, just as Mietta's partner Tom appeared at the doorway, wearing a concerned frown.

Tom virtually fell through the doorway and was followed by a man in a suit and then another. Tom looked at Daniel with a crestfallen expression and simply said, 'I'm sorry.'

The man standing beside him said: 'Is this him?'

Tom gave him a patently *fuck you* scowl and said nothing.

Three more men stepped over the threshold, one by one, and gathered in a semi-circle. There was five of them, all looking like insurance salesmen, or accountants, but with dour, grumpy faces. *Fuck! They were cops*, Daniel realised this even before the first of them glared at him and asked: 'Are you Daniel Hardman?'

He nodded dumbly, even as Tom stepped back through the doorway with his head bowed. He turned back and said 'Sorry Dan, I tried to get rid of them, but they insisted.'

Jesus, what the hell was this? Daniel's thoughts immediately jumped to someone – Audrey, or a family member perhaps – having died or been terribly injured, and police had come to break the bad news.

But why were there five of them? And they didn't look particularly friendly, or sympathetic. And not a police uniform amongst the lot of them.

The talking suit, who appeared to be in charge, told him his name: Detective Sergeant something, and asked him more questions, which didn't seem to make any sense. He answered them automatically without thinking. The suit showed him a piece of paper which he ignored, but would later find out, was a hastily drawn up warrant, which future advisers would say was one of the shoddiest legal documents they'd ever seen.

Why didn't they just tell him what had happened?

The Detective Sergeant – whose name turned out the be Doherty – shepherded him towards the table in the kitchen nook, and the others spread out around the squash court looking curiously at everything; which struck Daniel as being pretty rude under the circumstances.

In the kitchen, they sat down opposite each other, whilst the other men wafted around the studio like poorly-dressed ghosts.

The detective took a sheet of paper from a soft leather briefcase and laid it on the table between himself and Daniel. It was a picture of a woman who looked a lot like Audrey. She was standing side-on with a big parcel under her arm. It was hand-drawn, with coloured pencils.

'Do you recognise this woman?' Enquired the detective.

Daniel started to get a very bad feeling. He looked around at the other suits and saw one of them standing by the refrigerator. He removed a photograph, from the door and held it up at eye level for a moment, scrutinising it, then turned to his boss and nodded emphatically. Daniel knew it was a picture of Audrey, he'd stuck to the fridge months earlier.

Daniel looked again at the drawing in front of him and said: 'This looks a lot like my partner, Audrey Burke.' Even as he spoke he felt anger and affront rising up in him. Some fear too. 'Maybe you better just tell me what all this is about. Has something happened to Audrey?'

The talking suit said they were simply seeking his cooperation with their enquiries.

'Enquiries about what?' He raised his voice a bit...Involuntarily.

Doherty looked at one of his men and then back at Daniel. 'We're investigating the theft of the Weeping Woman from the National Gallery, by the Australian Cultural Terrorists.' The detective watched him closely for his reaction.

'What? ... What!' Daniel literally deflated as he let go an

enormous sigh, and a wave of relief washed over him. 'Is this some kind of joke? You have to be kidding. Fuck me, I thought someone had died or something.'

Doherty stared deadpan at the artist, for a long time, not giving anything away. But what was going on behind his detached face was anything but calm. *This wasn't right.* The artist had answered all of his questions without any hesitation or guile. Clearly he had nothing to hide. It hadn't even occurred to him why they were there – not until Doherty told him. He'd thought his girlfriend had been in an accident or something.

Shit! Not the reaction he was expecting at all. Something was very wrong. Right now, the suspect seemed genuinely relieved and bemused.

This particular lead had seemed more promising than anything they'd had before... A breakthrough. An eye witness at the railway station with a detailed description of a woman seen down by the lockers, on the very day – with a suspect-looking package.

But Hardman was genuinely oblivious. Could it be his girlfriend was involved – was actually one of the Cultural Terrorists – without him knowing? It seemed unlikely.

Maybe he was just a good actor. Doherty doubted this too, but the only course of action was to forge ahead. Put the screws on hard enough, he might still crack.

Mallory and Fink had retrieved some timber off-cuts from a big plastic bin in the corner of the studio, which they were holding up for Doherty's perusal. He gave them a nod and said to the artist. 'Our information is that you frame your paintings in a way that's almost identical to the way the returned Picasso was re-framed.' He had no way of knowing whether this was in any way true – but it sounded good. 'So if you don't mind we'll take some of these off-cuts with us, for forensic examination.'

'No problem, help yourselves.' Obliging tone – just a hint of sarcasm. No sign of angst, thought Doherty.

A couple of detectives had made their way upstairs to the mezzanine, where he and Audrey had their bedroom and office. They'd found Daniel's typewriter, and one of them was holding it up above the balustrade, almost as if he was getting ready to throw it over. Doherty nodded up at him.

'And we'll need to take a sample from your typewriter to compare to the ransom notes.'

'Of course,' said Daniel helpfully. Tone, a little condescending. *But again, no sign of panic.*

'And we'll be needing fingerprints from you and Miss Burke, for comparison.'

Daniel frowned at this, thinking it was now getting a bit invasive, and wondering about the legality of it. He'd be checking with his lawyer first; but he smiled and said. 'I'm sure that can be arranged – we have nothing to hide, and we're happy to help you clear all this up – the sooner the better.'

The relief at no one having died was starting to where off, as he watched the detectives helping themselves to stuff around his studio. He was starting to feel a little violated, and he was starting to wonder just why five detectives from the major crime squad were here in the first place. *What led them here? Where were they getting their information?*

He looked again at the drawing in front of him and it suddenly struck him as being really quite bizarre. Clearly this was nothing like a police identikit sketch. It just didn't look right – a full length drawing of Audrey standing in profile, with a big painting-sized parcel under her arm, the lockers in the background. They even seemed to have her shoes right. And it looked just like Audrey, except it wasn't a very flattering depiction of her. *Where the hell had the police gotten this drawing?*

He wanted to ask Doherty that exact question – not that he would've expected an answer – but at that moment, the phone in the kitchen started ringing.

He ignored it. But the detective sergeant looked expectantly at him and then at the ringing phone and raised his eyebrows. 'You can take that if you want to.'

I bet you'd like me to, he thought.

He picked up the phone, with a kind of belligerent devil-may-care attitude. *I really do have nothing to hide, so fuck you.*

Astonishingly the person on the phone was an ex-student from the art school in Geelong; one of those, he guessed, involved in the rumor mill. He was calling, he said, to congratulate him and Audrey on their audacity at sticking it up the art establishment by stealing and then returning the Picasso. He also said that he thought he and Audrey might be in a bit of trouble, and wanted to wish them luck.

Daniel felt like telling him the cops were there right now – all five of them – and wasn't that a funny coincidence. But he said nothing – just listened, then hung up. *Jesus!*

'That was short and sweet,' said Doherty. 'Anything interesting?'

'Only if someone down in Geelong having advanced knowledge of you being here – even while you're still here – is interesting. What do you reckon? Someone's pretty well informed aren't they?'

Doherty scowled at him like he'd committed some sort of faux pas, and Daniel saw his men exchange worried glances between themselves.

Doherty asked him who was on the phone, and what they'd said.

'I can't remember exactly; maybe you can play the tape back later – maybe even get your secretary to make a transcript.' He was being openly facetious now, and it was probably not a good idea, but the coincidental phone call had tipped him over the edge – from annoyed to seriously pissed off.

So when Doherty just kept scowling at him, he reeled off a few names; the guy on the phone and one or two others he knew also to be acolytes of the creep, Blackthorn.

'All these very well-informed people, been helping you with your investigation, have they?' His tone was thick with sarcasm, and he glared brashly at the head detective.

Doherty looked furious and worried all at once, and his minions had stopped whatever they were doing, as if frozen by some kind of spell; all looking at the artist and at their boss.

Daniel had returned his attention to the picture in front of him. Something about it kept drawing his eye, something beyond it being touted as evidence. He found himself picking it apart; analysing it with his artist's eye, almost as though he was critiquing it. The longer he examined it, the firmer became an intuitive bubble lurking just beyond his conscious cognition – something familiar from the past; something revelatory – but also murky and dire in some way.

Absorbed in his analysis, he was oblivious to the tension building in the room. Suddenly he had it... His intuition coalesced all at once into an epiphany of recognition. 'Blackthorn' he breathed.

'What?' Doherty screwed up his face.

Daniel looked up from the drawing with such piercing intensity, the detective recoiled slightly. Daniel demanded: 'Where did you *get* this drawing?'

Doherty clenched his jaw and returned the stare, mutely. But there was also bewilderment in his eyes, and the detective's mind raced as he reviewed the chain of events that had led to him acquiring that particular piece of evidence. He realised he didn't have an adequate answer to Hardman's question. It wasn't a police sketch – no such thing, it was a witness' description – but somehow, it had come in the form of a picture. No one on his team had questioned it, including himself. *Why not?* He winced inwardly... Because it was too good. A smoking gun gifted to him.

A wave of what could only be described as panic rippled from his gut up into his throat, and Doherty felt immobilised by the intense glare of the artist, as if *he* was now under interrogation. And he didn't like it – not one bit.

'I know who drew this!' The artist asserted abruptly, with his index finger stabbing into the centre of the drawing like a knife. 'Doug Blackthorn drew this!' His eyes took on an incendiary glow. 'I recognise his drawing style. He taught me, for Christ sakes! I'd recognise it anywhere.'

A sigh seemed to go through the posse of detectives distributed around the sprawling studio. Nothing audible, but the air seemed to press down, from the high vaulted ceiling.

Blackthorn? Doherty thought to himself, squinting at the indignant artist, still with his finger pressed accusingly to the picture. He knew that name. It was even on the office whiteboard somewhere – but just on the periphery – not a suspect. And as he racked his brain, he was sure he'd heard the name mentioned elsewhere too; by one or more of the callers to the anonymous hotline.

Blackthorn. Academic? Critic? Lecturer at the art school in Geelong – that was him. Geelong – where so many of the tip offs on the hotline seemed to have been coming from in the last week or so. Geelong...Wasn't that Hardman's home town?

Doherty had a sinking feeling that gelled into a conviction – that something really was all wrong – that Hardman and Burke were not legitimate suspects; just as his gut had told him when he'd first started questioning him.

His investigator's instinct was screaming that this was a stitch up.

He stomped on the idea and clenched his fists and his jaw. He had to save face at the very least, and at best, keep the pressure on this suspect, until both he and his partner could be excluded by hard evidence.

But all he could think was *dead end*. Another one!

And yet, this was different, and the suspect himself had hit the nail right on the head: *Where the hell had that drawing come from?* That question and many other related questions were top of his mind as he cast around and saw the expressions and body language of his men. He knew they were asking themselves the same question.

Had someone just tried to frame this artist and his girlfriend?

This Blackthorn character? What if Hardman was right about him having done the drawing? What possible motive would someone like that have – a respected academic and art critic – to take such a risk, giving false information to the police?

None of it made sense, and it was up to him to reassure his squad that the world hadn't just been turned completely on its head. Protocol first. Tick all the boxes. Forensic examination of the framing off-cuts, and typewriter, finger print both suspects. Solid evidence first. Only if all that draws a blank, would he have to face the awkward possibility that he had been deliberately misled.

He looked again at the drawing of the woman holding the very conspicuous package and he saw it in a completely different light now. *It had been too easy – that was obvious now.* He reached over and put a hand on the picture, wanting to slide it away and back into his file, but the artist's hand was still on it. Daniel pressed down with his fingers, pinning the piece of paper to the table. His eyes on the detective were indignant, demanding some kind of response or explanation.

Doherty just smiled and gently tugged the edge of the paper until Daniel eased his grip letting it slide away. The detective tucked it back into the file, and the file into his briefcase. He smiled banally and said, 'Did I tell you my wife's a painter?'

Daniel frowned and shook his head. He felt suddenly detached, like he was floating above the scene of his own interrogation.

'Wildflowers and natives mainly – still life, I suppose you'd say.' The detective was suddenly benign and social. 'I'm more of a figures in landscape man myself,' he said with a self-effacing laugh and looked around at some of the artworks scattered around the studio, as if seeing them for the first time.

'That drawing of my partner...' Daniel said deliberately, pointing a finger at the detective's briefcase and fixing him with a hard stare. 'Where did you get that?'

Doherty tipped his head sideways and gave a condescending smirk. 'I can't divulge anything like that, of course.'

'I'm telling you I know who drew that picture,' he said precisely. 'There isn't any doubt about it – Doug Blackthorn drew it, I'm one hundred percent sure of that.' He kept his eyes fixed on the detective, but Doherty dead-panned him in return. No reaction.

He became aware of some of the other detectives in the periphery, shifting their weight uncertainly. It was very quiet.

'Look,' said Doherty, 'the priority right now is to eliminate you and Miss Burke from the investigation; so the sooner we can get this material down to forensics and have you both in for fingerprints the better.'

Eliminate?... The detective's whole demeanor had changed. No longer belligerent and accusatory. *He knew... He knew they didn't do it.* Which meant he knew he'd been given false information and Daniel had just told him the source of that false information. It had to be Blackthorn. *That was a crime wasn't it?*

But Doherty seemed completely unfazed. *What the fuck was going on?*

Unperturbed, Doherty focused on rounding up his men and materials and making arrangements to interview Audrey and get them both in to be fingerprinted. He gave him a card – his business card with something written on the back of it – but Daniel wasn't paying attention. His head was spinning, thoughts tumbling over one another. *Had they just been framed for Melbourne's biggest ever art heist? By Douglas-fucking-Blackthorn?*

The detective seemed in a rush to draw the whole thing to a close. His men were funneling towards the door, no longer macho and aggressive; some of them even looking a bit shame-faced. Daniel shepherded them towards the door, in a confused state – half angry, half relieved – part of him not wanting them to leave until he got some sort of satisfaction or explanation.

Before he followed his men out, Doherty stopped and turned, coming quite close to him and said quietly; 'I wonder if there are people out there who might envy all this.' He waved an arm and looked up at the high squash court ceiling and National Trust skylights.

'You know this is a wild goose chase, don't you.' Daniel stated advisedly.

'Well, you're definitely the goose we were led to.' Doherty almost whispered it.

'Well if this leads to my arrest, you could be looking for a new job.' Daniel said just as quietly.

'You know it's all political now. The Police Minister wants heads on platters.'

'Well, bully for him.' Daniel said, fully po-faced now.

Doherty shrugged and turned to go.

'You know who you should be looking at, don't you?' He raised his voice a little and the detective paused. 'You should be looking at whoever misled you by giving you that false information. I told you who drew that drawing, didn't I? It was Blackthorn. Do you know who he is?'

Doherty looked at him with a cryptic and slightly troubled expression. Daniel went on. Just letting the words come, unbidden, like some fresh idea. 'Maybe you should look at Blackthorn, and whoever *he's* connected to. Maybe then you'd get somewhere. Maybe even find out who really did this.'

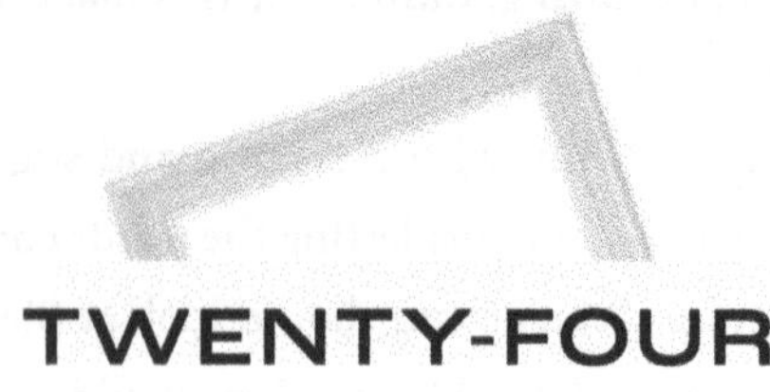

TWENTY-FOUR

Tuesday, August 25th, 1986

We've been taught to look outwards... convinced of the faulty nature of our own perceptions and opinions...
Angry Buddha, 2001

Doherty stabbed a pin into the offending drawing and impaled it to the cork-board, like it was the skin of some dread pest, pegged out as a warning to others.

'Well, where the fuck *did* it come from then?' He cast a leery eye around his team and scowled. 'Don't tell me ... please don't tell me, we're still no closer to finding out... Jesus!'

Mallory returned him a grimace. 'The desk sergeant at Russell Street took a statement from a woman who brought it in, but didn't get a phone number, and it looks like the name she gave might be fake – we can't find any record of her.'

'Are you kidding me? He didn't get a contact number or an address? That's bloody incompetent! Who was it? Who took the statement?'

Mallory gave him a long, glum look and said: 'Look Ted, you might want to ease up a bit. This bloke was on duty the day of the bombing, and he's only just back on deck; one of the few, I reckon. They've only just got the place operating at full stretch again, you know.'

Doherty sighed heavily and nodded, realising it had only been a few months. March this year. Horrific... Like something out of Beirut. A massive car bomb had pretty much destroyed the ground floor of police headquarters, killing a young police woman and injuring dozens. Terrorism right in the heart of Melbourne.

'Alright, fair enough. What did her statement say then?'

Mallory read from a piece of paper he had in front of him. 'Says she saw two women by the lockers at Spencer Street, *acting suspiciously.*' Mallory made air quotes with his index fingers. 'Says one of them was carrying a package wrapped in brown paper, and that made her think of the stolen Picasso, because she's heard *that art gallery guy...*' air quotes again '...on the TV saying the painting could be left in a locker at the railway station.' Mallory paused for a breath and gave his boss a doubtful look over the top of his reading glasses. 'Says she went right home and drew what she'd seen, so she wouldn't forget it.'

'Does that sound plausible? To Anyone?' Doherty scanned the faces of his men gathered around the small conference table, and was rewarded with an array of shrugs and pouty lips.

'Well, not after what Hardman told us. I mean he sounded pretty damn certain, didn't he?' Mallory looked around to gauge what the others thought. 'I dunno, d'you really think he could tell? D'you think he could recognise the drawing style?'

'Absolutely,' said Fink. 'I mean, it's technique, isn't it? Artists know about that kind of shit.'

'So have we heard from this Blackthorn character yet? I really want to get him in and stick this under his nose,' Doherty slapped the offending picture pinned to the board, 'with all the cameras rolling and see what sort of reaction we get.'

'We've left messages – three of them – he doesn't seem to be returning our calls.' said Fink.

'Maybe someone better get down to Geelong and interview him down there – put the wind up him.' He looked pointedly at Fink.

'Alright, I'm on it.'

'Take the picture with you. See if he shits.' Doherty pulled the whiteboard around to square it up to the men seated around the table. On it, he'd scribbled in a heavy line joining the names Blackthorn and Tate.

'Now just to recap... We already suspected a link here, but now we *know*... These two. Thick as thieves!'

'Do we?' Mallory looked puzzled.

'Yes – we do now. Absolutely.' He stared flatly at his second in charge. 'When I called Hardman, to tell him the fingerprints and the typewriter didn't match, and they were off the hook, I took the opportunity – you know while he was feeling well disposed toward us – to ask him if he knew Tate at all...'

All eyes were on their boss. Expectant.

'He said he did... Made some fairly uncomplimentary comments about him as an art dealer, not known for treating his artists particularly well, he said. And so then I asked him if he thought Tate and Blackthorn knew each other.'

'And...?'

'*Bloody oath they do*! His exact words. Said the two of them had turned up uninvited to one of his exhibitions and started causing trouble. He told me quite a bit more about Blackthorn. They've got history as it turns out. I'm preparing a file note about it, which you should all read. Anyway, turns out he's got motive in spades to try and put the finger on Hardman, *and* more particularly on his girlfriend, Audrey Burke.

'Interesting,' said Mallory.

'More than just interesting,' said Doherty. 'Hardman told me not only did this Blackthorn have a massive axe to grind with his girlfriend, but he reckoned Tate – being a big time art dealer – may well have cracked the shits with him too; for selling art direct to the public – because that's what he's been doing in their lovely little city studio and gallery. Selling art... Heaps of it, and no dealer. Cutting out the middle man.'

He paused and surveyed his crew. They were quiet, watching and waiting for him to continue. 'So I reckon there's a pretty good argument to make Tate and Blackthorn co-conspirators... Not just in fucking up our investigation, but maybe pinching the Picasso too. The real question now, is can we connect these two to our suspected insider at the NGV?'

'It's pretty damned likely, isn't it?' This from Thorpe, who'd been sitting quietly listening and ruminating. 'I mean we know it's all pretty incestuous, the Melbourne art world. Everybody knows everybody. Prominent Melbourne art dealer ... Almost certain to have contacts inside the National Gallery. And the same with Blackthorn, his main patch is Geelong but he's also been an art critic for a city newspaper... The gallery director Quinn, started off as an art critic too, didn't he?'

'Exactly. So they all move in the same circles,' said Doherty. 'They're bound to know each other. The question is, are they chummy enough to hatch some kind of clever little art heist conspiracy together?'

'But hang on... Surely not Quinn?' Asked Mallory with a hint of derision. 'He's got too much to lose to get involved in something like this, doesn't he?'

'Look, we know Tate and Blackthorn are linked, and we've got plenty of rumors – several different sources – about a Melbourne art dealer involved in moving forged artworks. We like Tate for that... I mean plenty of fingers have been pointed and having interviewed him a couple of times, I reckon he's as shifty as hell.

Blackthorn is a nasty piece of work by all accounts, and it looks like he's bloody perjured himself silly with this pretty little picture of Audrey Burke.' Doherty paused again to gauge the reaction of his team.

'So... Aspiring bloody art-world gangsters... All they need is someone on the inside... So, maybe not Quinn, but someone close to him, someone with access; selects a masterpiece off the walls of the NGV – lends it to Tate, just long enough to get a copy made, then Blackthorn... What's his involvement?' Doherty scratched his head. '...Some sort of enforcer, or maybe he's the salesman. Has some black market contacts or some such... Who knows?'

'Think about it, maybe it's not the first time they've done it, and all that's needed, apparently, is a nice little gallery card in place of the borrowed painting – put there by the ultimate insider, saying *gone for cleaning* or *gone to Canberra*, or something – then nobody's any the wiser.' Doherty rubbed his cheek, consulted his file open in front of him, then scanned the faces of his team. 'But who? Who's our insider? And where the hell *is* that little card? The card everyone saw on the wall on the Sunday – letting patrons and security know not to worry – the Picasso had gone to the ACT – to the sister gallery in Canberra?

'Probably *the* most vital bit of evidence in the whole case. But we don't have it, do we? Never sighted it, because it was gone before any police arrived at the gallery. We've only ever heard about it...

'What happened to that frigging registrar's card? That's the question I want to ask Quinn!'

There was a stunned silence amongst the other detectives for a moment or two before Fink piped up and said: 'But don't we think the Australian Cultural Terrorists put the card there? A.C.T. was their initials, wasn't it?'

'Was it?...Did they? Maybe. But if so, what happened to it; in between the alarm being raised on Monday morning, and the first police arriving hours later? Bloody vanished, didn't it?

'What I'm saying is, if the Australian Cultural Terrorists left it there for us to find, then who took it?' Doherty scanned the faces of his team-members. 'Maybe it was never the Australian Cultural Terrorists. Maybe there *are* no goddamned Cultural Terrorists... I mean we haven't been able to find hide or hair of them, have we?

'Maybe a *real* conservator's card was put up there, by someone wanting to cover the fact that the painting was off the wall... just to reassure everyone the Picasso was visiting the National Gallery in Canberra... Whilst these clever dicks were getting a copy made.'

A wave of restlessness went through Doherty's men. They were all thinking the same thing, but it took a moment before Mallory took it upon himself to voice it: 'Then who the hell's been sending ransom notes to the fucking newspapers all this time?'

A heavy silence fell over the room and Doherty screwed up his mouth as if the question had left a bad taste there. He looked from Mallory to each of his squad members, one by one. Finally he said: 'Maybe it was one of them one of the conspirators. Maybe something went wrong, and they needed to cover their tracks...'

'It's a pretty fucking big red herring to throw out there,' asserted Fink gently, 'The Australian Cultural Terrorists, for Christ's sake.'

'Yeah it is...' Doherty expression wavered between thoughtful and annoyed. 'Or maybe there was trouble in paradise – maybe a falling out – and one of them was trying to mess with the other members of their little gang...'

A wave of discontented grumbles went around the room.

'Anyway, three weeks and we've gotten nowhere: Blind alleys. Media manipulation by these so-called cultural terrorists... Dead ends all over the place. And all the while we've all been thinking the same thing, more or less... That it smells like some kind of inside job... That is, if it wasn't for the cultural terrorists and their bloody ransom notes.

'Now this bullshit with Blackthorn – some well-connected art academic – trying to frame a young artist who it turns out had nothing to do with it. What's that about? Why would he do that, if he's not trying to take the heat off of himself and his mates?

'I say it's time to forget about chasing these bloody phantom terrorists and focus our attentions closer to home. Start shaking the tree and see what drops. And I'm gonna start with the gallery director – see how he reacts to a few awkward questions, in particular about what happened to the conservator's card that was stuck to the wall.

'You might want to ask about his assistant...His intern, assistant curator, or something...' Thorpe was flipping back through his notebook. 'Hang on, hang on... There was something about that fella, I've got it down here somewhere. There!' Thorpe tapped his forefinger on the page he'd found. 'Travis McRae. He's...he's Quinn's *godson*.' The detective looked up and crinkled his nose in puzzlement.

'He's what!?'

'His *godson*, apparently.' Thorpe gave a little shake of his head and held up his notepad, as if to show them.

'Jesus!' Breathed Doherty. He reckoned all of them were thinking the same thing. *Why hadn't this little tidbit of information been factored into the equation before this?* 'Right, Fink, you and Mallory get down to Geelong and corner that friggin' art lecturer and put him under the grill. I want to see him sweating bullets about this drawing. Maybe we need to get a warrant – go through his whole fucken bureau – get forensics to match up his drawing style with this bloody picture...'

He slapped the picture on the corkboard again. Mallory gave

him a look, which seemed to say, *you might be getting a bit ahead of yourself there; about the warrant, boss.*

Then Doherty pointed at Thorpe. 'You and I, back out to the National Gallery...Interview Quinn again and get hold of this McRae character. Find out what *he* was up to on the night in question. Christ! Have we even interviewed this guy before?'

This last question was taken to be rhetorical, or too awkward to answer. Besides which, a consensus seemed to have been reached, that the meeting was over, and it was time to get moving; incidentally with a renewed sense of purpose, because something had shifted, and the investigation was, quite possibly nearing some kind of resolution.

As Mallory followed the rest of them out past Doherty he paused as if he had something he wanted to say to his boss, but just shook he head and said: 'Fuck me'.

'Yeah,' agreed Doherty, 'because we never really took it seriously until now, did we, the idea of an inside job? You heard what Hardman said to me as we left his studio?'

Mallory inclined his head in a way that bade him continue.

'He said we should be looking at Blackthorn and anyone connected to him. Said maybe then we'd get to the bottom of all this...'

Mallory shrugged and flicked an eyebrow.

'Thing is, I reckon he could be right.'

*

Penny put her coffee on the table and handed Jack his, before she plonked herself down bedside him on the couch and tucked her legs under her bum. She took a sip and snuggled into him, trying to get some of his attention away from the television. The news was on. He put a finger to his lips and pointed his other hand at the flickering box.

'Look, they said the artist whose studio was raided has been cleared.'

'A spokesperson for the major crime squad said police were no closer to identifying the Australian Cultural Terrorists, but the suspects whose studio was raided by police last Friday, have been eliminated,' said the TV announcer. *'A police spokesman said two people interviewed at the time of the raid had been ruled out as suspects and property taken for forensic examination would be returned to them.'*

The announcer went on to say police were appealing to the public for more help to identify the group believed responsible for the theft of a 1.6 million dollar Picasso painting from the National Gallery.

'Jesus, that's a relief.' Jack let out a short sigh and blew a stream of air over his hot mug of coffee.

He and Penny had been following the news all weekend, ever since it was reported on Friday night that a city studio had been raided. The news reports didn't say anything about who the suspects were, or whether or not anyone had been arrested, but the way it was reported in the media it sounded like the police thought they had finally caught the culprits; the Australian Cultural Terrorists.

Jack had been quite distressed. It took him completely by surprise how badly the news report affected him – a tsunami of guilt and remorse, together with a confusion of emotions hard to contain or even understand. Penny had tried to console him, but he could tell she was thinking the same thing. How could they arrest anyone for being the Australian Cultural Terrorists, when they were nothing but a figment of Jack's imagination?

It had been different when he was away in the country working on the painting. He'd felt like he was insulated from the whole thing. It had seemed like some kind of farce, being acted out far way; with Maynards' Keystone cops rushing around looking for his phantom terrorists. Meanwhile he'd been busy with his project. Working in his studio, away from the real world, all he really thought about was turning the tables on Tate and his cronies, and getting himself out of the shit. He hadn't thought that much about anyone else possibly getting *caught in the crossfire.*

Back in the city with the painting returned, an unexpected anxiety had kicked in. Every time the media mentioned the Australian Cultural Terrorists – which seemed to be every day, even after the painting was back in the gallery – it just got weirder and weirder. He started to realise he'd created a monster, which had taken on a life of its own.

He thought back to that hungover Sunday in the gallery when the idea had come to him - out of the blue, really. But with hindsight he questioned his use of the word *terrorists*. Terrorists were serious shit, and that was probably why the cops and Maynard, not to mention the media, all had their undies so tightly in a bunch. Maynard was on the warpath still – even after the painting had been given back. He'd seen him on the television news baying for blood. Clearly he wasn't going to be satisfied until someone was held to account.

And had he gone just a bit too far with all the ransom notes? On reflection, he probably had been having a little bit too much fun, and Penny agreed with him on that point, retrospectively, at least. But fun it had been, wreaking revenge down the years on his toxic high school art teacher, with little or no chance that Maynard would suspect or even remember him.

It had seemed like the perfect crime, and once the painting was safely returned that should have been the end of it. Until the police started homing in on their so-called *prime suspects*. How could Jack stand by and let someone else – some innocent artists – take the wrap for being the Cultural Terrorists and stealing the Picasso?

He'd fretted about it all weekend and in the end he got so agitated that anxiety gave way to anger. Anger at the naivety of everyone falling for his silly ruse in the first place; anger at Tate for exploiting him and backing him into a corner; anger at the entitled and pompous gallery director and most of all, anger at Maynard for provoking him all those years ago.

At some point during the agonising weekend, he'd come to the conclusion that he would go to the police himself, before he would let someone innocent be arrested and possibly charged. He would put the finger on Tate – he had the video evidence to prove his involvement – and he would confess to his own part in it. Maybe, Penny had suggested, he'd be able to do some sort of deal with the police... Offer them Tate and agree to help them figure out who else might have been involved, in exchange for a lighter sentence.

The word *sentence*, when it was said out loud, really brought home how serious the whole thing was getting, and that had sent him into a further spiral.

Maybe he'd been naïve thinking the whole thing would blow over once the painting was back. That got him thinking about the copy of the painting he still had, secreted in the studio back at the farm. Tate had dragged him into this mess in the first place, but part of Jack and Penny's solution had been to play a longer game... To go ahead and secretly make a copy of the Picasso. The longer game was, after all, the key part of their plan. They would just have to tough it out, through whatever twists and turns might still be to come.

Hence his relief – when he woke up hungover and moribund on

the Monday morning – to hear the suspects had been cleared, and the police were no closer to finding their culprits.

He'd given Penny a big hug, and said: 'Surely the whole thing is going to blow over now... I mean, they've got the painting back and they're chasing bloody phantoms... Just give it a rest, for fuck's sake.'

'Did you hear what they said about the finger prints?' Penny asked quietly, swirling around the dregs of her coffee.

'Hmm?'

'They said the fingerprints of the suspects didn't match the fingerprints on the paper packaging. ... Did you hear that?'

'Not really. So what?'

'I didn't think they could get fingerprints off paper. Those fingerprints they're trying to match... they're probably *our* fingerprints.'

'Shit!'

'Yeah...'

'But our fingerprints aren't on record, and there's nothing to lead them here...If there was...' He trailed off thinking, the police would have already come here. It was a big part of the reason he'd had such a shit weekend – a lot of the anxiety was him waiting for that fateful knock on the door.

Penny said: 'I heard one report said an eye-witness had given police a description of someone seen with a package down at Spencer Street, and that's what led them to raid that city studio...'

Jack knew what Penny was thinking: If some witness had wrongly identified the artist whose studio was raided, did that mean someone had actually seen Penny down there, with the package? How had the witness got it so wrong? What if another witness rightly identified *Penny*?

Penny knew there'd been plenty of people down at the railway station when she'd put the painting in the locker. Plenty of people who could have seen her, if they'd been paying attention. Penny gave Jack a little worried grimace and smiled weakly.

'Don't worry babe.' He rubbed her knee. 'We'd have heard something already. I reckon we're in the clear.' Jack wanted to believe it, but part of him was still very anxious.

The bloody fingerprints! Why hadn't they worn gloves... Jesus!

There was nothing for it but to hang tough and just try to wait it out. With the painting back, no further suspects, and the cultural terrorists being non-existent as they were, surely the investigation would run out of puff soon. Maybe Maynard would blow a gasket and pop his clogs. They could only hope....

*

In the end Daniel and Audrey decided to escape down to the coast. To decompress. Their friends Will and Lidia had invited them over for a meal, and the dinner had predictably turned into an intense de-brief, in which Daniel and Audrey re-told the story from every angle – themselves trying to make sense of it, even as they related the storm of events which had left them feeling shell-shocked and traumatised. Their weekend had seemed nightmarish and unnaturally elongated, from the raid on Friday until finally getting the call from Doherty late on Sunday, telling them they'd been cleared because their fingerprints didn't match and neither did the typeface of their typewriter.

Only then had Daniel exploded in rage. It had been building in him all through the weekend – a weekend tense and frantic with lawyer consultations and further interactions with the police – who'd quickly been frustrated by the lawyers' instructions not to cooperate or answer further questions. In some ways Sunday was the worst of it, when the phones went silent, as the lawyers and the enforcers enjoyed their Sabbath; leaving Daniel and Audrey to marinate in the misery of their seemingly shattered lives, in which nothing would be resolved until opening of business on Monday, or some ineffable eternity thereafter.

The telecommunications silence of Sunday was broken only by two bizarre calls from Geelong – just like the one that had come in the midst of the raid – both came from people Daniel would loosely describe as professional acquaintances, linked or suspected of being linked to Blackthorn.

His reaction to the callers was a forerunner to the blind rage he'd manifested when Doherty told him they were off the hook. He didn't know which was worse; the bloody-minded stupidity of the police, allowing themselves to be misled so blatantly, or the miserable, small-minded jealousy and gossip circulating in the parochial small town of his birth.

On the one hand, being accused of a major crime and subjected to the humiliation and shame of being questioned relentlessly, finger printed, forensically examined – all for nothing – all because a psychopath with an axe to grind had decided to try to get at them. It was infuriating. Somehow more infuriating because it had fizzled out so quickly. The futility of putting them through all of it, for no good reason was galling.

On the other hand, he knew how toxic the art world rumor-mill could be, and it was obviously already grinding away relentlessly in Geelong. He knew how quickly it could spread to the Melbourne art scene. It probably already had.

Implicated in a crime or the subject of malicious gossip; he and Audrey both knew how damaging that could be to an artistic career. The art world was not a nice place – he'd learned that long ago. And much of their obsessive talk throughout their Sunday of discontent had been around the damage possibly already done to his career – and just at the very moment it was taking off.

Whatever the outcome – Daniel told his old friends, while the dinner was cooking – there was no question at all who was behind it. Blackthorn, together with his bevy of disciples.

He could scarcely believe that not one or two, but three of them had called him – they just couldn't resist – all during the actual investigation, to either tell him how clever he and Audrey were for being the Cultural Terrorists, or to warn them that they might be in trouble, and offer fake camaraderie.

'How can you be sure it was Blackthorn?' Will flipped the tops off two more pale ales he'd gained from the fridge and slid one over to Daniel as he sat back down.

'Of course it was bloody Blackthorn!' he retorted. Audrey saw that some of the belligerence and anger erupting from Daniel intermittently over the weekend was bubbling to the surface again, under the influence of Will's supply of pale ale. 'All three calls came from known bloody Blackthorn associates'

'And the picture of Audrey...' Daniel went on to explain in detail yet again how the police had put it in front of him, and he'd thought: *What the fuck ... that's not a police sketch*. Audrey had started to notice, that the story was becoming more colourful and embellished with added detail, with each telling.

'They were all pretty smug, y'know – thinking we've got this guy dead to rights – one of them even got a picture of Audrey off the fridge and he's nodding to the chief detective, y'know, saying; *yep, that's her.*'

Daniel took a quick sip of beer. He enjoyed telling this part of the story. 'Meanwhile I'm just looking at the picture, thinking this doesn't look like any police identikit sketch I've ever seen... It was an artist's drawing, done with colour pencils...' He licked his lips and took another swig from his beer. 'Then all of a sudden I recognise the drawing style, I realise it's a Blackthorn drawing, I mean, y'know he taught me drawing, so of course I'd spot his style... What a fucking idiot.'

He had Will and Lidia's full attention. Audrey on the other hand was feeling a kind of discontented ennui. She'd heard this part of the story told several times already and she was really quite miffed that she herself was yet to see the offending drawing of herself.

'I'm like – I know who drew this! Doug Blackthorn drew this!' Daniel told of the resounding silence and all the detectives looking at each other, like someone had farted. 'I swear to God I'm surprised they didn't all shit themselves. You could've heard a pin drop; them all realising that they'd been had ... And I've *named* their bloody informant!'

Daniel reached for a cigarette, and looked questioningly at Lidia. Smoking was sometimes allowed inside; sometimes not. She smiled and nodded towards the open fire. 'Let's sit over here. The fire will draw the smoke,' she said, and then went on: 'Well, that's a crime – giving false information to police. What did the police say?'

'Nothing. Doherty – that's the head detective – he just started talking in circles... Small talk y'know, and then they wrapped it all up real fast. Couldn't get out of the place quick enough. Still wanted to fingerprint us mind you, and they still took the typewriter to test it.'

They settled themselves into the couch and the comfy chairs around the fire. The house was quiet and cozy, the fire glowing and drawing nicely. Will and Lidia's two young children were already away in their beds. Will asked, 'Will the cops go after him? I mean, Lidia's right, giving false information is a crime.... Perverting the course of justice, isn't?'

'Who knows?' Audrey said as she leaned forward for her wine, and then nestled back into the couch and took a thoughtful sip. 'I don't think the cops know what's going on. Been chasing their tails for weeks looking for cultural terrorists; then they get this *too-good-to-be-bloody-true* tip off that it's Burke and Hardman... And it blows up in their faces. They must be feeling pretty stupid right now... I mean imagine getting sucked in like that? And five detectives, no less? From the major crime squad – for fuck's sake? They're probably too embarrassed, to pursue it. I would be.' She smiled ironically and reached for Daniel's cigarette and took a drag.

Daniel frowned with mild offence, either for Audrey stealing his cigarette, or perhaps for suggesting Blackthorn not be held to account. 'Well, whether the cops go after him or not, we bloody will! He's not getting away with this. I'm gonna fuck him up.'

'What can you do though?' Will asked reasonably.

'I don't know... legally... Illegally. One way or the other, I want his fucken head on a pike. You don't get away with shit like this. We can't let someone like Blackthorn keep getting away with this stuff. Eventually someone has to take him down.'

Audrey saw Lidia give Will a sideways look and she was pretty sure she knew what she was thinking. Audrey herself was getting more and more concerned that Daniel's talk was turning to revenge, ever since they'd been cleared. All the way down to the coast in the car, he'd been going on obsessively about going after Blackthorn, and then the war metaphors had started to creep in, and that's when she knew he was really on a roll. *We might have to go to guns*, was the ominous metaphor with which he'd concluded, pretty much as they pulled into Will and Lidia's driveway.

'But Dan, maybe – as you've been completely exonerated, and pretty quickly – don't you think it might be wiser to let it go? I mean this Blackthorn is a nasty piece of work. It could be dangerous to go after him... And how would you even do that?' Will's tone was sensible and level – conciliatory rather than argumentative. As close friends, he and Lidia already knew the story about Audrey exposing Blackthorn as a predator, so the serious and frightening undertones of all of this was not lost on him.

'No, fuck that – he's gone too far this time.' Daniel said evenly. Calm, but with a steely tone and a cold hard stare. 'This could ruin my career. It doesn't take much in this fucking industry; and Blackthorn; he's an apex predator, or he thinks he is, and it really is the fucking law of the jungle... Kill or be killed.' Daniel drained his beer and gave a humorless grin.

'Jesus,' said Lidia, somewhat indignantly. 'Can we have a little less of the macho, fight to the death talk? I mean, really, this man is a rapist – the authorities at the university know about this now, don't they? They need to be encouraged to act on it... And now he's given false information to the police in a major crime. Surely this will be the end of him, without you challenging him to muskets at dawn.'

Audrey nodded her agreement and Daniel gave Lidia a peevish look like a child admonished. Lidia was a serious intellect and an experienced activist. Someone whose advice Daniel knew should be heeded. She was a force to be reckoned with.

'And besides Dan,' said Will lightly, 'That might not be how this goes down – I mean couldn't it just as easily be good for your career? You know what they say, any publicity is good publicity. You've been completely exonerated after all... In time, couldn't that be good for business?... *Talented up and coming artists framed by the real culprits for stealing Picasso.*' Will put on what he imagined to be a marketing voice and suggested a quote: '*The shadowy forces of the art world tried to shut him down – but good art prevails!*'

They all laughed at Will's nasally marketer's voice and there was a communal mumbling of support for Will's theory – that being framed and then cleared of a famous art heist might not necessary be bad for an artist's career, in the long term. All except Daniel – he was unconvinced. He scowled ironically at Will and screwed up his nose. 'Nah, I don't think you get just how bloody evil these mother-fuckers can be.'

Daniel thought about his long acquaintance with Blackthorn, ever since he was a student in the art school. And he thought about his gradual realisation of the alarming level of psychopathy of the man, and the terrible risk someone like that posed to young and vulnerable art students. And he thought yet again about the culpability and negligence of the powers-that-be in art education institutions who allow someone like that to remain in place. *It was fucked up.*

And he thought how he had encouraged Audrey to do what she had done. Try to expose Blackthorn for his crimes. It was the right thing to do, they had agreed at the time. Someone had to put a stop to the fucking prick. But he was still there – still the head of the art school – such was the inertia and cronyism in the establishment, that it would turn a blind eye to almost anything.

And now this.

He struggled in his own mind, thinking of a metaphor – them trying to defuse a bomb, to protect the wider community – and it now seemed it had blown up in their faces.

'You don't get how fucked the art world is, Will. It's like he's untouchable. He just keeps getting away with it – because everyone's afraid of him – even the useless bloody administrators of the art school, the chancellor or whatever idiot hired him. The same bloody idiots that are too scared to sack him.

'And now that he's got away with it, he reckons he can go after us... Because let's face it, he would have the biggest fucking grudge in all of Christendom against Audrey.'

Will took a swig of his stubby and smiled sympathetically and gave a little snort of a chuckle at his friend's colourful turn of phrase. Daniel continued.

'And you didn't see him and that fuckhead Tate together at our last Private View. Bloody nerve of the pricks to turn up there....' He looked from Will and Lidia to Audrey for support.

'Yeah. No shame. And the two of them together – that's a bloody sinister pair.' Audrey looked at Daniel and raised one brow.

They had talked about it quite a bit since that night – the worrying appearance of Blackthorn and Tate together. But now it seemed way more menacing. After all, as Daniel had pointed out, Logan Tate was the owner Helicon Galleries, making him one of the most influential art dealers in Melbourne. One of the many who had turned Daniel down, and so, one of the gate-keepers of the art selling business at whom he'd thumbed his nose, when they decided to try selling art direct to the public. And it had worked – it had worked almost too well – once Audrey had found them the perfect venue from which to do it.

'Someone like Tate wouldn't like what we've been doing up at Mietta's, wouldn't like it one little bit. Selling direct to the public, cutting bloody parasites like him out of the deal. I reckon he'd be pretty much having kittens of absolute jealous rage – seeing art going out the door without him getting his pound of flesh. Poor baby.' Daniel paused to light up another cigarette and Audrey took over.

'So put those two together, you've got the friggin' Zig and Zag of toxic retribution.'

'Yeah...' Daniel puffed his ciggie to life and flicked the match into the fire. 'Blackthorn wanting *your* guts for garters and Tate probably wants to fit me up with cement boots to set an example to any other enterprising young artists who might try to cut out the fucking money changers in the future.'

'But how's it going to affect your career?' Will demanded. 'I mean you've been selling shitloads of art, and there's nothing they can do about that, is there? You've hit on the perfect formula – private exhibitions at a fabulous city venue. Mietta loves having you guys there... It all works. Someone like this Tate freak is just gonna have to suck it up.'

Daniel shrugged. 'Well, that's working for now, but you might be surprised. Ultimately these people have a lot of influence – lots of creepy little fingers in lots of pies.' He took a drag and directed a stream of smoke towards the fireplace. 'The art world is a closed shop. Very incestuous and very cliquey. You've got to suck up to the right people otherwise they close ranks and freeze you out. If you don't play their game, you can very easily find yourself black listed. And then you're fucked.'

'Is it really that bad? Surely there must be some reasonable people in the business. Some reputable dealers?' Lidia suggested.

'Maybe. Who knows? But from what I've seen most of them behave like they've all part of some kind of brutal cartel, with the head honcho – whoever the hell that might be – feared and reviled by the lesser rats scurrying around below. And basically they all agree, the artists themselves – especially those trying to start a career – are the very bottom of the heap.' Daniel took a last drag and flicked his butt contemptuously into the fire. 'And half of them are bloody criminals anyway, I reckon. Wouldn't be the least bit surprised if these two were involved in stealing the Picasso.'

'What? Blackthorn and this dealer?' Will sounded a little incredulous.

'Why not?' Daniel switched a glance from Will to Audrey and back again. 'We reckon there might have been an ulterior motive for them trying to set us up, not just revenge. Maybe they were trying to cover their tracks, trying to deflect attention – maybe get the heat off themselves.'

'Really? What makes you think that?'

He and Audrey exchanged another somewhat conspiratorial look. 'A lot of people have been saying all along it seemed like an inside job. Something a bit dodgy about that gallery director, Quinn...Every time he's been interviewed... You know.'

'The bloke with the bow ties?'

'Yeah, but here's the thing... You know Travis – the guy we ran into when we surfed the Rock? He's got himself a job as an intern or something at the NGV, with Quinn. Someone told me he's related to Quinn in some way – a nephew or something – which makes sense because he's such a loose unit, I don't think he'd get any sort of job there otherwise.'

'Go on...'

'Well, remember Travis was the one told us about the fake Fred Williams being used to pay off a poker debt? And he would only know that because he's got something going on with Tate. I think they're in some sort of relationship, or something.'

'So, is Travis gay?'

'I don't know. He's such a loose unit I reckon he'd fuck anyone if it got him some sort of advantage. Maybe he's bi... That's not the point. Point is, suddenly Travis has access to all these priceless artworks at the NGV and maybe he and Tate decided to borrow the Picasso...'

Everyone's eyes were fixed on Daniel. Will put his wine glass down and exhaled: 'Whaoo, really?'

'You know, Travis takes the painting off the wall, says it's gone for cleaning or something... Then they get some clever dick forger – maybe the same one Tate's got faking the Fred Williams – to make a copy. Put the original back on the wall and no one's any the wiser, and off they go... Sell the copy on the black market. Maybe that's where Blackthorn comes in. He'd be their fence, I reckon. Probably got dodgy contacts all over the place...Overseas, black market, you know.'

Will gave him a stern and puzzled frown, which said... *You must be joking*. Lidia stifled a scoff.

Daniel shrugged condescendingly and stuck out his lower lip. 'Well, stranger things have happened... If they'd been copying Fred Willams paintings, maybe they decided to do the same with the Picasso – but something went wrong and de-railed their little plan – and suddenly they all had to scramble to cover their tracks, including trying to frame us...'

'But when you say something went wrong, don't you mean the Australian Cultural Terrorists went wrong?' Will's tone had a hint of irony. 'I mean they stole the painting didn't they? They're the ones been sending ransom notes anyway...'

'Hmm... did they really though?' Daniel asked sarcastically. 'I think you'll find Will, the Australian Cultural bloody Terrorists are a hoax, never to be heard from again, I'll wager, because I reckon they never existed in the first place.'

TWENTY-FIVE

Monday, August 31st, 1986

You can wake up any time.
Angry Buddha, 2001

Ted Doherty poured a mug of coffee and put it next to his wife's plate, just as she was cracking open her boiled egg.

'Thank you darling.... Perfect!' she said with genuine appreciation as she spooned a piece of soft-boiled egg onto a finger of toast.

He poured a mug of coffee for himself and sat down next to her. He was the master of the perfect soft-boiled egg, the one area of culinary practice in which Nancy deferred to him. The *eggspert*, she sometimes called him.

'So, you're really starting to think it *was* an inside job after all?'

Ted had been antsy all weekend, driving his poor wife to distraction, using her as a sounding board for his latest theories about the investigation. A whole week had passed without any progress other than eliminating the two young suspects that had been served up to them. Fink had drawn a blank when he went to Geelong to try to confront the art academic, Blackthorn, about the drawing of the female suspect. He'd refused to even see him.

Ted had finally got him on the phone once, and he was

completely belligerent and evasive; in the end, telling him to contact his lawyer, which had riled Doherty so much he was sorely tempted to have him arrested and get him in for questioning. But as Mallory had pointed out to him – unnecessarily – they had nothing on him other than the artist, Hardman's opinion that the sketch was Blackthorn's work.

His theory about an inside job was getting little traction, mainly because of the primacy in the Picasso investigation of the Cultural Terrorists and their stupid bloody ransom notes. The investigation was about to enter its second month and it seemed, to Doherty, it would never end.

Ted took a considered sip from his mug and smiled wanly at his wife. 'I just can't shake it. I mean I know it seems implausible on so many levels, but my intuition just keeps on screaming... *Inside job*.'

'And the Cultural Terrorists...?' Nancy mopped up some egg yolk with her last finger of toast, and took a bite.

'I'm so sick of hearing about the damned Cultural Terrorists. I mean, where are they? What evidence do we have of them, other than a series of stupid ransom notes, each of which sounds like a bloody joke?' He put his mug down. 'I think I'm about done with the Cultural Terrorists.'

'So... Take them out of the picture, it changes everything, no...?' Nancy licked her fingers and gave him a little smug smile. 'Without them, suddenly an inside job looks much more likely.'

'Exactly! We know Tate and this Blackthorn character are both dodgy and clearly as thick as thieves. If we can make a connection between them and someone at the National Gallery...' He paused and looked intently at his wife.

'You always say you should trust your gut more. And you've been saying all along, you thought something was fishy at the NGV.'

'Yeah... It's gonna be complicated though, controversial. Some noses could get properly out of joint.'

Nancy raised her brows ever so slightly. 'When did that ever stop you?'

'You're right.' He gave his wife an intently determined look, staring over the top of his glasses. 'I reckon it might just be time to start shaking some branches a little higher up the tree.'

'Trust your gut sweetheart. You know it's the right thing to do. And fuck the politics *and* the art world elites, if they don't like it; not your problem.'

Nancy hardly ever swore. Only when she felt passionately about something. But she was right. Fuck them all. He never wanted this bloody case in the first place.

*

Audrey clattered the plates into a stack and dropped them into the bottom of the cupboard with a crash that sounded like a firecracker going off. She was angry and hurt, and she was worried. The tension in their new abode had been ramping up exponentially in recent days. There must've been some Greek in her – smashing crockery seemed like a good way to let off steam and show her displeasure.

But the noise only irritated Dan even more. He paced back a forth in front of the dining table like a caged animal; a rollie in one hand and a beer in the other. 'Fucking academics!' He fumed. 'What do they say about teachers? And a fucking teacher who also happens to be a psychopath... I mean who hires these people? And that fucking evil child-molesting shit thinks he can try and destroy my goddammed career...? I'll have his fucking guts for garters!' He siphoned the last of the can and crushed it in his hand before flinging it across the kitchen and sinking it into the open bin, a three-pointer.

Audrey jumped at the sound of it hitting the other empties and glared at him across the room, a cup and a tea towel in her clenched hand. His belligerent manner and petulant stare pushed her over the edge and she flung the cup straight down on the tiled floor. The exploding crockery emphasised her exasperated expletive. 'For *fucks* sake!' She stamped a foot and then kicked a few of the cup fragments for good measure. 'Just stop! You've got to let it go, Christ! You can't let him get to you like this.'

Daniel stopped his pacing, shocked by the violence of the smashed crockery, and stood transfixed by the sight of Audrey so harried, momentarily overwhelmed with concern and guilt that he had upset her so.

But it only took a moment for his ire to re-surface. He was on a roll – had been for a week – unable to keep a lid on the fiery indignation that had infected him like a virus. And something about the hurt and the anger in Audrey's eyes, inflamed him even more. No one really understood... Not even Audrey.

'How can I let it go? That fucker, Blackthorn has probably fucked my career. That talentless piece of shit. Him, and that fucking prick Tate. All because of jealousy and conceit. The fucking shysters!'

'And what about revenge?' Audrey dead-panned him with a tired, drawn expression.

'Yes! Yes! That too. Petty, bloody-minded revenge. That fuck Tate, he's one of the biggest assholes, one of the gatekeepers. Just couldn't deal with the fact I was selling art without an agent... Without their fucking permission. And Blackthorn... he's always hated me ever since I was a student, and a better bloody painter than he'd ever be... And he knew I knew it too, the fucking bastard.'

We were selling art, together, thought Audrey. 'And revenge for exposing him.' She said pointedly. 'For exposing Blackthorn.'

Daniel calmed slightly and looked carefully at his partner. She continued: 'Might as well say it; he did what he did because of a grudge against me. *I* was the one who exposed him, so I suppose it's all my fault really, isn't it?'

'No...' Daniel hesitated, confused. Audrey's manner was a bit off kilter. 'But it's *my* career they're trying to ruin. It's *me* they're targeting.'

'Yep, it's you, isn't it Daniel? Fuck me, it's always you, you... You!' Audrey's eyes flared and her posture – deflated a moment before – became erect. 'I was the one who was framed! It was *my* picture plastered all over the evening news. All my family, all my friends, work colleagues... Everyone saw it. I'm the one who gets recognised in the street. *Oh, there she goes. She one of those cultural terrorists...*'

There was a momentary stand-off while they glared at each other. In that moment, Audrey sensed a fundament shift in the energy between them, and Daniel's eyes narrowed slightly as if sensing something adversarial – even threatening – in her.

'I'm the one whose reputation's in tatters. I'll never live this down. I've been fucking-well defamed in the worst possible way. But it's always *your* career that we have to worry about. Daniel the Great. No need to worry about anyone else's professional reputation.'

Daniel looked shocked by her invective. 'But it was *my* career we were working on... Together.'

'Yes, thank you. Yes, *we* were working on it *together.* And it's not past tense, by the way, we are still working on it. But you've got to let this go, and move on, get back to the core business, because business was going so well...'

'It was...' Daniel glared and a sulky, dark expression descended on him. 'You can already sense the difference in people's attitude. I can almost fucking taste it. Even Mietta and Tom. The last time I saw her, she wouldn't even look at me, cold as fucking ice.'

'Oh Jesus! This is what I'm talking about. It's your attitude.

Stomping around the place like some kind of vengeful, bloody deity, ranting and raving to anyone who'll listen. If you want to create a self-fulfilling prophesy, then you're going about it the right way. And we can't afford to piss Mietta off, you know that.'

'Yeah, but you can't fight this kind of character assassination. I reckon she's already gone. We're persona non-grata *already*. She doesn't want the association to rub off. That's how it starts. Everyone just starts shying away. No one says anything, but you end up black-listed, and that's it... Career fucking tanked, all thanks to that fucking piece of shit, Blackthorn.'

'It doesn't have to be this way,' Audrey gave a weary sigh.

'But it is this way. They wanted to shut me down and they've probably succeeded.'

'Don't you mean shut *us* down? He framed *me*, for Christ's sake! Me! It was *my* picture! It was *my* character they assassinated.'

'Ok, yes, I know. I know!' Daniel sounded exasperated, pissed off. 'But they were just using you to get to me. To stop me selling art...'

'Oh, for fuck's sake...' Audrey left the expletive hanging as she flung the tea towel at the sink and walked out of the kitchen without another word.

*

Quinn placed the receiver deliberately into the cradle of the speaker phone on this desk and kept his hand on it for some time, almost as though he was afraid it would jump back up. Then he lent back on his cushioned high-backed office chair and rubbed his chin, whilst his top lip massaged his bottom lip.

What could this possibly be about? Doherty, the crime squad detective investigating the Picasso theft, was coming to interview him... Again. Tomorrow morning.

It had crossed his mind to put him off – put him off indefinitely. He had a packed schedule, and it wasn't going to get any better, right up until he left for his new job in London in six weeks. Could he have kept him at bay for six weeks? Probably not. Best to nip it in the bud – whatever *it* was.

But what could he possibly want with Quinn? He'd answered all of Doherty's questions with tact and candor. On the phone the detective had invoked the standard police double-speak; *a few routine questions, some loose ends to tie up.* He'd also asked where he could get in contact with Travis.

Damn! Throughout the entire debacle Quinn had suppressed the creeping suspicions he'd had about Travis. Eventually he'd have to admit, he'd been in denial. Because the sinking sensation had been there all along, like a shadow, a nebulous spectre. He'd never liked Travis, far less trusted him. But he'd put his misgivings aside for Rosalyn. Rosalyn's oldest friend, Betty – Travis' mother – had been desperate to find something solid for the kid, something serious to give his stalled career a boost.

After the theft, he had put Travis out of his mind; that's when the denial had set in, he supposed. It just didn't bear thinking about – that Travis might be involved – his mother being so respected within the highest echelons of the justice system.

He exited his office and wandered around the corner towards the European gallery. *Walking would help him collect his thoughts.* At first it had been easy for him to ignore the niggle of suspicion; after all the Cultural Terrorists had been taking all the blame. But then, naturally enough, the alarm bells really started to sound, after Travis' extraordinary late night tip-off. *How did he know? What did he know, exactly?*

But with the painting returned and no harm done, it had again seemed preferable not to dwell on questions about Travis, in much the same vein as Quinn preferred – as a general rule of thumb – to know as little about Travis' doings and lifestyle as possible.

But now with the trail gone cold, and the very existence of the cultural terrorists in doubt, it appeared Travis was right; the authorities had turned their attention to the possibility of some sort of inside job.

He sighed heavily as he walked quietly amongst the few visitors, a perverse realisation dawning on him, that he might actually come to miss those damnable terrorists – fakes and phantoms that they were – because without them he might finally have to confront the real possibility of an enemy within his ranks.

Did Doherty have new information? Surely no real evidence... Probably just speculation, and with a bit of luck, it really was just loose ends on his mind.

As he rounded the corner, there she was; the riotous green framed by dark timber, like a beacon against the magenta wall.

The gallery was quiet, and there were only two people looking at the painting.

One of them was his chief conservator, Derek Tillery. *What was he doing here, away from his conservator's lair in the bowels of the building?* He looked intent, transfixed by the painting, like a punter seeing it for the first time. This struck Quinn as being quite strange and a prickly sensation crept over him – even more so, when Derek noticed him come up beside him and he gave a little startled jolt.... Not like Derek at all.

'She looks better than ever, doesn't she Derek?' Quinn stood beside his conservator and looked at the Weeping Woman, and gave him a little sigh. 'I don't know about you, but there were times I thought we might never see her again.'

'Hmm...' Derek said nothing, just stared at the painting as though trying to decipher a puzzle. 'Why?' he said finally turning his head slightly towards the director, but not taking his eyes off the painting. 'Why steal it? And then just give it back?'

'Who knows? Maybe we'll never know. Thank God at least, they didn't damage her.'

'Indeed...Indeed.' Derek said wistfully. 'In fact, she's in absolutely perfect condition.'

'Yes, she is.' Quinn glanced at his conservator, but Derek's gaze stayed on the painting, a barely perceptible furrow troubling his brow. 'All's well that ends well, I suppose,' he said quietly, then exhaled deeply, as if some kind of spell had been broken. He looked up at his director and smiled with his mouth, but his eyes remained troubled.

Derek's oddity moved Quinn to confess: 'I'm up for another inquisition. That detective, Doherty, he wants to talk to me again – Christ knows about what. He's coming down tomorrow.'

'Interesting,' Derek said airily. 'I don't envy him his task, do you?'

'Well, no, I suppose not. What do you mean, exactly?'

'The lady vanishes...' Derek turned back to the painting and performed a gesture with his hand like a magician making something disappear. His voice was a little breathless and his manner even stranger; quite out of character for his normally staid and pragmatic conservator. Quinn started to wonder if Derek had gotten a bad mushroom in his morning omelette, or some such. 'Then she reappears, out of the blue, after two and half weeks away – God knows where – and all the while these mysterious cultural terrorists leading everyone on a merry dance.'

'True enough.' Quinn said with a non-committal grunt.

'Spirited away. The so-called culprits nowhere to be found. And now she's back – delivered to Spencer Street *as requested*, you might say – and still no answers. A mystery.' Derek gave him a sideways glance, before returning his gaze to the painting, which seemed to captivate him. 'Maybe the detective's getting desperate, running out of options, and that police minister, Maynard, he wants heads to roll, doesn't he? Doherty's got to be under a lot of pressure.'

'Well, yeah... You're quite right, wouldn't want to be Doherty for quids.'

'Do you think he suspects?' Derek's question took him by surprise. It startled and annoyed him in equal measure.

'What do mean? Suspects who?' He tried to sound nonplus. *What the hell had gotten into Derek?*

'Well it's his job *to suspect*, I suppose...' The conservator trailed off.

'Just wanting to tie up some loose ends was what he said.'

'Yes, loose ends,' said Derek vaguely. 'I expect that's it.' He turned and gave Quinn a suddenly quite pointed stare. 'Loose ends like the backing board, and the missing providence labels, perhaps.'

Jesus! This was the first time Derek had brought up the problem of the missing labels head on, since they first noticed they were missing. It still wasn't common knowledge outside of Derek's department and a few trusted confidents around the NGV. It had become like a dirty and embarrassing secret that no one wanted to talk about.

'That's not what they're concerned about Derek. Not even on their radar, I'd say; and that's probably for the best, don't you think?'

'Well...' Derek said dubiously, 'maybe we *should* be concerned ... I mean aren't you, Ellery, even a bit?'

The director and conservator exchanged another one of their looks. Non-verbal concurrence, tinged with a suspicion of disparity.

'Of course.'

'Why keep the labels?' Derek asked with a worrying intensity and gave him a hard and harried look, like something inside him was hurting.

'We'll probably never know.'

Derek returned his attention to the painting, absorbed again by the Picasso, leaving Quinn to wonder anew, what fascinated him so. Quinn cleared his throat and said 'well'; getting ready to move on.

'It really is perfect, isn't it?' the conservator mused breathlessly.

'Yeah well, I've got to get along.' Quinn set off towards the inner reaches of the European gallery.

'Good luck!' Derek called after him with an almost merry lilt. When Quinn looked back, Derek had moved right up close to the painting, as though he was examining the minutiae of the brushstrokes right there on the gallery wall, instead of in his lab.

*

Back down on the basement level, as he made his way back to the lab, Derek Tillery, ducked into the bathroom up the hallway from his office and locked himself in the nearest cubicle, just in time, as he felt the bile rising hot and fast.

The gastric tsunami that followed didn't let up for several minutes and still he continued to retch and gag, until he was completely spent and sprawled beside the toilet bowl in the tiny stall. The small space smelled like a plague house. He listened for any sound outside the cubicle, hoping no one had witnessed his wretched commotion.

Once he was sure it was over, he washed his face and dusted himself off and returned to his office, where he sat, straight-backed at his desk and watched the shadows move across the high slit window of his subterranean office. If anyone had seen him there, they might have imagined him meditating, or pondering the meaning of life, or perhaps working up the nerve to take some kind of drastic action.

As the shadows lengthened, he finally stood up from his desk and went to his filing cabinet. His hand went straight to the file – the one he'd hidden two weeks prior – the one that now attested to his sin, his sin of inattention. He opened the file and extracted the incriminating evidence – the report in his own hand – so carefully compiled only last year, when the Picasso had arrived at the gallery.

He slid the sheaf of papers into the open briefcase on his desk and fastened the clasp. The old incinerator in his backyard was already loaded up with last year's fruit tree prunings, all dried and ready to ignite. It would burn hot and hellish once it got going and there would be nothing left of the damning papers, nothing but smoke and ash. Nothing to bear witness to his appalling oversight.

*

Travis turned off the highway and up the long gravel driveway. It was lined both sides by ancient, looming Cyprus trees. The unnatural shade they threw across the long laneway at mid-afternoon, gave the approach to the old farm a peculiar, spooky atmosphere. He couldn't help feeling that such plantings – so popular with the colonising settlers of the recent past – were an affront to the natural order of things. Or perhaps he was already spooked by the message Blackthorn had left on his answering machine. He hadn't heard from Blackthorn for weeks and there was no particular reason he would expect to, now that it was all over. But the message left on his machine had unsettled him. Blackthorn had been clearly drunk. In fact he'd sounded totally shit-faced. Shit-faced and ranting. Ranting about Hardman and Burke and about the Weeping Woman. Ranting about being wronged in some way, and ranting about retribution.

Normally he wouldn't have let it get to him. Normally he would've ignored a manic, drunken phone message from Blackthorn. If he'd thought hard about it, he probably could've recalled several others in the past. But there was something about Doug's strident tone on the recording – and the extremity of what he was proposing should be done – that had alarmed him.

And he hadn't just sounded drunk; he'd sounded like he was having some sort of existential meltdown, which was why – when he tried twice to return his call and got no answer – he'd decided, on impulse, to drive out to the farmlet Doug rented on the western outskirts of town, on a little hill they called Mount Morgan.

He crunched to a stop on the wide driveway in front of the dilapidated old farmhouse and killed the engine. He was barely out of the car when he saw Blackthorn stagger down the front steps, the fly wire door banging shut behind him. He had something long and straight in his hands, which he brandished at Travis. For one heart-stop moment Travis thought it was a gun. But it wasn't. It was a garden rake.

'Fuck off!' He shouted hoarsely, swinging the rake in a wide circle as if Travis was standing twenty feet closer to him than he was, unbalancing himself precariously as he followed through with the swing, then turned back to face the young interloper.

Travis backed away.

Blackthorn chewed the air and dipped forward as though he was about to fall flat on his face; recovered and squinted hard at Travis, as if trying to spot something in the distance.

'Dougy...' Travis greeted him in a perfunctory way, and frowned.

Blackthorn frowned back, a hint of recognition crossing his otherwise ornery features. 'Huh...You!' he huffed and nodded his acknowledgment. He turned and staggered back towards the house, beckoning him to follow with his free hand, the rake still clutched in the other. 'Better come in for a drink, then.'

'Yeah, great,' said Travis reluctantly following the old coot into his abode and checking his watch. Ten minutes before noon. *Looks like another drink is exactly what you need.*

Blackthorn leaned the rake in the hallway and it fell to the floor, but he didn't notice, negotiating the hallway like he was at sea, until he reached the kitchen table and held onto it for stability.

'What's with the rake, Dougy? Been doing a spot of gardening?'

'Thought you were won of those bloody narcs, come to ask more bloody stupid fuckin questions.' Blackthorn lunged for the kitchen bench like it was a moving target and reached for a third-full bottle of whiskey. 'Fuckblits...' he slurred, without any further elaboration.

Travis looked around the old farm kitchen, taking in the alarming state of disarray; unwashed dishes piled up in the sink and some even stacked on the floor; two rubbish bins full of empty beer cans and assorted bottles, the excess overflowing into the adjacent laundry. Strangely there were papers strewn around amongst the kitchen debris in such a random and messed up way, it appeared someone's office in-tray had exploded in the vicinity.

And the place stank, like something gone rancid, or something dead. The various troubling stenches all overlain with the yeasty sweet smell of spilled alcohol.

Blackthorn anchored himself to a kitchen chair and slammed two empty glasses onto the table. He started filling them from the whiskey bottle with a measure of dexterity that belied his wasted condition. 'Bastards,' he mumbled vaguely, then, 'shit!' as he slopped whiskey onto the table. He slid a glass over to Travis, who had taken a seat opposite him, and raised his own unsteadily.

'Cheers... fucken'...' he mumbled into his glass as he took a sip.

'Bastards... fucking bastards. They're all bloody jealous, they are, the fuckers...'

'Yeah. Bastards.' Travis agreed obligingly, raising his glass, thinking; *and how's drinking half a distillery helping your paranoia, Dougy?*

'Fucking think they can outsmart me.'

'The cops?'

'Yeah... Blackthorn looked a little uncertain... Confused. 'Yeah... I'll fucken kill em...'

'The cops?' Travis sounded alarmed. 'That's probably not a good idea.

'No NO! 'Blackthorn yelled belligerently. 'That fucking Hardman cunt!'

'What's *he* done?' Asked Travis. Oblivious.

'What's he done? What's he fucken done?' Blackthorn wiped his chin where some spittle had gathered, and glared with hostile affront. 'I'll tell you what he's done...' Blackthorn put his shot glass down on the table like he was operating some kind of precision equipment, trying that hard not to spill it. To Travis he looked so far gone, he'd be hard pressed to even remember what exactly Hardman *had* done to earn his ire.

'Bloody sold me out to the fucken plod he has!' He let out a kind of hiccoughy belch and continued. 'Bearing false bloody witness to that fuck-ass detective investigating the y'know... the Picasso thing...' The drunk academic flung his arm out towards the kitchen window, as if the investigation was going on in his back paddock.

'Fucking liar. Fucking lying prick he is!' He was suddenly more animated, alarmingly so and he leaned forward breathing volatile fumes all over Travis, who recoiled, thinking, *no one better light a match.*

'Huh?' Travis gave him an exaggerated look of puzzlement and tipped his head sideways.

'Tellin' the police I drew that fuckin picture!'

Christ, thought Travis, having something of an epiphany. He hadn't thought about where the picture had come from when he saw it broadcast. But now, he remembered Tate telling him that Blackthorn had had an idea to take the heat off them – he just hadn't connected the two.

Jesus!

'That picture?' said Travis He'd seen the picture, all over the television news and the newspapers. Everyone had. And anyone who knew Audrey Burke, had immediately recognised her. And some people – Travis included – knew Blackthorn hated Audrey Burke.

Travis was shocked, remembering the drunken conversation with Blackthorn in which he'd mischievously, suggested that Hardman and Burke might be the Cultural Terrorists. He remembered now, how Blackthorn had liked the idea. He'd quite taken to it.

He eyed Blackthorn now, slumped in his kitchen chair, lost in thought and staring into the distance, his whiskey glass resting on his big belly. If there was anything cognisant going on inside his head, he looked like he might have been composing his defense – and struggling at the task.

Now it all made sense: Blackthorn drinking himself into oblivion, protesting his innocence and denying having drawn it... In Travis's estimation, that could only mean that was exactly what he *had* done. It *had* been a pretty good likeness, after all. The implications started to pile up in Travis's head. Meanwhile Blackthorn was looking at him suspiciously, as if even in his inebriated state, he could read his mind, or see it on his face.

'Well I didn't fucken do it!' Blackthorn shouted belligerently. 'Why the fuck would I?'

Travis thought again about his planting the idea in Blackthorn's head a few weeks ago. Just a harmless lark, really. Now he felt a sharp pang of something that almost felt like remorse. 'You mean that picture of Audrey Burke? The one that was all over the media a week back?'

The mention of Burke seemed to light a fuse under the already volatile and deranged lecturer. 'That fucking bitch!' His eyes blazed as though he was suddenly sober. 'She deserved to go down, the lying fucking bitch! And who says it wasn't them? Why not? They both fucking deserved it!' Spittle flew across the table and a bit of it hit Travis in the face. He wiped it away and scowled.

'But you didn't draw the picture, right Doug?'

'Of course I fucking didn't! But that Hardman prick is saying I did. He's got that bloody detective convinced of it, and somehow it's got back to the University. The fucking Vice-Chancellor asked me about it the other day!' In his drunkenness he somehow managed to look both aggrieved and astounded by this.

'Are you sure you didn't draw the picture Dougy?' Somehow Travis just could resist poking the bear. After all, when it was all said and done, Blackthorn was one of the most obnoxious reprobates he's ever known, even if he was a useful one to know. But it looked like Blackthorn may have cooked his own goose – and it amused Travis to think maybe the old bastard was about to go down for all his shit-fuckery – and that that in turn might take the heat off himself and Tate. The irony was quite exquisite, and if he were brutally honest, he'd have to say Blackthorn deserved it.

Blackthorn gave him a dark and foreboding look of disgust, and abruptly shoved his chair back and staggered to his feet, violent intent erupting from his mangled visage.

Travis was already on his feet, ten times more nibble than his adversary and sober to boot. At the door he turned and said: 'Because it sure as hell looked like one of yours... What the fuck were you thinking?'

Travis got to his car before Blackthorn was even down the front steps. He heard a string of slurred expletives directed his way as he jumped in the car, and in the rear-view mirror he saw that Blackthorn had reacquired the rake, and was swinging it wildly at his car, from a comically ineffective distance.

His spinning wheels sprayed gravel up towards his would-be attacker, and through the dust he glimpsed Blackthorn throw the rake after the car and then stumble and fall.

Travis laughed as he zoomed down the driveway and wondered whether Blackthorn would drink himself to death out on his depressing little farm. The twinge of guilt he'd felt earlier – remembering that his own facetious suggestion might have caused Blackthorn to put himself in the shit – had already turned to humour and he laughed again, as he turned onto the highway and headed for Geelong.

Blackthorn verses Hardman, in a fight to the death... That was something he'd pay good money to see.

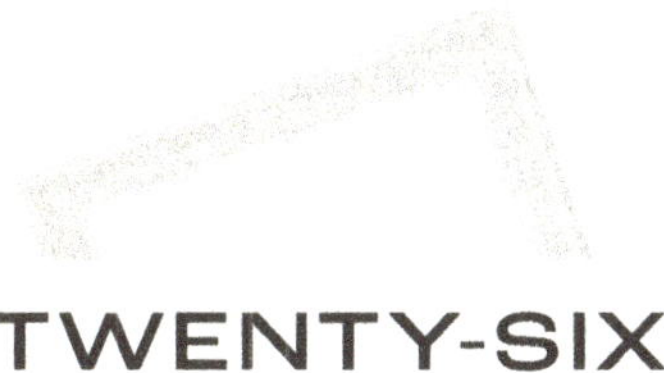

TWENTY-SIX

Tuesday, September 1st, 1986

Never open an umbrella indoors.
Angry Buddha, 2001

Quinn cupped his tumbler of single malt in his hands, as if it was radiating actual warmth, and stared out through the window of his darkened study at the Southern Cross. Rosalyn had retired an hour ago, but he himself was still wide awake. Restless. He rarely took strong alcohol this late at night.

The visit from Doherty, the detective, the previous morning had unsettled him; unsettled him deeply. He sipped his whiskey and an image crossed his mind of the detective as a terrier, locked onto his trouser cuff. He needed to shake him off, metaphorically. But how? He was bloody relentless. Right from the very start of the debacle he'd gotten a weird vibe from Doherty, a sense that he was suspicious of everybody – even of Quinn himself. He'd ignored it at first, written it off as the man's professional constitution. It *was* his job to be suspicious.

But something had shifted. He'd noticed a distinct change in the detective's demeanor this time. He seemed almost cocky, more sure of himself, and more tenacious. Quinn had played him with a straight bat. The usual aplomb. Not giving an inch, nor allowing any chink to show in his own amour.

But it seemed like Doherty knew something. His questioning had changed both in content and timbre. A lot of questions about Travis this time; his role at the gallery, his security credentials (what a joke), access to the gallery, and so on.

And he'd persisted with an annoying and repeated line of inquiry about Travis's association with the art dealer Logan Tate, from Helicon Galleries (*You'd have to ask him about that*) and whether he himself knew Tate and the art lecturer Douglas Blackthorn.

He surmised from the totality of the detective's questions that Blackthorn had somehow gotten himself in Doherty's sights... *What do they say? A person of interest.* And it seemed like it might have had something to do with the artist whose studio was raided a week ago, and subsequently cleared of involvement. Quinn had no idea how the two might be related, and the detective had played his cards very close to his chest – at pains not to enlighten him.

There'd been an invigorated barrage of questions covering all the old ground; the special snake-eye screwdriver needed to remove the painting, his own movements on the night in question and the *mystery*, as Doherty called it, of the *vanishing conservator's card*. Quinn didn't care for his tone or the innuendo, but he held his tongue and stuck to his story... That he'd seen the card attached to the wall when the missing painting was first discovered, but not since. It had, apparently, been lost.

And what about your young protégé, McRae*? Any chance he may have come across the missing registrar's card by any chance?*

And what did the card say, exactly? Removed to the ACT? Removed by the ACT? Sent out to the cleaners, perhaps?

Not entirely sure, had been Quinn's reply. Strangely, in truth, he couldn't recall the exact words. He'd only see the card once, and the only thing that stuck with him was the disconcerting similarity of the hand-writing to his own.

'The human brain can be so unreliable recalling detail, even after a few weeks, don't they say?' Quinn had been deliberately smarmy. 'I'm sure you find that's often the case in your line of work?' Doherty had been visibly miffed at Quinn's allusion to the detective's own craft. *Teach your grandmother to suck eggs, do you?* And from there, the interview took another turn for the worse.

He started asking whether he, Tate and Blackthorn had had any business dealings together, and whether or not Quinn had heard any of the rumors going around about forged artworks being moved through the Melbourne art world. In the end Quinn couldn't help but show his annoyance at the obstinacy of the detective's interrogations – which only added fuel to the fire of Doherty's self-righteous and distrustful manner.

Finally, Quinn had pleaded an urgent board meeting – which wasn't actually occurring until the following day – and dismissed the detective, but not before Doherty responded by threatening *to invite him downtown* to continue the interview at a later date. He'd given Quinn his card and said he'd be needing to talk to Travis as soon as possible, and asked him to get Travis to call him at his earliest convenience.

The whole thing had left him feeling annoyed and a little shaken. And for the first time some fear had crept in, at the thought of Travis actually having some sort of criminal involvement in the whole thing, and – heaven forbid – that Doherty might actually be able to come up with some sort of evidence.

It wasn't lost on him that – if it did transpire that Travis was involved in some way – it could even appear that Quinn had been covering for the little bugger the whole time...*Unthinkable!*

Did Doherty not know who Quinn was?... And shouldn't someone have this investigative terrier on a leash of some sort?

With this thought in mind, he took a rueful sip of single malt, and it was at that very moment – ungodly hour that it was – his study telephone started ringing. It almost made him spill his Scotch. *No one rings at this hour. Someone must've died.*

*

'Ellery.... Ellery?' His father's voice sounded distant but insistent at the same time, and a little irritated.

'Christ! Is everything alright? Is mother Okay?"

'Yes, of course she is. Why wouldn't she be?'

'It's just...very late. It's... Why are you calling at this hour?' Quinn glanced at his watch. It was eleven fifteen. 'And I can't hear you properly. Are you holding the receiver funny?'

'That better?' His father's voice became clearer. 'I was going to call you tomorrow, but you're always so hard to catch. And anyway, I decided this couldn't wait. Been keeping me awake. We need to talk about it now.'

'Talk about what?'

There was a somewhat extended pause, as if his father was composing himself, or not sure what to say. Very out of character. 'What's been going on down there at the NGV? All this... This Picasso thing. I thought it was all resolved, now that you've got the painting back.'

'Yes... Yes it is. She's back in her rightful place in the European Gallery. Everything's good in the garden.' Quinn felt a distinct sinking sensation and a flutter in his gut – a vestige of childhood scoldings – at the strangeness of his father calling him late at night to ask him this. And... just after his recent run in with Doherty.

There was another awkwardly long pause on the other end of the line.

'Well, I've had a very strange visitor this afternoon.... Came out to see me here, at Government House. Very unusual. In fact somewhat inappropriate in a way. But he came after work... *Unofficially*....and so off the record, if you will.'

Ellery breathed into the handset, but he couldn't form the words he wanted to say – *Who? Who came to see you?*

Sensing his discomfort, his father continued, after another brief pause.

'The Chief Commissioner – You know Geoff. You know he's a member of my club don't you? Came out to see me... Here.' Another pause 'It was really rather embarrassing... For both of us.'

'What did he want?' recovering his composure somewhat, Ellery tried to sound blasé.

'He said one of his detectives – the one investigating the Picasso thing – has become convinced the whole thing was an inside job, and that senior staff at the gallery could be involved. He's told the commissioner he thinks you might know more than you're letting on.'

Quinn felt a burst of heat flush his face, and he clutched his whiskey tumbler, with a sudden urge to take a big swig, which he resisted. Something in his father's tone elicited a long-buried feeling – something old and vestigial, like some forgotten gene. It felt like shame. And with it came flashes of memories. Memories of guilty revelations. Always his brother telling on him, and blowing the whole gig, just when little Ellery thought he'd covered his tracks so well... *And besides; so what? He hadn't done anything wrong.*

'That's preposterous!' He tried to summon all his indignant incredulity. 'I know who you mean. Name's Doherty. He's delusional, possibly even deranged. Probably been in the job too long. Got a bee in his bonnet about, Travis – you know, Betty's son – I've got him out here doing a twelve month internship with me. And well, you know Travis, he a...umh...'

'Bad egg,' his father said pointedly.

'Well, y'know. It's fine. Betty and Rosalyn... you know. It's fine. Doherty's got the bull completely by the tits, I assure you P'pa.'

'You're sure about that?'

'Absolutely!' Again, the remnants of childhood patterning put the slightest quaver in his voice. And he knew his father heard it.

'Because the way Geoff tells it, he's got the police minister breathing down his neck and a senior detective who swears he can find no trace of the culprits – the ones sending all those ransom notes – what were they calling themselves?'

'The Australian Cultural Terrorists,' Ellery intoned dryly, as he stared bleakly into his whiskey tumbler.

'Yes. Well he says he doesn't believe they even exist anymore... The detective that is, not the commissioner. Thinks it was all part of some elaborate hoax to cover up some kind of *inside job*. There can't be any truth in this, can there? Please tell me there's not... He's barking up the wrong tree, no?'

'I told you, he's mad. Bull by the tits... Barking up the wrong tree; use whichever metaphor you like. Doherty's delusional.'

Something about Ellery's defensive manner – a bit of belligerence creeping in – made his father hesitate. And Ellery recognised the pause. A father knows his son. There was no fooling the governor. There never had been. There was another long and uncomfortable pause between father and son, a faint hiss of static on the line, then an audible sigh from his father's end.

'Okay, well look Ellery, in the end I've assured Geoff that there is absolutely nothing to see here, alright?' Another pause. Ellery said nothing. 'You understand what I'm saying don't you? I've given

Geoff – one of our oldest and dearest friends, who just happens to be the chief commissioner of police – my own *personal* assurance that you were *not* involved in anything untoward in this whole Picasso incident.'

The hissing on the line seemed to get slightly louder.

'Right?'

'Right.' Ellery's voice, even to himself, sounded small, like his ten-year-old self. A plethora of childhood incidents were flashing through his mind's eye now; misdemeanors from his childhood. He felt incendiary annoyance that his father might be alluding to such ancient history; the insubordination of youth. But he also felt an unexpected and really quite crushing sense of humiliation, which neutralised his anger and took away his voice.

'So... Geoff's going to take care of this over-zealous detective. I just hope there won't be any more talk of an inside job...'

More hissing.

'Ellery, I need your assurance there won't be any more embarrassing revelations come to light along those lines...'

'Don't worry, there won't be.'

'We're quite sure, are we?'

'Yes.'

'When are you and Rosalyn leaving for this new appointment in London?'

'In about six weeks.'

'Not a moment too soon, perhaps.'

'Yes, father.'

The hissing stopped. The line was dead.

*

The foyer of police headquarters still looked like a construction site, where the repairs were continuing, after the bombing. It sent a shiver around Doherty's midriff as he hurried through, trying to look like he belonged; heading towards the lifts at the rear.

By the time he reached the fifth floor, the tingling feeling persisted, and this, together with a tightness in his gut, told him he was having an attack of nerves; understandably really – being summoned downtown to see the police commissioner.

Another first.

Well, he'd survived his pre-emptory audience with the odd-ball police minister a few weeks earlier; so he supposed he could handle the Commissioner of Police. Although deep down he knew this would be a much tougher gig. At least this time, he was armed with better and more information, and a concrete sense that the investigation was progressing towards a possible conclusion.

After his last interview with the gallery director Quinn – and given the bizarre and evasive behavior of the critic, Blackthorn – he was more convinced than ever of some kind of conspiracy involving someone at the gallery and high-up members of Melbourne's art community. It was the only thing that made sense. All he needed was some hard evidence, or for someone to talk. And he needed to get hold of that McRae character, and grill him; but for the moment, he seemed to have gone to ground.

He and Mallory had already developed a promising strategy. Mallory had formed a very low opinion of Blackthorn's integrity and ethics and so, he reckoned, given the right encouragement, he could be coerced into shopping his co-conspirators.

Mallory – playing bad cop – would tell him they had found the informant who had presented the drawing at police headquarters – even though they hadn't – and that she had fingered him as the author of the drawing. *Perverting the course of justice*, was what he'd be charged with, unless he cooperated. They'd offer him immunity, in exchange for the names of everyone else involved.

He'll roll over on the other rats for sure, Mallory had opined, *because from what I've seen, I reckon he's the biggest rat of the bunch.*

So, Doherty reckoned, he could confidently tell the commissioner they were close to closing the case.

The commissioner's secretary – middle aged, ex-police Doherty guessed, precisely spoken and authoritative – bade him sit on the big leather couch opposite her desk, while she buzzed her commander. But his bum had barely touched down when the speaker phone reactivated and a gruff and gravelly voice said, *send him right in.*

Even sitting behind his desk, the commissioner was a tall and imposing man. He was balding with greying dark hair around the temples. He gave Doherty a brief and perfunctory smile, and gestured to indicate where Doherty should take a seat in front of the large solid desk.

'Thanks for coming in detective.' Formal, no first names, the faint smile vanished to be replaced with a dour expression. Doherty didn't know the commissioner personally, but everyone in the force knew him to be a non-nonsense lead-from-the-front commander.

'My pleasure, sir.' Doherty sat himself down and gave the police chief a brief formal smile in return. The commander remained impassive, a hard and unyielding stare. It made Doherty remember what he'd heard of the commissioner's war record; a Vickers machine gun operator. The police boss seemed to have Doherty in his sights now, from the behind barricade of his wide oak desk.

'We'll get right to the point, shall we detective?'

'Of course, Sir.'

'The Picasso investigation... You've been running it for quite some time now haven't you? Must be going on a couple of months so far, yes?'

'Five weeks, Sir.'

The chief gave him a deadpan scowl. 'You must be aware the whole business has caused a lot of embarrassment to the government and in particular to the Police Minister, Mr. Maynard.' Something about the way he said *Mr. Maynard* left Doherty in no doubt the commissioner was not enamored of the Labor minister currently overseeing his police force. He doubted the ex-machine-gunner was left-leaning when it came to voting.

'Yes Sir, I am aware of that, but our investigation has thrown up some important new...'

'And it hasn't helped that no arrests have been made.' The head man apparently had no compunction cutting Doherty off mid-sentence. 'If I'm not mistaken, even after all this time there are still no serious suspects and – correct me if I'm wrong – the trail on these so-called cultural terrorists has gone cold.'

'Well that's true. It's my belief that the Australian Cultural Terrorist are not real in any concrete sense. We now think that all along they may have been a ruse to throw everybody off the scent, but...'

'So, it's bullshit. No bunch of dangerous radicals, stealing priceless bloody paintings to fund their nefarious deeds and bring down civilization as we know it... A hoax. Probably students or something; stole the thing for a lark and now they've given it back. And two months down the track we still haven't found hide nor hair of them. Is that what you're telling me detective?'

'Well not exactly, Sir. The investigation has shifted away from looking for these cultural terrorists, and we do think we now have some legitimate suspects that we're...'

'You know what I think? I think these damned punks – students, down and out artists, or whoever the bloody hell they are – they'll be lucky I don't get hold of 'em. Pulling a prank like that is one thing, but calling themselves terrorists is asking for trouble – real trouble – given the state of the world. Bloody idiots.'

'Actually sir, we don't think it was students, or artists... we actually think it might have been certain senior people within the art industry, and we think it may have been an inside job, possibly involving someone at the National Gallery itself.'

'Inside job you say, detective? That's sounding a bit Hollywood isn't it? Seems a bit implausible to me. Do you have any hard evidence?'

'Not yet, but...'

'Listen, son, the painting's been recovered, hasn't it?'

Doherty nodded with an unhappy expression, but sensed he should not interrupt.

'No damage done to it... No one's dead or injured. No apparent evidence *anywhere* of who did it. The national gallery people are happy and relieved, the insurance companies are off the hook... Everybody's happy, no?

'The police minister, Mr. Maynard wasn't ...not the last time I saw him.' This just slipped out, before Doherty could think better of it, and he bit his lip as he watched a dark cloud descend on the commissioner's brow. His cold expression made Doherty feel like the old soldier might be just about to squeeze off a burst of the Vickers at him without a hint of compassion or regret.

'Listen Ted, not to put too fine a point on it; the force has suffered a lot of embarrassment over this whole affair, and if we're not careful it could really harm our reputation. I mean it hasn't looked good at all has it? These activists, or whoever the hell they are – ridiculing the Police Minister; our members running around and let's face it, at times, being made to look plain silly... Teams of police searching art galleries; then there was that debacle in Adelaide, and no suspects, no arrests... And it didn't really help

– didn't look good at all – when the painting was recovered without the police being involved. It was the bloody Age newspaper and that gallery director, who got it back. Frankly it's embarrassing. Doesn't reflect well on the force and it particularly doesn't reflect well on the detective in charge of the investigation.' The commissioner looked pointedly and gloomily at the detective, who seemed to have shrunken into the chair opposite, a chair that was no doubt already staged several inches lower than the commander's.

Doherty's heart sank. This was not going well – nothing like he'd anticipated. It didn't help that the commissioner kept talking right over the top of him. 'Well, sir that's exactly the point I was trying to make. We think people at the gallery itself, might be involved...'

'You think... That doesn't sound like evidence to me, detective. Sounds more like supposition and innuendo.' The top cop gave him a condescending look over his glasses. 'Let me spell it out for you Ted. This isn't looking good for you. It's not going to end well; not if after two or three months, this is all you've got. I'll be honest with you... I've seen unsuccessful investigations like this ruin careers. It happens.'

'But with respect sir, we really do believe we're very close to a breakthrough...'

'Ted, Ted... Am I not making myself clear? Trust me detective, I'm trying to do you a favour here – I'm telling you, I've seen it happen. One senior investigator I knew years ago, ended up a desk sergeant up in Dimboola, all because he couldn't let go of an investigation gone sour.' The two policemen eyed each other quietly for a few moments. The commissioner eyes were impassive, cold. Doherty imagined his trigger finger itching.

'It's a dead duck, Ted. I know it's a hard one to swallow after you've put so much time and effort in, but it's been decided. We can't waste any more police resources on this one. It's time to let it go. I'm pulling the pin on it.'

The chief's tone gave no quarter. It was final. But Doherty could feel all the frustration of the past weeks bubbling to the surface. His gut was certain he was on the right track, finally. How could he let it go? 'Sir, I understand what you're saying and I respect your decision, but I have to object; I'd like it on the record that I object to closing the investigation, because I believe we have solid leads, leads which could plausibly lead to arrests.'

'No Ted. No... You don't want to *object*. Trust me, you really don't.'

Ted held his gaze. The commissioner was impassive and stern, as if carved from stone. 'You know that sergeant in Dimboola? I think he might have retired recently...I could put in a word for you. All it would take is one call.' His boss' airy tone left Ted in no doubt of the veracity of the threat. 'Trust me Ted, it's over.'

The commissioner put his palms on his big desk and stood up, signaling that the meeting was at an end.

'Yes, sir.' Doherty sighed and got up reluctantly, but then gathered himself and straightened his back, then, unaccountably found himself giving the commissioner a formal police salute. 'Thank you commissioner.'

He left the commissioner's office without another word, and descended back into the lobby and floated through the foyer without even noticing the repairs going on to the broken building. He descended the steps to street level and was finally roused from his trance-like state by a blast of cold air. Even though it was early spring, Russell Street was being swept by a ferocious hailstorm.

*

Ross Maynard was fuming. Not that anyone would know by looking him; standing right in front of the large picture window beside his desk, he seemed to be admiring the view of the tree tops of Treasury Gardens.

Meditating perhaps. Or enjoying the changing vista of Melbourne's mutable spring weather. It had been hailing a moment ago, but now it was sunny; the rolling billows of cumulonimbus already chugging away into the eastern skies.

But he was far from calm. He was repressing his rage.

He sighed deeply and returned to his desk and sat motionless for a moment, staring at his speaker phone, as if it might be some sort of small, skittish prey, crouched on his desk, about to leap away at any moment. After some time he let go a small exasperated gasp and snatched up the phone and spoke quietly but tensely to his executive assistant, at her desk in the outer office: 'Get me the Premier on the phone, please June.'

'Yes, I know he is June, but it's urgent, I need to talk to him, this morning.'

'Yes, well get a message to his chief of staff or one of his media people – there has to be a break in proceedings at some point. Tell them it's urgent, first chance he gets. It won't take long.'

He sat at his desk with his head in his hands for a time, then. Brooding... And fuming, still. Quietly. He stood up and went to the window and checked the progress of the weather, then returned to his desk and shuffled some of the files collected there, waiting for his action, without any real interest or intent.

Before long there was a knock on his door. No heads up from June. He had a pretty fair idea who it would be. 'Come in.'

'Morning minister...' His chief ministerial advisor flashed him a token grin and allowed himself in.

'Russell. How are you?'

'Very well minister. You?'

'Dandy.'

Russell sat himself down and treated Maynard to one of his oft used expressions – sycophantic condescension, with an overlay of measured thoughtfulness. 'I understand we're trying to get hold of the premier?'

'Well, *I'm* trying to get hold of him Russell, yes. Nothing for *you* to worry about.'

'May I ask what it's about?'

'I think you probably know what it's about. You probably had it on your jungle telegraph, even before I was told.'

'The Picasso investigation? Being put on pause by the chief commission's office?'

'Put on *pause*? It's been canned, for Christ's sake. Shelved indefinitely – now and forever more. Geoff told me himself, this morning – in no uncertain terms. Paused? No. It's been bloody euthanised.'

'Hmm, yeah.' Russell showed his white teeth – half grin, half grimace – and sucked in a short breath. 'Maybe for the best, though? I mean it really did seem to have run out of puff. Painting's back, all in one piece. Police resources wearing a bit thin on it, not to mention patience, and still not a single Kalashnikov-waving art terrorist to be found anywhere in greater Melbourne.'

'It's a bloody disgrace, Russell. If we let these people get away with this, with no repercussions we might as well declare open season on every gallery and valued institution in the city. There has to be some consequences, otherwise...We're capitulating! It's the thin end of the wedge, Russell.'

His chief advisor knew how invested his minister was in the Picasso investigation. How could he not? No Minister of Police – nor Minster of the Arts – had ever been shoved into the public domain like Maynard had by the Picasso theft, and so Russell, as his ministerial minder had been faced with unique challenges and frankly, one of the most problematic times in his public service career.

When he first landed the job with Maynard, he'd found it exciting and challenging. Such a strange and interesting mix of portfolios – Police and Arts. He had never really got his head around why the premier had chosen to appoint Maynard into both. But then, the stealing of the Picasso had been like a perfect storm – rocketing his minister into an arena of unprecedented public and media scrutiny. A nightmare, really, especially with the supposed culprits, right from the start, targeting the minister directly with such personal and persistent vitriol.

He understood only too well why his boss was so invested in bringing the culprits to justice. But equally he understood that Maynard was, of course, way too triggered to make any objective decisions on the subject. It was a conundrum of horrendous and inescapable proportions. He felt great empathy for his boss, but he never lost sight of where his own priorities were, in terms of preserving his own skin.

And this was why, when he'd been contacted by his contemporary at the Chief Commissioner's office, he knew the jig was up. No one wanted to keep flogging this deceased horse. Not the police, who'd been made to look embarrassingly inept through the whole thing; not the National Gallery, who were no doubt thoroughly mortified by their own carelessness at having lost the thing in the first place; and not even the media, who had finally – thank God – started to lose interest.

Only Maynard was still brim full of righteous zeal to bring the culprits to account and, if he were completely honest with himself, Russell doubted his own resolve and diplomacy was up to the task of talking him out of it.

'Thin end... In what way minister?'

'We allow a crime like this to go unpunished, we might as well forget all about the rule of law. I mean it's all about consequences, deterrent... It's what our justice system is based on. Without it we'd descend into a lawless jungle.'

'Yes minister... But doesn't this one really stack up as a victimless crime, in a sense? And with the painting back where it should be, it's almost as if no crime really happened at all. At least that's the way the insurance people I've spoken to seem to view it. They say that quite often a stolen painting is recovered by insurance investigators... No questions asked and quite often, no charges laid, because it's usually returned anonymously, just like the Picasso was.'

Maynard frowned petulantly at his advisor. 'Well that's not what happened in this case. I mean, the damn thing wasn't even insured.'

'Yes – but it came back nonetheless. No harm done. Bogus terrorists vanished like phantoms. Public losing interest. Gallery people happy as Larry. And the Commissioner's office getting twitchy as hell, the more it drags on. Probably really is time to cut our losses.'

'Bugger me, Russell...' Maynard's eyes flared and his frizzy grey hair seemed to get even bigger. 'Why has everyone around here gone soft on these criminals, for Christ's sake? They're calling themselves terrorists and holding the state to ransom, and everyone seems to want to just treat them like a joke – give them a slap on the wrist, and send them on their way.'

The passion in his boss' voice and the intensity in his gaze, drew an unaccustomed silence from his normally loquacious advisor.

'Well, I'm not having it. I'm not going to rest until these

reprobates are brought to justice, and I don't care what the Chief Commissioner thinks about it. He answers to me. And I don't care if the bloody gallery, or their insurers – if they even have any – are satisfied with the outcome, because I'm bloody well not; not until I see some heads roll. One way or another these insolent bloody scum-bags are going to regret the day they crossed swords with this state's Minister of Police, you mark my words Russell.'

Jesus, they really got under your skin with all that bullshit in their ransom notes, didn't they? Thinking this, Russell found himself, again, uncommonly lost for a counter argument to console or advise his minister. Maynard went on, pointing at the phone on his desk. 'I'm on a call-back with the Premier and I'm going to tell him, we either re-open the investigation, or he'll be looking for a new Police Minister, because this shall-not-stand!'

Russell's resume, if not his actual professional life started flashing before his eyes, and he felt the onset of a bit of panic now, and so he drew breath to speak, not even quite sure what he would say. But he was saved by the bell. The minister's phone began to ring.

Maynard snatched it up. 'Yes? Yes, put him through.'

Russell heard a distinctive voice, faintly in Maynard's earpiece. The Premier.

'Yes, exactly.'

'No.'

'No, Bob. No, I won't. Not as long as I'm Minister.

'Really?'

'Yes. I understand, but...'

'Alright, yes. Yes, if that's what you want.'

'No, I'm not. Not one little bit.'

'Alright. Goodbye.'

The conversation was over all too quickly and Russell looked at Maynard with questioning expression, confused and a little perturbed at having witnessed the seemingly ominous one-sided conversation.

'The premier?' he inquired solicitously.

'Get out!' Maynard's eyes flared fierce and aggrieved under his bushy eyebrows, and he pointed at his office door.

*

Daniel stood back the full length of the studio to view the large and imposing self-portrait. This space was more cramped than the expansive squash court studio he'd had at Mietta's, but still, adequate for his needs.

He smiled at what he'd done. *Portrait of an artist as a young fucking head-kicker.* He looked appropriately cantankerous in the self-depiction. Ready to have someone's head off. Perfect. He looked at the semi-encrypted text along the bottom edge of the painting, which he'd re-jigged at the last minute to read CORRECTION, over the top of MONGOOSE.

Yes, perfect. He would enter it in the Archibald. Portrait *by* the artist, *of* the artist who was framed for stealing the Picasso. The textual epithet along the bottom had originally read FUCK THAT, but he'd painted over it... twice.

As he stood against the back wall examining the work from a decent distance, and rewarding his tired neurons with a surge of nicotine, he was finally satisfied. It was done. It had cost him more than most projects. But the result was striking, confronting and a little bit disturbing. A statement, no doubt. And it had, as they say, *historical context.*

Outside the studio, Smith Street was already buzzing with early punters, heading for the pubs and eateries all around the narrow laneway that concealed his workplace. It seemed strangely busy for a Tuesday night in late winter. But then again, he realised, it was the first day of spring, and the evening gloaming was still washed with an orange hue to the West.

He strode through the back streets in the chill of the spring evening, invigorated by the clear skies and deliberately forcing the pace, to get his heart rate up a bit. He was home in no time, flushed and a little breathless, enlivened by the exercise and yet still mentally exhausted by the long days he'd spent on the portrait. From the front porch he could hear the phone ringing, but he didn't rush, thinking Audrey would get it. When she didn't, he hurried down the hallway to the kitchen and grabbed the receiver before it stopped.

'Hello?'

The voice on the other end of the line was mysterious to him, but the name, when the caller introduced himself, was vaguely familiar. A friend of a friend. He said he was a journalist, which normally would have put Daniel on the defensive. But their common acquaintance was an old and trusted friend, and there was something about the man's voice that sounded genuine and sympathetic. He worked for Melbourne's leading broadsheet, and so, Daniel supposed he'd probably read something under his by-line before.

The journalist explained that he'd heard about the raid on Daniel's studio. And he'd heard about the drawing of Audrey. He even knew that Blackthorn was suspected of having drawn it. And by implication, he seemed to know something about the history between Blackthorn and Audrey. He was very well informed.

Rather than be disturbed by this stranger, a journalist, knowing all of this about them, he felt strangely comforted by it. Such was the confidence inspired in Daniel, by the soft-spoken and empathetic voice on the phone, that he happily filled in some of the gaps, and told him a little about the impact the events had had on himself and Audrey.

Where was Audrey? He looked around the kitchen – it was uncommonly clean and tidy – and peered into the dining nook, where Audrey often set up to work, but there was no sign of her. What he really wanted to do was put this guy on speaker, so they could both listen to him. He was already thinking that having a sympathetic well-placed journalist on their side could help to counteract some of the damage done to his career. And not far below the surface lurked another thought; maybe this guy could help them nail Blackthorn, and bring him to account for his maleficence.

As if reading his mind, the journalist started to explain that he had a special interest, and was something of an expert in the new Freedom of Information laws enacted by the state government.

Even though he had a vague sense that he might be taking some kind of bait, he had enough confidence in the journalist to tell him a bit about their history with Blackthorn and the extent of the grudge he surely held against Audrey. And he told him about his conviction that it was Blackthorn who had done the drawing.

'You see, I was student of his, back in art school. Years ago. I recognised his drawing style, y'know, when the cops showed me the picture. I *told* them... I *named* him.'

'Fucking hell. Like you named their informant.'

'Yeah... Fuck me, you should've seen their faces.

'I would've liked to...' The journalist hesitated. 'Do you think they knew *then* that he was the author of the picture?'

'I don't know. They were pretty cagy. But they back-pedaled their way out of my studio at double-time. It was pretty funny I suppose.' Not for the first time, Daniel saw the humour in what had otherwise been a confronting and disturbing experience.

The journalist gave a small chuckle in return and said: 'Would you like to find out for sure if it was him? I mean that's a pretty fucked up thing to do to someone. And it's a crime too... He should be held to account don't you reckon? He sounds like a complete bastard.'

'Yes and yes. He is an absolute fucking arse-wipe. And yes, we'd like to nail him, not just for what he did to us, but for all the other shit he's gotten away with over the years. You've got no idea.'

'Actually, I have heard; some anyway.' Another pause.

'Here's the thing Daniel, just to put you in the picture. Full disclosure... My interest in all this is sort of academic, in a way... Because of my interest in FOI.'

'Go on...'

'You see these laws are quite new. They haven't been tested in a lot of ways, and your case could be very interesting. Could be like a test case.'

'I don't follow you.'

'What I'm suggesting is, we could put in a Freedom of Information application to get the police to divulge where they got the drawing from.'

'Jesus, really? Would that work?' Daniel's head started to spin at the possibilities.

'No idea. It's never been done before. One thing I can tell you for sure though; the cops are going to shit themselves sideways, because essentially, we'd be using untested FOI laws to try and get them to reveal the name of a police informant. It's unprecedented, and quite frankly, a little bit scary.'

Daniel was hooked immediately. 'Fuck, I'm in. How would we do it?'

'Well I can put in a FOI application. It's pretty straight-forward. The thing you have to realise though, is the police will contest it. They'll fight it tooth and nail, because it would set such a legal precedent if it worked – kind of a dangerous legal precedent.'

'How do you mean?'

'Well... Your case is one thing. Very unusual. But can you imagine? Every gangster and thug using Freedom of Information to get the names of police informants? That's why it's scary. Frankly I'm not even sure it should be done. But it's interesting isn't it? That's why I say my interest is partly academic. I'm just curious to see if it's even possible.'

'Well I say let's give it a go. I don't feel like we've got a hell of a lot to lose.'

'Hmm...' He heard the journo blow out a long puff of air. 'The thing is, if we do it, the police will fight it hard. They'll throw all their legal resources at it... So we'd need help, and plenty of it. Heavy-duty legal help.'

'Jesus!' Daniel let out a long sigh. *There was always a catch*. 'Well that pretty much counts us out. We can't afford lawyers. We can barely pay the bloody rent.'

'Okay, yeah, of course, I understand that. But that might not be a problem.'

'How so?'

'I know someone, a colleague... Actually a very old friend, he might be able to help. Knows his way around the legal system pretty well. I've told him a bit about your situation, not too much, no names or anything; just enough to pique his curiosity, but I think he might be interested.'

'So who is it, this friend of yours?'

'Well, I'll introduce you if you want. He's a QC, actually. Very well regarded. Very skilled. He's already curious, because of the precedent and the context... And he's an art lover. Once he meets you, all being well, he might be willing to act pro bono, y'know just because of the precedent, just because it could be a very significant test case.'

'You really think he'd represent us for no fee?'

'I think he could be convinced. Actually, he's a bit of a fan of yours, Dan, and he's a collector. If everything panned out, maybe in the end, you could gift him a painting or something. He'd be pretty chuffed with that.'

At this point Daniel was sufficiently intrigued and excited by the journalist's proposal that he wanted to tell Audrey all about it. She would be fascinated, but also skeptical and critical. He needed her advice. *Where the hell was she?* 'I'm gonna need some time to think about it, and brief my partner. Interesting idea, no question, but there's a lot to think about.'

'Of course. Take your time.' The journalist gave him his contact numbers at work and home and said to call him anytime. He suggested they might meet next time, together with the QC and Audrey and 'throw around the idea' a bit more.

Once he hung up, he was impatient to tell Audrey all about the conversation and he found himself puzzled and even a little annoyed that she was out, somewhere. She didn't have anything on, not that he was aware of.

He went out the kitchen door to the back deck, and looked out at the empty clothes hoist, centered in the small backyard, with the branch of the big old lemon tree weighing it down on one side; his newly cultivated veggie patch on the other. Back in the kitchen he stopped and listened – for what, he didn't really know – a sound of movement, her voice? But there was just silence, and suddenly, unaccountably, the quiet sent a small chill through him. He went down the hall towards their room, and as he did, the creeping sense of disquiet grew. He didn't know why he was feeling such a sense of foreboding.

As soon as he entered the bedroom he saw it – a small white square, out of place and conspicuous on the dresser – an envelope, with his name on it.

He knew right away, before he even reached for the letter. He knew by the quiet, and the tidy emptiness of the room. Everything of Audrey's was missing, and so was she.

Audrey was gone.

TWENTY-SEVEN

Thursday, September 8th, 1988
(Two years later)

I sleep on and wish myself awake in the bright, repetitious and miraculous day that is to come.
Angry Buddha 2001

Walking down William Street, approaching the court, Daniel could feel the wind at his back. A north-westerly, with a hint of warmth at the end of a cold winter. His ever-present surfer's instinct, told him the surf would be banging. But surfing was the last thing on his mind. He had important business to conduct – at the big end of town.

He saw the dusty green Victorian dome first, atop the solid sandstone edifice; straight and staunch on the corner of Lonsdale – the protective ramparts of the city's justice system – open to all, provided you could afford the premium. As he waited to cross Lonsdale Street he thought about the ferryman on the Styx, and that made him think about the Titan Wars and battles in general. *Who really does pay the ferryman in the end?*

Ostensibly, this was to be the last of so many legal proceedings; all of them to date, managed pro-bono by the friendly Queen's Counsel recommended to him long ago. A QC with an interest in legal precedent. A QC looking to make a place for himself in legal history, perhaps. But a man of utmost integrity nonetheless; Paul Chambers – his very own legal amigo, and supposed counsel to Her Majesty – had become a close friend and confidant to Daniel in the two years since Audrey left him, and he and Paul had set off to cross their own legal Rubicon.

Daniel always knew he was in the realm of the privileged, as soon as he entered the shadowy ambience of the plane trees, overhanging the salubrious addresses of William Street. Around the court itself he often felt he'd stumbled into an alien world, peopled by a covert elite and their legal functionaries. On the corner, a rotund gentlemen in his penguin black and whites, was having a hushed but intense conversation with a troubled civilian. For some reason, as Daniel passed by, he was transfixed by the neat row of coloured fine-liners in the breast pocket of the man's bar jacket. He followed a group of three young women down the hill, towards the entrance of the Supreme Court. Their synchronised somewhere-to-be gait, as much as their skirted business suits and sensible shoes, told him they were going to the same place he was.

This was to be the conclusive act in their long-running legal drama; his fervent hope at least, and one no doubt shared by Paul, his long-suffering legal representative. It had gone on for far too long, and there had been many casualties along the way; the first being his relationship with Audrey, closely followed by his own peace of mind, and more recently his sense of personal safety. Finally Paul had come up with what he believed would be a winning gambit. In this, the final of many proceedings – which had worked their way inexorably to the highest court in the land – Paul had arranged an ambush for the police legal team, by subpoenaing Blackthorn himself. Paul said it was a *fait accompli*. It would leave them nowhere to go. Blackthorn would be declared a hostile witness, and the opposing legal counsel would have no alternative but to instruct their client to answer the vital question, or risk perjury charges.

Did you draw the drawing? Did you give false evidence to police? Did you pervert the course of justice? And are you a reprehensible piece of shit? Guilty on all charges your honour!

As usual, Daniel had arrived early. Different court, different day; same routine and same cloying anxiety and dread. Outside the front entrance, he paced up and down the long portico, tracing the artful geometry of sandstone pavers. His pacing probably made the security guys at the front entry nervous, but fuck them, he was a veteran of waiting and pacing. The elegant symmetry of the long cloistered verandah, was like some sort of idealised Roman forum. Its old-world columns and arches and potted palms, reminded him of the stylised elitism of his school days; and not for the first time he thought, with a mixture of resentment and guilt, about his father's disappointment that after all those school fees, his eldest son had picked up a paintbrush instead of a quill or syringe.

He waited and paced, and kept waiting, until well past their agreed meeting time, and well into the allotted time for their case to be called. Surely they needed to be inside, waiting outside the courtroom. He started to panic. *Had he got the instructions wrong?*

As time grinded on, he started to worry that something drastic had gone wrong. Had he missed Paul? Come to the wrong entrance? Surely one of Paul's team would have come out to get him. He stalled. Paralyzed from action. The security guys were eyeing him suspiciously.

How long had he been pacing?

He started playing possible scenarios in his head, and replaying his own recent traumas.

The first death threat had come six months ago. The last one, just two days ago. There was no question his pursuit of Blackthorn

– and of answers, and some sort of satisfaction – had upset some important people; people who obviously felt they had a lot to lose.

He'd been shocked of course, but not really surprised the first time he played back his messages and heard the distorted, threatening voice: *I'm going to kill you.* In the end, the threats had become so commonplace that once, when his new partner – unflappable and sanguine ally that she was – had picked up the phone to the now familiar gravelly voice, promising deadly retribution, she'd simply held up the receiver and yelled out; *Daniel, it's for you!*

But the threats had crept into his psyche and gradually eroded his stability, if not this resolve. This was evidenced by the builder's jimmy bar he kept under his pillow, and the unregistered shotgun on top of the wardrobe. Paranoia had gradually set in. How could it not?

He didn't doubt that Blackthorn has capable of making threats. After all Daniel had gone after him relentlessly, ever since the police raid on his studio. To this day he was in no doubt that the drawing was Blackthorn's work. And he'd dragged him through the courts, impugned him and accused him. He'd gone after him with a ruthless vengeance that he knew was damaging to his own soul, and probably an affront to the laws of karma in general. But he seemed strangely incapable of modulating his own response to what had been done to him. He just couldn't let it go. That was the meaning of the 'MONGOOSE' text across the bottom of his self-portrait. The mongoose goes after the cobra, gets it by the neck and nothing will make it let go; not until the serpent has been dispatched.

But he suspected there was more to it, more at stake. And his gut told him it wasn't Blackthorn making the threats at all. He'd become convinced that senior figures in the Melbourne art world had been involved in the theft of the Picasso. And he was convinced Blackthorn was mixed up in it too, somehow. Why else would he have tried to frame him?

And so, no doubt, him and Paul going after Blackthorn, represented a threat that the rest of them might be exposed too.

He remembered saying to Doherty on the day of the raid: *Why don't you look at Blackthorn, maybe he'll lead you to the real culprits.* And yet, what had happened instead? The investigation had just stopped. Stopped dead, almost immediately after the raid. One minute the police had been vowing to leave no stone unturned. The next minute the police investigation, into the biggest art heist in the history of Australia – a crime supposedly done by people calling themselves terrorists – was simply dropped like a hot potato.

To Daniel, this was the surest sign that well-connected people had been involved. They – or perhaps Blackthorn, off his own bat – had tried to frame him and Audrey, to take the heat off themselves, and it had back-fired when Daniel had recognised Blackthorn's handiwork.

Now, with the police obligingly dropping the investigation and the case long cold, the last thing, any of them wanted – and possibly players within the police too – was someone stirring the pot. He was sure, this was the real reason he was getting threats; because at the end of the day, he didn't really think Blackthorn had it in him. He may have been a disgusting person, but behind all the bluster, Daniel reckoned he was all just piss and wind.

'Excuse me, Mr. Hardman...' The quietly assertive voice came from a petite woman standing behind him. He'd been lost in thought, staring out at the streetscape between the pillars of his cloistered cage. He turned to see a woman he recognised from Paul's office, one of the paralegals.

'Where's Paul?' He demanded a little too stridently, after glancing along the portico and seeing she was alone.

'He sends his apologies. He's really very sorry. Something's come up and he can't attend.'

'Can't attend? That's impossible! We've got a hearing scheduled in the Supreme Court. And we're late! What could come up? ... This... This is too important...' He looked at the small well-dressed woman, bewildered. Her face showed mild sympathy but little else. 'Someone better have died!' He immediately regretted this and the young woman's expression darkened, as if perhaps someone had.

'Well what are we going to do? We can't just not show up, can we? What happens next? Do we reschedule?' Daniel was perplexed and aghast that Paul had stood him up and sent a junior staffer to tell him. *How could he not be here? He'd never let him down before.*

'I'm sorry,' the woman repeated, without further elaboration.

'What?' Daniel left panic turning to anger. 'What's going on? What's this about?'

'I'm sorry, but that's all I've got. Mr. Chambers just wanted me to convey his sincerest apologies.' She turned to go. It suddenly occurred to him that Paul had been got at. If Daniel was getting death threats, maybe they'd started on Paul too.

'Wait!' His voice sounded plaintive and out of place and echoed loudly in the stone portico.

She began walking away. Over her shoulder she said, 'Mr. Chamber's office will be in touch.'

'No!' He took a few quick steps after the young woman, then hesitated. 'He's been got at, hasn't he?' he yelled. He glanced around and saw the security men at the entry were looking at him like he could be a problem they might have to solve. He watched the young woman primly descend the steps to the sidewalk and turn up the hill. She didn't look back. He leaned against the column at the top of the steps and watched her until she disappeared around the corner. He felt like he was glued to the pillar and wondered whether he could hold himself up without its support.

A strong gust of wind funneled down the city street, caught him in the face and he smelled the rain in it. His weather sense told him a change was coming, maybe even a storm. And he thought again about how the surf was probably pumping, and his mind gave him an image of a great roiling grey cloud loaded with rain and hail, churning in from the southern ocean the way they did sometimes, ahead of a change. And then he found himself sitting down on the fancy pavers, because he'd slid down the polished sandstone pillar that was supposed to be holding him up. And then the rain came in sideways and hit him in the back of the head like a fusillade of bad luck; and he thought darkly about the shotgun on top of the wardrobe and about Blackthorn's farm outside Geelong, where he'd been once in his student days.

The bouncing rain was misting up the Roman forum, and through it, he saw one of the security guys standing over him. 'Are you alright, Sir?'

'Just resting,' he said. And with that he knew it was time to retreat. The world had closed in, and there were just too many bad people in it.

He would go to the coast. He would find a tin shed – as he was wont to do – and he would paint.

Paint and go surfing.

*

Travis crunched along the gravel path toward the treated pine viewing platform. He could already see the swell lines, like corrugations stretching out to sea, and the strong off-shore breeze buffeted and tugged at his jacket. The surf was going off, and he'd come down to check the tide at his favorite break. He'd already estimated it would be the perfect tide for Seal Rock in about an hour, and so all bets were off – fuck doing any work today – he was going for a midday surf, and it looked like it was going to be *all time*.

He sauntered down the track toward the look-out, noticing a line of four people hogging the observation deck – all standing abreast of each other, in their loud, rip-off surf shop clothing – staring out to sea; heads on them like mice, chattering excitedly amongst themselves. *Fucking tourists*, he hissed under his breath, but none too softly, as he went past them and gave them an unfriendly scowl. None of them even noticed, because they were all too busy pointing and making excited comments about the big waves.

He swung to the left and went down the steps descending to the beach. After about twenty steps, he stopped on the landing, jutting out over the high buttress, where the remaining steps switched back the other way, hugging the cliff all the way down to the water. The little square platform gave him a good view of Seal Rock, to see how it was breaking, as the tide started coming in.

Good; only four guys out. He stood and watched a small set of waves break over the shallow reef. He reached into his pocket for a joint he'd rolled earlier, and scanned the stairs up and down to see if there was anyone around. He looked up at the tourists. They were all looking down at him like he was an exhibit in the surf zoo. *Bloody kooks*. He lit the joint and puffed it too life – giving the holiday makers a dead-pan death stare – then flicked the match out over the cliff.

He scanned the horizon and he could see there was a decent set of waves coming. The ribboned ocean was a deep steel blue, reflecting the stormy grey sky. There were still some white caps out to sea, although the unseasonably warm north-westerly had suddenly dropped off, after getting quite strong through the morning. In the lee of the cliff the water was glassy and calm, and the waves were starting to barrel nicely over the reef, as the tide filled in. It was strangely humid for spring, and Travis reckoned it smelled like rain, which wouldn't be a bad thing. He quite liked surfing in the rain.

As the herb started to take effect, he felt relaxed and at peace with the world. He heard a rumble of distant thunder and he looked up and saw a faint flash somewhere inland, away in the rain-forested hills. The tourists on the landing looked around, spooked, like they'd never heard thunder before. He smiled and returned his attention to the waves, and as he did, for some reason he thought about his artistic adversary and sometime surfing buddy, Daniel. He hadn't seen him down on the coast for a while and he wondered how he'd been getting on.

The last time he'd seen him had been a bit of a shock. He'd seemed irritated and a bit distraught. It was at some sort of gathering – a book launch, in the city – and Dan had been more than a little drunk, and more than a little pissed off with the world. In the end he'd had a rant to Travis about the whole Picasso thing, and it was only then, he'd realised just how much it had affected him.

In fact, it almost seemed like it had fucked up his entire life, or at least that's how it seemed from the fraught state Dan was in on that particular occasion. His girlfriend had left him, he no longer had the funky studio in the city, and it sounded like he wasn't selling much art – after having been killing it for a while – with his private exhibitions and fancy city-centre shop front.

In all honesty, Travis would have to admit he'd been jealous as fuck. For that reason he'd felt a moment or two of invidious satisfaction, seeing his erstwhile high-flying competitor on the rocks. Back then, his own career had been going nowhere – part of the reason he'd gotten involved with Tate, and everything that had followed from that – but Tate, of course, had been full of shit, and had only wanted to get into his pants; and ultimately use him as his insider in the Picasso scam.

But when Dan started banging on about Blackthorn, he'd found it hard to listen. He said Blackthorn had tried to frame him and Audrey by drawing *that picture* of Audrey as the Picasso culprit. Travis knew this was true, but of course he said nothing, not wanting to implicate himself. In fact, he'd felt a rare moment of shame, remembering how he'd started the rumor mill in Geelong, and more particularly, how he'd planted the seed in Blackthorn's stupid head to do what he did.

He was even more shocked when Daniel had started talking about some court case – or it sounded like a series of court cases – in which, somehow, he was going after Blackthorn – trying get him held to account for giving false evidence. *Jesus,* Travis had said. *That sounds fucken' heavy.*

He wasn't sure, why he thought of Daniel Hardman at that moment – perhaps because he hadn't seen him in the surf for a while.

The surf was looking good, and two surfers had gotten out. *Perfect, only two guys left in the water.* There was another flash, this one brighter, and a loud rumble of thunder soon after. The storm was getting closer. A couple of fat rain drops hit Travis on the head and spattered about the on the timber deck; but then the rain stopped, as if the thick, humid air was holding off for a moment before letting fly. *Better go up and get into my wetsuit,* he thought, *before the rain sets in...* It didn't matter how much it rained once you were in the water. *Surfing in the rain was kind of fun.*

He flicked the spent joint out over the railing and watched it tumble down for a moment, then turned to go back up the stairs. But as he turned the landing seemed to sway unaccountably and a strange sensation rose up in him, almost like a bit of static electricity, from the charged up stormy air. And in that moment he thought again about Hardman and Burke. And he thought about Blackthorn too... And Tate as well. But not just them. Somehow or another, he was thinking about everyone he'd ever known, all at once – all of his family and friends, colleagues, school friends; even strangers, like the tourists above him; even his ancestors – some who he'd never known existed.

It should have seemed very strange – but it didn't. He knew with implicit clarity he was having a mighty epiphany. In this state, he understood why Blackthorn was the way he was. Deep inside his own waters he experienced and felt the terrible abuse Blackthorn had suffered as a child, and he felt perfect empathy for him, and also for three-year-old Tate; broken hearted at the loss of his mother. In fact, he instantaneously experienced the pain and trauma and joy of everyone he had ever known. He even felt the joy and happiness of the colourfully dressed tourists, having their first real holiday from their oppressive country of origin. He loved them all, unconditionally...Even the holiday-makers.

Travis felt he was standing outside his own body. And at the same time, he was at the centre of a luminous universe of balance and peace. And all at once, he understood his true inner self, with absolute clarity of knowledge. And it was all infused with a wonderful sense of forgiveness. Forgiveness of himself and everyone who had ever wronged him.

He was in fact, experiencing his timeless, elemental self. He was connected to everything and every sentient being, in the most intimate and perfect way. The connections were like the neurons in his own brain; in fact they *were* the neurons in his brain, they were one in the same... As were the strings of dark matter connecting the stars and galaxies throughout the universe. It was all part of one perfect whole.

A primordial mind deep, deep inside himself – which he'd always know was there, and yet had been a mystery to him his entire life – smiled quietly, in divine satisfaction, and he was filled with transcendent love for all things.

He would never be the same. He had been utterly transformed.

It was perfect.

From the point of view of the tourists on the upper platform, it had appeared as if sword of light had burst out of the top of the man's head. At least that's was what one of the witnesses told the young police constable taking her statement.

Like a Star Wars light sabre, another one said: *Bright, bright, white and bluish. And blinding.* Another of them said it was pink and red, with a greenish tinge at the end. Strangely, they all agreed the light seemed to emanate from the top of the man's head – and out of his ears too – then shot upwards, to merge with a dazzling bolt of lightning as it descended from above.

The constable wondered how reliable their accounts could be, after all, the event had necessarily happened at the speed of light, she reckoned.

In any case, the flash and the bang, they all agreed, had been simultaneous; temporarily blinding them, and the shock wave knocking them all off their feet, and scorching the forearm of one of the hapless holiday makers.

The police constable dutifully took it all down, as if getting the exact colour of the lightening flash, and the sequence of events, were important details. The truth of it was, she was looking to distract herself. Anything to take her mind off what she'd seen when her and her partner had descended to the blackened, scorched landing to look for signs of life, as they were obliged to do.

She wondered if she could ever forget what she's seen there, on the landing – like some kind of horrendous human sacrifice gone wrong – or if she'd ever get the smell out of her nostrils. She would go on to be a life-long vegetarian.

Did anyone know who the deceased person was?

None of them did. A surfer they thought.

Should they try to find some kind of identification?

No way. Her partner had been quite adamant. *Better to wait for the forensic people and the coroner.* Neither of them wanted to go back down to the landing, and the charred and broken wreck that was all that remained of Travis; who had, for the briefest moment in time, known all the secrets of the universe, before his eyes exploded out of their sockets and his feet burned foot prints into the treated pine deck, a visible reminder to all, for years to come, of the grisly incident at Seal Rock.

*

Below him, the deepest aquamarine seemed to go on forever. The clarity was awe-inspiring and filled him with a sense of wonder and bliss. He was weightless, for a moment or two, before buoyancy took over. He swam against it, swimming down. Half a dozen purposeful strokes, until he thought he could see the sandy bottom, still far below him in the impossibly clear waters.

He arched his back – this time giving in to buoyancy – and gradually rising to the surface, blowing out a stream of bubbles as he went. He broke the surface and gasped, filling his lungs and shaking the water from his eyes. Treading water, he scanned the horizon. Nothing but the vast expanse of the Indian Ocean.

He was right in the middle of it. *Amazing!*

He rotated ninety degrees until the island came into view, with its *Robinson Crusoe* palms curving out over the white sandy beach. He followed the line of the surrounding atoll, until he could see the small group of surfers, sitting off the end of the coral point, waiting for waves.

He kicked his legs and pushed at the water, coming around another ninety degrees, until *Cry Baby* came into view; resting at anchor in the deep calm water off the end of the atoll, in the lee of the island. He kicked furiously to stay afloat, and waved his arm above his head.

Penny waved back.

In his mind, Jack took a postcard snap-shot. *What a picture.* Penny, tanned and gorgeous in her bikini, standing there, *amidships* on their little boat, smiling and holding up two glasses. Clearly, she'd decided it was cocktail hour. In the distance, the blue waters stretched away in the distance, reflecting a perfect sky of a lighter hue, marred only by bourgeoning pavilions of tropical thunderheads vaulting up above the distant horizon.

He swam back towards the boat with a leisurely stroke, enjoying the cool waters of the open ocean, so refreshing after the mid-afternoon equatorial heat. She met him at the stern as he dragged himself up onto the small dive platform and threw him a towel; and when he'd dried his hair, handed him a gin and tonic. 'Cheers!'

'Is it gin o'clock already?' he enquired solicitously, taking a sip.

'It is somewhere in the world.' Penny grinned. 'How's the water?'

'Fabulous. Why didn't you come in?'

'I'm pretty tired. Two big sessions this morning.'

Penny had become the resort's surf coach for the guests' children. If the kids wanted to learn to surf – while the fathers were surfing the gnarly barrels on the point, and the mothers were enjoying some down time on the beach – her job was to look after them in the shore break at the end of the lagoon; show them how to stand up on the big foam longboards supplied by the resort.

Jack never could have imagined Penny as a surfer. She'd never tried it, growing up in Melbourne. But here in the Maldives, she'd taken to it like a duck to water. And she'd even started having a go at the challenging left-hander off the end of the point, but only on small days. It was an advanced and technical wave, which broke fast and hollow over a shallow and razor sharp coral reef. Tiger's, as the surf break was known, attracted surfers from all over the world, and so Jack was very impressed that Penny's surfing had progressed to the point that she was able to handle it.

He himself had never really taken to surfing. Instead, he'd found a passion for scuba diving, and he'd trained and eventually got himself rated as an instructor. When the surf was flat – as it sometimes was for fairly long stretches – the resort paid him to take surfers on informal dive charters, to help ameliorate the disappointment of no waves, after guests had come so far and paid so much.

It was a pretty good earner, and between the charters and the surf coaching, they were able to make a good enough living to support their far-flung tropical life-style. And if the resort was short-staffed, they sometimes got extra work on the island; Penny in the kitchen and Jack working the bar.

After their drink, Jack got to work preparing the fish he'd caught earlier. He did it with a salad of fresh julienned vegetables and a spicy lime and ginger dressing the chef at the resort had given them to try. Their latest anchorage was an almost ideal situation; living on the *Cry Baby* moored in the shelter of Tiger Moon Island Resort. They were able to source fresh food through the resort kitchen, they had all the work they needed, and if they wanted company they could always go over to the resort and socialise with the visiting surfers; have a drink at the bar, eat at the restaurant or go to the outdoor cinema on Wednesday nights. It was a pretty good gig.

They took their dinner up onto the deck and ate it at the little table they rigged up in the cockpit, whenever they weren't at sea – which was most of the time – and had a glass of white wine, watching the sunset over the mirrored waters. It was a riot of colours – all oranges and pinks and lilac – as the setting sun reflected off the towering columns of tropical cloud which often accumulated at the end of the day.

They'd been invited over for a drink on the big surf charter boat moored a bit further up the point, but Penny said she was too tired. They both knew the surfers always invited Penny, because they thought she was pretty cool, and they weren't used to seeing girls out surfing Tigers. Penny knew it irked Jack a bit, even though he never said anything.

They watched the calm waters darken to purple and red as *Cry Baby* rocked almost imperceptibly, and a crescent moon brightened in the western sky.

Penny sipped her wine and stared contentedly at Jack. 'We've got a pretty bloody good life haven't we?'

'We do. People'd fight fire-breathing dragons to live like this.' He gave her a faintly ironical smile, to go with his hyperbole, and raised his glass. She clinked hers against his and they both smiled, and sat quietly, watching the darkening waters, and the lights coming on at the resort, and also reflecting across at them from the charter vessel off their starboard bow.

'Do you believe in karma, Jack?'

'Yeah, I suppose. Why?'

'I dunno... I just wonder sometimes. Did we do the right thing? I mean you know, back in Melbourne, and then, selling it in Bangkok, the way we did?'

'Selling what?' He gave her a little cheeky smile.

'Funny.' Penny slapped his arm gently. 'I suppose we must've though, for everything to work out the way it did. I mean look at us. We kind of landed on our feet, didn't we?'

'We did.'

They sat quietly for a few more moments and both took a sip of wine, just enjoying each others company and the tranquility of the tropical evening.

Finally Jack said: 'I'm not sure I believe in karma, but I believe in consequences.

'Those people were nasty, greedy entitled humans of the worst kind. They didn't give a fuck who got hurt as long as they got what they wanted. What we did, we did to protect ourselves from them, and, as it turned out, to put them in the shit at the same time, for being complete assholes. They got what they deserved. And if we lucked out along the way, then maybe that is karma, or maybe it's just the flip side of consequences. Maybe that's what people mean by *making your own luck*.'

'That's really what we did I suppose, isn't it? ... Made our own luck.'

'Yeah.'

After a while Penny said: 'Are you ever going to tell me?'

'Tell you what?'

'You know what... Which one was it?

'Oooh...You already know the answer to that one... If I told you...'

'I know, I know... Then you'd have to kill me. Ha ha!' Penny gave a miffed chuckle. Jack smiled, and they sipped their wine and watched the planets and stars appear between the clouds in the indigo sky.

ACKNOWLEDGMENTS

Thanks to my sons, Sam, Luke and Harry for identifying this as the story that needed to be told, and for their encouragement, love and inspiration. To my wonderful partner Lisa for her support and love, and for her advice and insightful feedback throughout the project. Gratitude and esteem to Margaret for her generosity in trusting me with her story. Enormous appreciation to Gisela for her engagement and expertise throughout, and her generosity in reading, advising, and remembering. Thanks also to Corrin for his early encouragement, and indeed, to him and Mark for 'setting the cat amongst the pigeons' with their brilliant documentary. Thanks also to Sally for her acceptance and trust.

And to my sister, Judy for her solidarity and support through the hard times, and for her trust, invaluable advice and archival mastery, in the sensitive and delicate task of teasing this 'true-life fiction' from the tangled and often painful strands of the past.

ABOUT THE AUTHOR

An ex-science journalist and naturopath, Stuart Rosson lives in Torquay, where he runs a guesthouse, writes fiction and surfs. His previous books form two parts of a post-apocalyptic action trilogy. His third book, *Framed*, is a fictionalised exposé of the theft of Picasso's Weeping Woman in 1986.

Throughout the mid 80's he was the science writer for the *Sun News-Pictorial*, covering news and features on science, health and medicine. Moving to the Surf Coast, in the early 90's he worked as an operations manager, for a global surf company until 2001. After leaving the surf industry he studied natural medicine, and went on to practice as a naturopath until 2009.

His first book, *East* – a post-apocalyptic action adventure – was published in 2018. His second book, a prequel to *East*, and set in mid-21st century Melbourne, was all but completed, when he switched track to write *Framed*; the fictionalised 'true' story of the theft of Picasso's Weeping Woman from the NGV in 1986 – a crime for which his brother was framed.

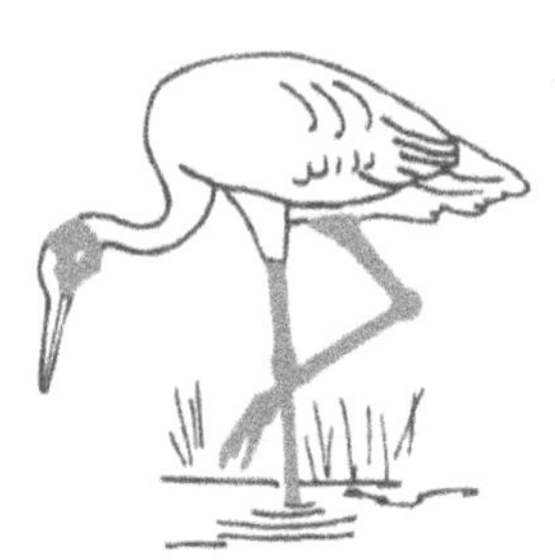

Be Published